W9-CBJ-212

TEACHING FOREIGN LANGUAGES IN THE BLOCK

Deborah Blaz

30970000112969

PROFESSIONAL LIBRARY
ROUND ROCK ISD

EYE ON EDUCATION
6 DEPOT WAY WEST, SUITE 106
LARCHMONT, NY 10538
(914) 833–0551
(914) 833–0761 fax

Copyright © 1998 Eye On Education, Inc.
All Rights Reserved.

ISBN 1-883001-52-8

For information about permission to reproduce selections from this book, write:
Eye On Education, Permissions Dept., Suite 106, 6 Depot Way West, Larchmont, NY
10538.

Library of Congress Cataloging-in-Publication Data

Blaz, Deborah

    Teaching foreign languages in the block / by Deborah Blaz
        p. cm. — (Teaching in the block)
    Includes bibliographical references
    ISBN 1-883001-52-8
    1. Languages and languages—Study and teaching.   I. Title.
 II. Series
    P51.B545   1998
    407—dc21   97-49633
                                          CIP

10 9 8 7 6 5 4 3 2

Editorial and production services provided by Richard H. Adin Freelance Editorial
Services, 9 Orchard Drive, Gardiner, NY 12525 (914-883-5884)

Other Books on Block Scheduling

Teaching in the Block
Stategies for Engaging Active Learners
edited by Robert Lynn Canady and Michael D. Rettig

Block Scheduling
A Catalyst For Change in High Schools
by Robert Lynn Canady and Michael D. Rettig

Middle School Block Scheduling
by Robert Lynn Canady and Michael D. Rettig

The 4 X 4 Block Schedule
by J. Allen Queen and Kimberly Gaskey Isenhour

Action Research On Block Scheduling
by David Marshak

Teaching in the Block, the series
Robert Lynn Canady and Michael D. Rettig, General Editors

Supporting Students With Learning Needs in the Block
by Marcia Conti-D'Antonio, Robert Bertrando, and Joanne Eisenberger

Teaching Mathematics in the Block
by Susan Gilkey and Carla Hunt

Teaching Foreign Languages in the Block
by Deborah Blaz

For more information on Teaching in the Block, contact us at:

Eye On Education
6 Depot Way West
Larchmont, NY 10538
phone (914) 833-0551
fax (914) 833-0761
www.eyeoneducation.com

Also Published by Eye On Education

Performance Assessment and Standards-Based Curricula
The Achievement Cycle
by Allan A. Glatthorn

The Performance Assessment Handbook
Volume 1: Portfolios and Socratic Seminars
Volume 2: Performances and Exhibitions
by Bil Johnson

A Collection of Performance Tasks and Rubrics
Middle School Mathematics
by Charlotte Danielson

Upper Elementary School Mathematics
by Charlotte Danielson

High School Mathematics
by Charlotte Danielson and Elizabeth Marquez

The School Portfolio
A Comprehensive Framework for School Improvement
by Victoria L. Bernhardt

Research on Educational Innovations, 2d ed.
by Arthur K. Ellis and Jeffrey T. Fouts

School-to-Work
by Arnold H. Packer and Marion W. Pines

The Reflective Supervisor
A Practical Guide for Educators
by Ray Calabrese and Sally Zepeda

Instruction and the Learning Environment
by James Keefe and John Jenkins

The Educator's Brief Guide to the Internet and the World Wide Web
by Eugene F. Provenzo

FOREWORD

Block schedules provide opportunities for teachers to change their instructional strategies so that students become more active and successful learners. There is a growing body of evidence from experiences with high school block scheduling that strongly supports the notion that with proper staff development and careful schedule design the overall school environment becomes more positive and productive. There is also evidence that many teachers increase their personal contacts with students. Furthermore, when curricular and instructional issues are addressed appropriately, achievement in many schools improves, as measured by factors such as reduced failure rates, increased number of students on honor rolls, and higher test scores.

Because we believe that instructional change is the key to successful block scheduling, we are sponsoring this series of books, written primarily by teachers who have been successful in teaching in block schedules. While we believe this series can be helpful to teachers working in any type of schedule, the ideas should be especially useful for middle and high school teachers who are "Teaching in the Block."

The idea of scheduling middle and high schools in some way other than daily, single periods is not new. We find in educational history numerous attempts to modify traditional schedules and to give the instructional school day greater flexibility. In the 1960s, for example, approximately 15% of American high schools implemented modular scheduling, which typically combined "mods" of time to create schedules with instructional periods that varied in length from between 15 minutes to classes of 100 minutes or more.

Many reasons have been given for the demise of modular scheduling as practiced during the 1960s and 1970s. However, two of the primary reasons often cited are that (1) too much independent study time was included in those schedules and school management became a problem, and (2) teachers in many schools did not receive training designed to assist them in altering instruction in the longer class period (Canady and Rettig, 1995, pp. 13–15). Current models of block scheduling do not include significant built-in independent study time and, therefore, school management problems are not exacerbated, but helped. We have found, however, that in schools where block scheduling has been implemented successfully, considerable attention has been paid to adapting instruction to maximize the potential of available time.

We repeatedly have stated that if schools merely "change their bells," block scheduling should not be implemented. We also have contended that if teachers are not provided with extensive staff development, block scheduling will be a problem. "The success or failure of the [current] block scheduling movement will be determined largely by the ability of teachers...to improve instruction. Regardless of a school's time schedule, what happens between individual teachers and students in classrooms is still most important, and simply altering the manner in which we schedule school will not ensure better instruction by teachers or increased learning by students" (Canady and Rettig, 1995, p. 240).

Deborah Blaz, a French teacher at Angola High School, in Angola, Indiana, and the 1996 Indiana French Teacher of the Year, is the author of *Teaching Foreign Languages in the Block*. Since block scheduling gained serious consideration in high schools, many foreign language teachers have expressed concern as to whether or not foreign language instruction was an appropriate "fit" for the block. In the A/B schedule, foreign language teachers complained about the lack of daily instruction, and in the 4/4 schedule teachers feared that lower retention of material would occur because instruction did not continue for the entire year.

Not only does Ms. Blaz masterfully respond to these issues, but she also provides foreign language teachers with a significant "hands-on" guide for active instruction during the block. Specific illustrations of how to adapt more than 25 strategies for the instruction of foreign language form the centerpiece of the book. In addition to lesson plans and instructional strategies, Ms. Blaz also shares her experience with the 4/4 schedule and how it has enhanced student achievement in her school. Various plans for sequencing foreign language classes within the 4/4 schedule also are addressed in detail.

We highly recommend this book to all middle and high school teachers of foreign language regardless of their schedule. However, we feel teachers in all block schedules can benefit greatly from this significant contribution to foreign language instruction and the block scheduling movement.

Robert Lynn Canady
Michael D. Rettig

Please share with us...

Eye On Education is interested in learning about your experiences teaching in the block. Please let us know about:

◆ a lesson plan that worked especially well

◆ a strategy that harnessed the potential of the extended period

◆ an anecdote that shows how block scheduling influenced the learning process

Please write, phone, or e-mail us at:

Eye On Education
6 Depot Way West
Larchmont, NY 10538
(914) 833-0551 phone
(914) 833-0761 fax
block@eyeoneducation.com

ABOUT THE AUTHOR

Deborah Blaz, a French teacher at Angola High School in Angola, Indiana, is a native of St. Charles, Illinois. She received her B.A. in French and German from Illinois State University, a *diplome* from the Université de Grenoble in Grenoble, France, and, in 1974, an M.A. in French from the University of Kentucky. Ms. Blaz has taught French and English to grades 7 through 12 for the past 19 years in Indiana.

Her exposure to a block schedule began when she taught conversational English at a private high school in Grenoble, France, and continued with teaching a special blocked class at the University of Kentucky. Later, she taught a summer school Foreign Language Elementary School (FLES) program in Indiana. She has now been on an accelerated block (4/4) schedule for three years at Angola High School, which was named Indiana's Most Outstanding Successful High School for 1996–97 by the Indiana Association of Teacher Educators and the Indiana Association of Colleges of Teacher Education. This was attributable, in large part, to the block schedule and its many positive effects.

Ms. Blaz, who was honored as the Indiana French Teacher of the Year in October 1996 by the Indiana chapter of the American Association of Teachers of French (IAATF), has actively promoted the block since it was first proposed to the staff, serving first on the school restructuring committee and then on the faculty action committee. She was a presenter at summer workshops held in Angola on the block schedule and successful block teaching strategies during the summers of 1996 and 1997, and has done numerous inservices on those topics at schools in Indiana and Michigan.

She may be contacted at Angola High School, 755 S 100 E, Angola, Indiana 46703.

ACKNOWLEDGMENTS

There are many people at Angola High School who were helpful in this undertaking. I'd like to thank all my colleagues, especially Cynthia Jones (fellow foreign language teacher) and Dave Snyder for his help with statistics and computer advice. My principal Dr. Rex Bolinger was the driving force behind both the school's successful move to the block schedule as well as the chain of events that led to my writing this book. I am indebted to him for his support and assistance throughout this process.

I'd also like to thank Beth Portela, Dee Friel, Jocelyn Raught, Audrey Havard, Sari Kaye, and Patsy Hattori who shared ideas with me for this book.

Many thanks to my capable editor Robert Sickles for answering all my questions, and to Robert Lynn Canady and Michael D. Rettig for their assistance.

The blind faith in me shown by my family—Walter Best, Mary Blaz, and my children Nat and Suzy—was most amusing and satisfying.

And finally, I am grateful to my husband Mike for his assistance with research, technical advice, and especially for his understanding and preternatural tolerance (his choice of terms) throughout this project.

TABLE OF CONTENTS

1

MEETING NATIONAL STANDARDS: FOREIGN LANGUAGES AND THE BLOCK SCHEDULE

"Nothing will ever be attempted, if all possible objections must be first overcome."

Dr. Johnson, *Rasselas*

Not long ago in the United States, learning a foreign language was considered to be merely a part of a good liberal education, or an intellectual exercise recommended for only the brightest students. It was automatically assumed that anyone studying a foreign language wanted to be either a teacher or an interpreter/translator. Fortunately, many business, political, and educational leaders are belatedly realizing that the whole world does not speak English, and a second language is now becoming a vital part of the basic preparation for an increasing number of careers. At a job interview, applicants are often asked what languages they speak, and even when a language is not a job requirement, applicants report that foreign language skills have improved their chances for promotion as well as enhanced job flexibility and mobility.

Finally, foreign languages are no longer regarded as a frivolous option. According to the authors of *A Nation at Risk* (1983), foreign language proficiency is vital to the national interest, in politics, the military, and business, as well as in education. As a result, foreign language instruction is being required to change its focus from teaching grammar and literature to an emphasis on language proficiency and communications skills.

The response from educators has been swift. National standards for foreign language instruction have been established, which have been translated into policy at the state level. Most often, these newly written or revised state policies take the form of proficiency-based curriculum guides. In addition, states such as Nebraska and Indiana have established special diplomas for students who take a more challenging academic load that requires three or four years of foreign language. States such as Texas require one or two years of study as a prerequisite for graduation. Schools, as a result, are offering more foreign language classes and to students of more varied ability levels than ever before.

THE NEED TO ADAPT

Our task has been to study, learn, and adapt to meet these new goals. Foreign language teachers know that oral experiences are critical to the development of proficiency; students need all the contact they can get. For decades, immersion (e.g., the famous Berlitz course) has been shown to be the best way to facilitate learning another language. In schools where immersion is not an option, but that wish to improve the atmosphere in which foreign language learning takes place, adaptations must occur that afford more teacher-student contact time. As we all know, expecting any teacher to teach for 5 or 6 hours per day in formal class settings and be responsible for 150 to 180 students per day is not conducive to high-quality teaching. The great problem seems to be the incessant interruption of the bell—the movement of students in and out of classrooms every hour; the feeling that the class is over just as learning has begun. For foreign language teachers, there is insufficient time to set up tapes, engage in extended conversation, or write anything longer than a paragraph. With more contact time as our goal, the block schedule is ideal for teaching foreign languages; in some cases it doubles the amount of time per day spent listening, speaking, reading, and writing the language.

Schools that only offer six or seven class periods per day usually find that very few students continue language studies beyond what is required because of scheduling conflicts or graduation requirements. Still, we all know that students will not be proficient enough for the business marketplace after only one or two years of foreign language. For foreign languages, this may be the most important contribution a block schedule can make: more students finding they have time to continue their language studies. Enrollment in the upper-level classes increases under a block schedule, with students able to take (theoretically) up to eight years of language in four years, or possibly even earn college credits in the language while still in high school. Due to its structure, the block provides more opportunities for taking elective courses, or for acceleration, than a six- or seven-period schedule can offer.

However, it is also true that the urgent need is not just more time, but better use of time. The need for new teaching strategies that minimize the old grammar-and-vocabulary emphasis and provide more interaction possibilities is also indisputable; it is mandated in the new national standards. Reflecting the modern emphasis on communication, a foreign language classroom must be dynamic; changes in curriculum also must be accompanied by changes in instruction and in assessment. By changing the role of the classroom teacher from "sage on the stage" to "guide on the side" via cooperative learning, for example, we can profoundly change the learning process in our classroom. While it is possible to try new things in any schedule, the block schedule obviously offers a longer period of time in which to try out new methods.

In this change, the role of the individual teacher is of paramount importance. Teachers need a strong sense of professionalism and a belief that they have the time and resources to be as effective as they are capable of being. This should be easier to accomplish with an environment where more time is available for planning. Now, with longer preparation time each day for the teacher and the generally decreased amount of paperwork, teachers on the block report that the pressure to develop excellence in the classroom via new activities becomes much more manageable and less stressful.

THE NEED TO INCORPORATE TECHNOLOGY

Technology is also playing a larger and larger role in foreign language education: language laboratories are new and improved and funding for purchasing them is becoming more available; televisions and VCRs enhance cultural presentations; and video cameras enable the students to produce more interesting reports and projects than ever before. In addition to supplementary videos, many new textbooks come with interactive software programs through which students can not only view video clips, but also hear foreign speakers, construct sentences, drill vocabulary, practice speaking, or create a skit/play with characters that move. They can even record their own voices for the dialogue of the play.

For foreign languages, the Internet opens myriad new possibilities. The Internet offers us current events as they are happening (for example, we watched part of the Mardi Gras live, as well as a bank fire in Paris), up-to-date information on cities and sights (how much an Eiffel Tower ticket costs, what hours the Prado is open, what events are planned for the Oktoberfest this year), keypals (penpals via computer) in the target language, and many opportunities for research on various topics, often in the target language.

Adding all this wonderful technology to a shorter class period is difficult. For example, time spent going to and from the computer room, setting up the links, explaining the project, and logging on to the network, often leaves students with very little time to accomplish anything, in a standard 45- or 50-minute class period. With the extended time offered by a block, however, it becomes not only feasible, but even fun, with many rewards in terms of learning. (The Internet is discussed more fully in Chapter 4.)

To summarize, the block offers foreign language teachers many opportunities to fulfill the requirements to adapt their curriculum, instructional methods, and assessments to meet the demands of students, parents, and society. This chapter explains what the block schedule looks like, discusses the benefits and difficulties each has for foreign language teachers, and refutes common criticisms and fears about block schedules. It also discusses the national standards and how the block can help schools achieve them.

Chapter 2 deals with curriculum and pacing issues, as well as with several other steps to be taken before going to a block schedule. Chapter 3 shows how to construct a good, solid, workable lesson plan (with samples to be found in Chapter 6). Chapter 4 deals with teaching strategies that work well in the block, with examples for French, Spanish, and German classrooms; and Chapter 5 talks about assessments in their many different forms. All are written specifically with a foreign language classroom, and its particular needs, firmly in mind.

WHAT IS A BLOCK SCHEDULE?

"In a progressive country, change is constant; change is inevitable."

Benjamin Disraeli

The block schedule has been used for many years in different countries; I taught English in France on a modified block schedule over 25 years ago. In America, the block schedule has been used successfully at the university level for years; didn't you have at least one Monday–Wednesday–Friday class that met for two hours, for example? The high school and middle school, however, have traditionally only taught summer school programs on the block; for instance, academically troubled students might have English for three or four hours a day, five days a week, for four or five weeks. Driver Education is also traditionally taught in blocks in the summer.

ALTERNATE-DAY

One form of block scheduling being used today is called an Alternate-Day schedule (Canady and Rettig, 1996, Chap. 2). In this schedule, rather than every class meeting daily, students and teachers meet every other day for a longer "block" period of time. Alternate-Day schedules also are called "A/B," "Odd/Even," "Day 1/Day 2," or "Week 1/Week 2" schedules. There are several different variations of the Alternate-Day schedule, offering either six, seven, or eight courses. A typical six-course schedule offers three courses each day for approximately 120-minute blocks; seven-course schedules typically have three alternating blocks of approximately 100 minutes each, and one block (usually including lunch period) that meets every day for 45 to 55 minutes. An eight-course schedule has four courses meeting for approximately 90 minutes on Day 1 and the remaining four courses on Day 2. Many schools name this schedule after their school colors: Monday, for example, would be "Red" day, meeting blocks 1, 2, 3, and 4, while Tuesday is "Black" day, meeting blocks 5, 6, 7, and 8.

PLUSES AND MINUSES OF A BLOCK SCHEDULE

Here are some advantages offered by this type of schedule for foreign languages:

♦ The teacher has more time to teach.

Foreign language classes of 80 minutes or longer make it possible and easier to: do significant research; engage in a prolonged conversation or seminar; view a movie-length video; complete a whole set of learning centers; do a lengthy cultural simulation; or have a guest speaker. In short, teachers are motivated to employ a variety of instructional activities other than lecture. (Note: Doing so also makes the 80 minutes much less tiring for the teacher!)

♦ Usable instruction time increases.

Because of fewer class changes and the unavoidable class opening and closing activities, students will spend more actual time thinking, speaking, and so forth, in the target language. More time on task, especially in such a concentrated fashion, should translate into more learning taking place. The block also offers time for a greater diversity of activities, such as field trips, guest speakers, student speeches and skits, and for better use of audiovisual and computer-oriented resources, as well as for getting involved in community service opportunities (such as teaching English to Spanish-speaking people with a literacy coalition, or helping at a grade school with Spanish-speaking children).

♦ Students are more likely to continue taking a foreign language, because the block increases their options (number of classes they may take).

If they were having trouble fitting your class into their schedule when they had only six choices, with eight they now have room! HINT: Try to have your upper-level classes scheduled during a block that does not have any AP classes offered, or on a day that has the least high homework classes to conflict with it.

♦ Fewer class changes have unexpected benefits.

Less time in the hall means less time to create conflicts that spill over into the classroom (Have you ever had a girl come into your room crying and remain inconsolable for the entire period?). There will be an automatic reduction in the number of tardies and fewer disciplinary referrals. For example, experts recommend that students with attention problems should have a limited number of teachers, a limited number of physical relocations, and a limited number of disruptions throughout the school day. The block is ideal for these students.

♦ Teacher and student have time to "cool down" after classroom incidents occur, because one or more days elapse between classes,

It is easier to confront problems rationally with an extra day to think them over before meeting again. The idea of seeing "problem" students or classes only on alternating days appeals to a lot of teachers. Students report the same feelings about problem teachers.

> Some teachers think the kids need to practice every day in class M-T-W-Th-F to be successful. I think that kids get VERY tired of it and don't participate as much as we would like to think. It becomes routine and boring, so they don't do it. When the practice is every other day, kids are more willing to do things.
>
> Dee F (August 1997, FL-TEACH archives; see References for the Internet address)

♦ Students will do more homework than in the past.

With fewer classes each day, students have less homework to do each evening. They are more likely to do it, and to do a better job of it. Students also have some leeway in planning to do reports and other work. For example, if they have a big game or date one night, they can complete extra work on another night.

♦ Morale will improve.

One teacher reported that she no longer felt as if she had been "hit by a steamroller at the end of the day." Teachers of 30+ years say the block has "energized" them. The combination of less stress (fewer students, less paperwork) and enhanced potential for creativity is "a winner."

Of course, the Alternate-Day schedule has several issues or concerns that must be dealt with for it to be successful. One is the need for balance. Teachers must have a planning period each day. This is easy in an eight-block schedule, but more difficult in a six- (when a teacher is teaching five courses) or seven-block schedule. Suggestions to handle this can be found in Canady and Rettig (1995, Chap. 7) or in Tanner et al. (1995).

> Teacher planning time is a VERY IMPORTANT ISSUE. We came back in the fall and found out that we were to have a prep period every OTHER day. It is EXTREMELY EXHAUSTING to teach four blocks in one day with no prep. When you add before- or after-school meetings and hall or cafeteria duties, it is almost physically and mentally impossible to get through the week. My colleagues, even the energetic and young ones, are complaining of stress all the time. If your school is still in the talking stage, be sure to guard your prep time.
>
> Janet B. (February 1996, FLTEACH archives)

Students also must have carefully balanced schedules so that all their difficult classes do not fall on the same day, or all the benefits of the block may be lost! At our school (and many others), teachers rate their classes as High, Medium, or Low homework, and the guidance staff endeavor to schedule students with no more than two "high homework" classes per day.

Another issue is deciding what to do if school should be canceled due to something such as an electrical problem or inclement weather. For example: Should the school stick to the schedule or "slide" the schedule based on the number of days missed? Sliding may make problems for guest speakers, field trips, and other activities, so most schools choose to just consider the day canceled, making up any inequalities in Day 1/Day 2 numbers toward the end of a grading period (Canady & Rettig, 1996).

Teachers often are concerned with how to fill a longer period of instructional time and maintain students' attention. The answer is to provide a variety of activities, especially of the cooperative learning type. Chapters 3 and 4 deal with this concern in great detail.

Teachers on the block schedule also need to have a well-planned method for helping absent students catch-up on work missed. Students with poor attendance suffer more on a block schedule, as they miss more work than on a traditional schedule. Remember, though, that the students have fewer teachers to check with, and fewer classes to catch-up with, which should benefit both the teacher and the student who was absent.

Teachers also are often worried that, with a day off between classes, they will need to spend more time reviewing what was taught, because students have had more time to forget what they had learned. While some teachers report an increased need for review, it is not crippling; many teachers design lessons that have a built-in review activity at the beginning of each day. A majority of the teachers who replied to my posting on the Internet were quite positive about the Alternate-Day block, stating that they believed the extended period of time spent learning compensated for other concerns.

> It is important to give specific and SUBSTANTIAL homework, more than they can finish in one sitting, to encourage them to interact with the L2 on a daily basis, though the class only meets twice weekly.
>
> Carolina M. (March 1995, FLTEACH archives)

> I'm in a middle school that has ALWAYS had foreign language on an A/B schedule. I've got 75-minute classes every other day for the whole year, and I love it. I find that the kids don't forget their homework, and it's such an advantage because I can let them do more "hands on" learning and activities. This is the 2nd year that we've been on the block. It's really worked out great for us!
>
> Susan 4361 (July 1997, FLTEACH archives)

> It took me a while to trust myself and the students enough to let them struggle with activities while I circulated and gave pointers. The atmosphere, both in the classroom and the school at large, became more centered and less frantic and constantly confrontational. Basically, though, the block schedule forced me to improve (or at least vary) my teaching. I think it's also fair to say that while we may have "covered" somewhat less, what we did was better absorbed by most.
>
> Jim (July 1997, FLTEACH archives)

Teachers also are concerned that going to a block schedule will increase class sizes. Most foreign language teachers do see a small increase in class size, but primarily in the upper level classes, which were not overloaded to begin with. More students taking more advanced classes is a good thing!

> It (the block) has helped our upper level course enrollment since the students don't have to choose between a language and something else. Singleton courses can now be scheduled at different times so that students CAN take them.
>
> Beth D. (November 1996 , FLTEACH archives)

Some of the pluses and minuses for a block schedule, based upon lists from Yorktown and Springfield High Schools, are found in Figure 1.1.

To summarize, the Alternate-Day schedule offers many advantages over daily, single-period schedules. A few additional positive aspects of this schedule can be found at the end of the section on the 4/4 Semester Plan. However, in order to contrast this schedule with the next type, consider these facets of the Alternate-Day schedule, which remain unchanged from the daily, single-period schedule:

- Teachers still work with 100–180 students and must keep records on that many students for the entire year.

- Teachers still have just as many (up to six) different preparations, every week, all year.

- Students still have six to eight different classes to be responsible for, all year long.

- Students have few opportunities to accelerate; in four years, they can only take four levels of foreign language.

If they are failing the class, even early in the year, students must either remain in that class for the rest of the year, or drop it and wait until the following school year to take it again.

THE 4/4 BLOCK

The 4/4 block, or semester/semester plan, or "accelerated" schedule, deals with some of these issues not addressed by the Alternate-Day schedule. In a 4/4 schedule, students enroll in four classes that meet for approximately 90 minutes each day. Typically, teachers teach three classes and have one preparation period. A class that was formerly offered over a year's time is now condensed into one-half of the school year; classes that were formerly half-year classes now take only one-fourth of the school year. Halfway through the school year, the student takes four different classes during Semester II.

FIGURE 1.1. PLUSES AND MINUSES OF A BLOCK SCHEDULE

Teacher Positives

A longer prep every day
Only three classes per day
Interdisciplinary teaching possibilities
Not as many preparations each day
More one-on-one time with students
More time for cooperative learning, class
    discussion, projects, speeches, use of AV
    resources
Fewer students each day
Longer lunch periods
Two days to grade papers
More opportunity to assist students
Review and reteach on the same day
Less stress for preparation
A chance to know students as individuals
Students every other day
Less time lost moving from class to class
Fewer disciplinary problems
Mini-immersion element
Planning time to get things done

Teacher Negatives

Increased class sizes in some
    classes
Make-up work for absent
    students
Greater creativity from teachers
    required
Only see students every other
    day
First year on block required
    many adjustments
Homework
Need to be very organized

Student Positives

More time to organize and prepare for classes
Two evenings to complete homework
Less stress to prepare fewer classes each day
Extra day to prepare for tests
More time to finish tests
Fewer opportunities to be tardy
More comparable to college schedules
More individual help from teachers
Boring classes every other day
Different classes every other day
Longer lunch periods
Don't see same teachers every day
More in-depth discussions on subjects and
    studying

Student Negatives

Friends in class only on alter-
    nate days
Longer classes sometimes boring
    or tiring
Things forgotten between days
Homework put off too long be-
    cause of extra day
Lots of homework when absent

This list, from comments received from both Yorktown H.S. and Springfield H.S., which are on an A/B or Alternate-Day schedule, was compiled from surveys given to teachers. It does not list all the possible positives or negatives, but gives a good feel for how the block is regarded.

I find it interesting (and somewhat amusing) that teachers list seeing students every other day as both a positive and a negative aspect of this form of the block! Also note that the positives list is much longer than the negatives, for both students and teachers.

It may be easier to visualize a 4/4 schedule if you can picture an Alternate-Day schedule. Instead of being offered on alternate days, classes are offered on alternate semesters. The four classes on a "red" day become the student's schedule for the first half-year; the student finishes that set of classes and then changes to the other set of classes ("black") at the second semester.

Once again, classes are designated High, Medium, and Low homework classes, and students' schedules must be balanced from semester to semester so that they are not taking all the difficult classes at once. The original idea for this sort of schedule came from summer school studies, where marked achievement was noticed when students had longer, more "intense" classes. It was originally dubbed the Copernican schedule because, like Copernicus, it seemed to fly in the face of tradition (Carroll, 1994).

The 4/4 block offers these advantages to a foreign language teacher:

♦ You work with fewer students.

During each half-year (roughly half), you will keep records on only half the number of students and grade half the number of papers and final exams. You only have to learn half the number of names and faces at one time. This makes it easier for you to get to know students more quickly and to develop a good working relationship with them.

♦ You have (usually) fewer preparations each "semester."

You will teach only three classes at any one time. Because the 4/4 schedule does involve rethinking the pacing of your curriculum and possibly redesigning some lessons; and because you are teaching for a longer period of time each day and need to cover a year's work in a semester; a caring administrator would see to it that you have no more than two preparations at one time.

♦ You have a longer and more useful planning time (usually an entire 90 minutes).

This makes it much easier to rethink and redesign, as well as to develop a more varied lesson plan.

♦ Fewer texts are needed than on other schedules.

With fewer students during any one "semester," your school will need fewer books. This could be used, by a resourceful teacher, to justify the purchase of some needed videos, software or supplementary texts. Use your powers of persuasion!

♦ Classes still meet every day (some teachers want this, and some do not).

> For two years we were on a partial block schedule. Three days a week we ran our regular 7-period (50 min.) classes. The other two days we taught half the amount of classes for 90 minutes each. The biggest complaint teachers had, including myself, was the fact that we didn't meet with the students every day. We didn't even consider the A/B schedule as a result of this.
>
> Beth D. (November 1996, FLTEACH archives)

♦ Students take only four classes at one time.

This means that the foreign language class should be one of their two more difficult classes. The students have more time to concentrate on learning the foreign language, and with fewer distractions. More homework will be turned in than before. This means that students also will feel less stress, less pressure than when taking six or seven classes at once. (I recently heard from a foreign language teacher whose school is on a 10-block (5/5). They have shorter block periods, but feel that the 5/5 format offers more options for students. She says her foreign language program enrollment has increased significantly since they went to the block.)

♦ Students can take MORE foreign language classes.

With eight options per year instead of six or seven, it is easy for students to double-up on foreign language classes and stay with the language longer because they have more choices in their class schedule.

♦ Teachers and students have two "fresh starts" each year.

If you have the "class from Hell," you can say good-bye to them at midyear and start anew with a different group. If a student rubs you the wrong way, it is much easier to tolerate the situation; just keep saying, "It's only ___ more weeks."

There are also some educational ramifications to the "fresh start" idea. First, if a student is failing the class, he or she may audit for the remaining time and retake it the next semester, if it is offered, instead of having to wait until the following school year; or the student may drop the class and try again at the next possible opportunity. Students also may elect to retake a class for better understanding—mastery learning. This is also a possibility for students who have poor attendance due to situations beyond their control such as illness or accident. Although they might be capable of doing the work in a 4/4 block schedule, the pressure on the teacher to spend hours helping these students catch up is lessened; it is just as easy for them to audit, or drop and retake, just like students who are failing. My daughter's friend was in a similar situation her senior year. She dropped out for several weeks, came back the following semester, healthy and with a renewed determination to succeed, re-enrolled in her required classes, and was still able to graduate with her classmates. In a traditional or an Alternate-Day schedule, that would have been much more difficult for her to accomplish.

Also, more states and school districts are mandating extended learning time (XL) for slower students. On its Internet home page, Wichita North High School lists this need for more XL time as its primary reason for choosing a block schedule for the 1997–98 school year. (This Internet address is included in the References section at the end of the chapter.)

Another wonderful aspect of the "fresh start" is the opportunity for acceleration for students who do NOT have problems. Your students could, and should be advised to take Level 1 and Level 2 classes consecutively. An interested student can take as much foreign language as he or she wishes, and if there is a college or university nearby, the student could possibly proceed directly to the college's program to earn college credit while still in high school. The upper level classes will have more students enrolled in them, and there is a possibility of adding more classes (or more languages) to your school's curriculum.

> I teach in the block schedule (4 X 4) in high school, and have found my students to be working a lot harder than in the previous traditional schedule.
>
> Karina (January 1995, FLTEACH archives)

> We have found that the pace works well for the cognitive level of the middle school student as well as for the program....We consistently hear from high school teachers that the students who go through this middle school program are far better prepared for their level II classes than the students who wait until high school and do level I in a single year. The ones who were never terrific foreign language students in the middle school always have the chance to repeat a level I class in the same or a different language (many more choices in the high schools) and have gotten a good foundation.
>
> Shar H. (February 1997, FLTEACH archives)

> Last year was one of my best in 16 years of teaching. STRESS level was WAY DOWN, in addition to ILLNESS among faculty and students. The most challenging thing for me was keeping up with the papers. It's a must that they get graded and returned A.S.A.P. with this type of schedule. I saw a change in many of the students in terms of their taking on responsibility for their learning. They learned very quickly that if they fell behind, it was difficult to catch up.
>
> Beth D. (August 1996, FLTEACH archives)

Acceleration is where the 4/4 block has a lot to add to a foreign language curriculum. It is possible for a student to take eight years of language in this schedule. What a student should do about acceleration possibilities depends on what the student's reasons are for taking the language. A student whose desire is to take the AP (Advanced Placement) examination should take a minimum of five years of a language; it is a very difficult test. Students whose desire is merely for proficiency in a college requirement could take less, but they should take the language during the senior year so they are still well acquainted with it. Figure 1.2 (found on pp. 16–17) shows how a student could choose to accelerate language study on the 4/4 block schedule.

As you can see in Option A of the illustration, a student who really needs to be fluent (perhaps in order to be an exchange student) could double-up on classes and take all the levels offered. If, as in our case, there is a local college or university, then the possibility of continuing coursework at the college level is open to that student. However, if that is not the case, then that student would perhaps rather take a schedule such as the second one in Option A of Figure 1.2, which would maintain the student's study of the language throughout high school. If a student wishes to pass the AP exam, or even place well in a college entrance placement test, he or she should take the language during the senior year so that it remains fresh because of recent study.

Acceleration also makes it possible for a student who is good at languages to double up or even triple up on language study. Option B of Figure 1.2 shows a possible schedule for a student wishing to study two languages. This occurs fairly frequently in the block schedule, with some schools reporting students who take three or four languages, as shown in Option C. There are several bits of advice I offer to students who take two or more languages. Several studies indicate the existence of interference between languages; for example, Italian and Spanish, or Spanish and Portuguese seem to be subject to negative interference, whereby students forget which language is which, and mix up words and verb endings. An additional point to consider is that taking more than two languages means less proficiency in both, since the student cannot take the uppermost levels of either. However, for a student who wishes simply to be conversant with several languages, the block offers more elective time in which to pursue this interest.

OTHER CONSIDERATIONS

There are a few negative aspects to the 4/4 or intensive block schedule that particularly affect foreign language teachers. The first is the issue of holidays. Note that in the 4/4 schedule, students in the first half of the year are able to celebrate Christmas, Oktoberfest, and el Día de los Muertos, while students in the second half will not; however, students in the second half are able to celebrate Mardi Gras/Fasching/Carnaval, Cinco de Mayo, and other winter or spring events. Some teachers feel strongly that all students should experience every holiday; I feel that videos or the foreign language club can make up in part for what is missed.

The second issue is the foreign language club. Students are much easier to contact and involve in a French/Spanish/German club if they are currently taking a class in that language. Some adjustments may need to be made so that students not enrolled in a language for the full year are still informed of activities and are able to participate in fundraisers and other traditions you have established for your students.

Another consideration is transfer students. If your students transfer to a nonblock school, they will be way ahead due to the nature of the block, so no problem; but students coming into your school will probably be so far behind that placing them that semester will not be feasible. Hopefully, they would be able to resume their studies the very next semester, but if that level class is not offered, they will have a very long wait, and they may forget quite a bit. They may wish to audit the class for no credit rather than sit out for a whole year.

TRIMESTER PLANS

The trimester schedule is an attempt to address both the need for blocks of time in which to teach, and the need for time in which to provide extended learning opportunities for slower learners. The trimester plan involves shorter, more intense classes, with students taking six to nine classes a year. In a trimester schedule, students take two or three classes for a period of approximately 60 days, then a different two or three for another 60 days, and then a third set of classes to finish the school year.

This option provides extended learning time as follows: if a student is not doing well in a class, instead of receiving a failing grade at the end of the first trimester, the student just continues to take that class during the next portion of the trimester; the instant repeat without the stigma of an F seems to help many

Figure 1.2. Possible Student Schedules to Maximize Foreign Language Study on a 4/4 Block Schedule

OPTION A: Intensive study of a single language.

OPTION A, 1: Continuous language study:

	Semester 1	Semester 2
Year 1	Spanish 1	Spanish 2
Year 2	Spanish 3	Spanish 4
Year 3	Spanish 5	Spanish 6
Year 4	Advanced Placement	

This student could also enroll in college courses after Year 3 if that option is available, or could participate in an exchange program during Year 4.

OPTION A, 2: A similarly focused schedule, but one that would not use up as many student electives, is:

	Semester 1	Semester 2
Year 1	Spanish 1	Spanish 2
Year 2	Spanish 3 either semester	
Year 3	Spanish 4 either semester	
Year 4	Spanish 5	AP Spanish

OPTION B: Two languages, with AP for one and college proficiency for both.

OPTION B, 1: Uses only one elective option per semester

	Semester 1	Semester 2
Year 1	Spanish 1	Spanish 2
Year 2	Spanish 3	French 1
Year 3	French 2	Spanish 4
Year 4	French 3	AP Spanish

OPTION B, 2: Uses more than one elective at times:

	Semester 1	Semester 2
Year 1	Spanish 1	Spanish 2
Year 2	French 1	French 2
	Spanish 3 either semester	
Year 3	French 3	French 4
	Spanish 4 either semester	
Year 4	French 5	AP Spanish

OPTION C: Study of as many languages as possible.

	Semester 1	*Semester 2*
Year 1	Spanish 1	Spanish 2
Year 2	French 1	French 2
Year 3	German 1	German 2
Year 4	Japanese 1	Japanese 2
	and Level 3 (or 3 and 4) of favorite language*	

*Students wishing college proficiency would be advised to take these levels during the final year of high school.

students succeed, especially ninth graders, with whom this type of schedule seems to have been quite successful (Canady & Rettig, 1996).

The trimester schedule continues to provide the benefits of a large block of time in which to teach, as well as plenty of opportunity for either acceleration or remediation, and, like the 4/4 block plan, has the same issues or problems to deal with. In the trimester schedule, a motivated student could take 12 years' worth of language instruction. Figure 1.3 is shows how an accelerated language schedule could look on a trimester plan.

GENERALLY OBSERVED RESULTS ON A BLOCK SCHEDULE

Here is a summary of the findings from schools across the country; of course, not all schools experience each and every advantage or problem listed:

- ◆ Teachers in schools that take a year to research the change, followed by a year of planning and training, experience some success their first year on the block. Teachers at schools that have less time and training to help them adjust often have a mixed experience, with some initial drop-off in some areas. Give yourself and the new schedule more than one year before beginning comparison studies.

- ◆ Initially, there may be greater stress for teachers learning how to plan for a larger block of time, but eventually the school environment becomes less stressful for both teachers and students.

FIGURE 1.3. FOREIGN LANGUAGE ACCELERATION OPTIONS ON A TRIMESTER SCHEDULE

OPTION A: Student takes 3 levels of 4 languages

The student wishes basic knowledge of as many languages as possible.

NOTE: Any fluency in the first language taken (Spanish in this model) will be lost by the end of the fourth year due to interference between languages and the time that elapsed since study; however, basic knowledge should survive.

	Trimester 1	Trimester 2	Trimester 3
Year 1	Spanish 1	Spanish 2	Spanish 3
Year 2	German 1	German 2	German 3
Year 3	French 1	French 2	French 3
Year 4	Japanese 1	Japanese 2	Japanese 3

Option B: Student takes 3 levels of 3 languages

Option B, 1: The slower student could take a remediation class between first and second year would ensure learning the basics. Other students who took "time off" between levels of language could also take the remediation class before continuing.

NOTE: This type of retake/remediation option is one of the great strengths of the trimester plan!

	Trimester 1	Trimester 2	Trimester 3
Year 1	Spanish 1	Spanish remediation	Spanish 2
Year 2	Spanish 3	German 1	German remediation
Year 3	German 2	French 1	French remediation
Year 4	French 2	German 3	French 3

Option B, 2: The stronger student, who wishes to retain both more of the languages taken and more fluency, spreads language study over several years.

	Trimester 1	Trimester 2	Trimester 3
Year 1	Spanish 1	Spanish 2	German 1
Year 2	German 2	Spanish remediation	Spanish 3
Year 3	French 1	French 2	German remediation
Year 4	German 3	French remediation	French 3

Option C: Student takes 6 levels of 2 languages

The student wishes extreme fluency in two languages. This student would be able to pass the Advanced Placement (AP) exam in both languages.

	Trimester 1	*Trimester 2*	*Trimester 3*
Year 1	Spanish 1	Spanish 2	Spanish 3
Year 2	Spanish 4	French 1	French 2
Year 3	Spanish 5	French 3	French 4
Year 4	Spanish 6/AP	French 5	French 6/AP

Option D: Student takes 4 levels of 3 languages

The student enjoys languages and wishes to take as many languages as possible while remaining fluent in them.

	Trimester 1	*Trimester 2*	*Trimester 3*
Year 1	Spanish 1	Spanish 2	Spanish 3
Year 2	German 1	German 2	German 3
Year 3	French 1	French 2	French 3
Year 4	Spanish 4	German 4	French 4

> All in all, I think it [the block] worked very well in the foreign language classroom. There always seemed to be time to get going in a skit or with an activity. In one class, a concept could be presented, practiced, used, and even tested before the bell rang. There seemed to be time for the students to "get into" the language—and often I heard them comment about how it took them a while to operate in English again after 100 minutes of French!
>
> Marfam (May 1995, FLTEACH archives)

♦ On a block schedule, opportunities increase for interdisciplinary teaching.

♦ No report mentions any increase in discipline problems; many mention lower rates.

♦ Both student and teacher attendance will improve. Unless special plans are in operation, students will experience some difficulty recovering from absences. There is, however, some evidence that the "more motivated" students are absent less frequently on the block.

For the ones who hate school, we need to do a lot more than provide a block schedule.

> I can also offer information from our students' point of view. I had the pleasure of having the top two seniors....Both of them are college-bound seniors and both agreed that under the "old" method they would not have been able to take "fun classes" like art, music, weight-lifting, etc., because they would have been too busy trying to get in all the college prep courses. They probably couldn't even have taken Spanish 3 because there would have been no room. They also liked having two days to do the work because if they worked on it the first night and ran into problems, the next day they could visit with that teacher and try to resolve the problem rather than go to class unprepared.
>
> Dee F. (August 1997, FLTEACH archives)

♦ About 80 percent of teachers on the block lecture less and gradually engage students in more active learning structures. In one 1995 study done in Minnesota, students in longer (block) classes had a higher engagement rate than did students in the shorter, traditional schedule. (Note that teachers at this school received training in developing lessons to engage learners.) (Curry, 1997)

♦ The majority of students will say they like school better; the majority of teachers, after experiencing the block for two years, will report that they favor it and would not choose to go back to the traditional schedule.

♦ Curriculum adjustments need to be made with block schedules, especially with the 4/4 or trimester plans: to accommodate pacing issues (i.e., scheduling Level 1 and Level 2 of a language consecutively); to accommodate student need for more sections of one level due to retakes; or for enrichment (more elective options often means adding more course offerings). Many schools on the 4/4 block have added a fifth-year level foreign language class due to demand; my school now offers a sixth year).

♦ Students who are less passive in learning earn better grades. The number of students with A's and B's will increase. On a 4/4 block, there may also be an increase in students earning F's, until they adjust to the block and its demands (Curry, 1997). This did not happen in our case; Figure 1.4 shows our school's foreign language results on the 4/4 block.)

FIGURE 1.4. FOREIGN LANGUAGE RESULTS FOR THE PERIOD ENDING JUNE 1997

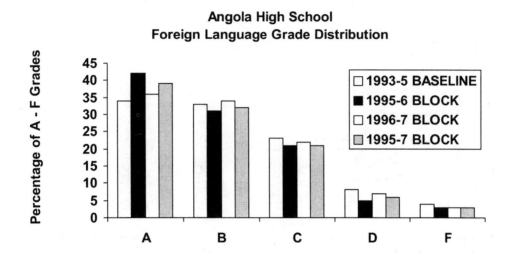

Angola High School
Foreign Language Grade Distribution

- ◆ In both the A/B and 4/4 plans, some foreign language teachers report difficulty covering the equivalent of two classes of material during a double-length period. (Curry, 1997)

ISSUES

WHAT ABOUT RETENTION?

A number of concerns arise when teachers consider a block schedule. The biggest seems to be the issue of retention. It is always normal to begin a new school year with some review of the prior year; but with an Alternate-Day schedule, will students remember what was being done in class two days ago (or, on some Alternate-Day schedules, from Thursday to the following Tuesday)? With the 4/4 block or the trimester there is the potential of having the summer *and* another semester to forget what they have learned. Will extra review or remediation be needed?

Psychological research in the field of learning should reassure us on this issue. Ebbinghaus (1885) memorized lists of nonsense syllables—what could be more similar to what a foreign language is to a first-year student?—and then tested himself on how many he remembered, first every hour for several days, then every day, and then monthly for several years. His results are called the forgetting curve (or the memory curve) in most Psych 101 texts (see Figure 1.5).

FIGURE 1.5. THE MEMORY CURVE (EBBINGHAUS, 1885)

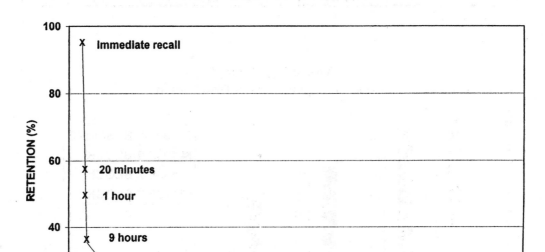

Ebbinghaus found that the most rapid forgetting occurs in the first 9 hours after exposure to new material. However, the rate of forgetting then slows down and declines very little even after many days have passed.

These results show that most forgetting occurred in the first nine hours, with the amount of forgetting slowly tapering off until the second day, and leveling off after a week. The amount of retention at 7 days and at 30 days is virtually the same, and this level continues for several years. Basically, according to this curve, there should be little difference between how much is forgotten over the summer and how much over a summer and a semester.

Any experienced teacher knows how much is forgotten over a weekend, over Christmas break, over spring break, and over the summer. Just mentally apply that as well as Ebbinghaus' study to the block: in an Alternate-Day block, 24 hours' worth of forgetting would have taken place between classes, and a corresponding amount of review would be needed. This could be a legitimate concern for some teachers who also are worried about being able to cover enough material; nevertheless, many teachers view the extended learning time offered as so rewarding that they are willing to make the trade. In addition, even in a traditional schedule, most teachers begin every class with a review activity, so no major changes need to be made.

Teachers going to an accelerated schedule, either the 4/4 block or trimester, are worried about the extended periods of time spent away from the language if students choose to take only one foreign language course per year. Experienced

4/4 block teachers (myself included, though not in this particular study) report that there is little noticeable difference between students who just took the preceding course and those who had a bit more time off between courses (Sessoms, 1995). Again, Ebbinghaus' curve shows little difference in retention between those two lengths of time.

Ebbinghaus' study was a long time ago, you could say, and there was only one subject used. Yes, but scores of graduate students working on masters' and doctoral programs have replicated this study, with many more subjects, and often with the question of whether modern students—the video generation—would perform differently. The first results still hold true today. There is more loss over a longer period of time, but it is slight, as the curve shows. For example, one study in cognitive psychology discovered that students retained 85 percent of major concepts they had studied after a hiatus of 4 months, and 80 percent after 11 months (Semb, Ellis, & Araujo, 1993).

A study often cited by opponents of the block is Smythe et al. (1973), where a small group of students studying French in rural Canada were tested after the summer (three months) and after a summer and a semester off (eight months). This study showed a decrease of four percent in total score as a result of a summer plus a semester off. Yes, according to statistics, that is a "significant difference," but in statistics there is also a concept called "power," in this case based on how many questions there were on the test. With the tests used in that study, that percentage (four percent), in some sections, is actually only one additional question missed! The final words of the study are: "It has been demonstrated that only relatively small changes in second language performance were recorded over reasonably long periods during which students were not receiving instruction. This in turn suggests that the foreign language teacher may not need to mount a particularly extensive programme of review for the skills measured by these tests" (Smythe et al., 1973).

The most important factor in retention seems to be "depth of learning," or how well students learned the material in the first place. An interesting study on language loss (Oxford, 1982) looked at three factors: age, the cognitive aspects just presented above, and the role played by attitude toward the language. The study found that those who began a language in elementary school were superior to those who began in college, but warned that this reflected the advantage of more time for study, not an advantage of youth. The Smythe study was cited in the second section, again with the conclusion that "the results of the two studies do not necessarily suggest that the observed performance changes are large enough to be practically significant."

ATTITUDE IS EVERYTHING

It is the third portion of the study, "Implications for Foreign Language Teaching," that most interests me. It says: "Even in its rudimentary state, research on language loss has already shown that attitudes and motivations toward L2 learning are very important in the maintenance or loss of the language; summer breaks in language study are not necessarily detrimental to L2 maintenance; practice of the L2 in a supportive environment is essential if the L2 is not to be lost" (Oxford, 1982, pp. 167–168). This seems to state quite clearly that what goes on in the classroom is of paramount importance: First, methods of instruction that test only low-level recall, for example, do not encourage depth of learning; a "supportive environment," however, is what is needed. Second, the teacher's attitude is crucial to being successful.

Another aspect of language skill attrition then is, obviously, the instructional factor: Students whose instuctors focus primarily on oral skills show more rapid and extensive loss (attrition) than those whose course of study also included comprehension and writing skills (Reilly, 1988). This factor has heavily influenced the new ACTFL national performance standards, which are discussed later in this chapter. Teachers, while stressing communication, must not neglect the other aspects of the language. The block schedule gives more time to cover all the different aspects of language.

> For grad school at Monterey, CA, I had to complete a research project and chose to look at "The consequences of language attrition on a high school four-period day." I will only give you the "nutshell" version here. Those students who had a "summer-only break" scored much better on an exam given the first day back in French 2 than did those students who had a "semester plus summer break" or those who had a "semester plus summer plus semester break." However, at the end of French 2, when final grades were averaged for each of the three groups, it was discovered that all groups were at the same place. There was a range of .47%, less than 1%, in their scores.
>
> Stephanie P. (September 1996, FLTEACH archives)

Finally, and most importantly, the accelerated block schedules, both 4/4 and trimester, offer another attribute found to be vital to learning and maintaining recall: intensity of instruction. Studies show that the distribution of foreign language study over time is very important. Results from the Ottawa-Carleton Project, for example, indicate that students enrolled in a program where they studied French for half of every day made a lot more progress than students who had the same number of hours of study spread over two years (Stern,

1976). Intensive programs of instruction have been reported again and again, all yielding better results than less intensive programs with the same number of hours of instruction (Edwards, 1976; Williamson, 1968; Larson & Smalley, 1972). These studies suggest that students in a more intensive instructional format use adaptive language acquisition processes that are different from those used by students who learn a language in a traditional schedule (Reilly, 1988). In other words, students who have a longer, more intensive burst of language seem to function better, and they maintain the gain over a longer period of time. The longer block of time in which to teach *is* more intense, and quality learning does take place. This is what I am seeing in my students, and it is my favorite aspect of the block schedule.

There are now hundreds of articles, case reports, and research studies about block scheduling, and "the vast majority of them are positive;…there are no major studies from the United States that are negative to block schedules" (Curry, 1997). However, with that said, I would like to include one caveat to that statement. Every foreign language teacher I spoke with before I went on the block told me that it was absolutely obligatory to have Level 1 and Level 2 classes scheduled consecutively, with no break longer than a summer between them. I have not yet seen or found a study to support this; these teachers were just sharing their own experience. The theory they had developed to support the evidence they saw is that because all the groundwork for comprehending the tenses, sentence structure, and other grammatical needs is not normally covered completely by the end of Level 1, it is very important that Level 2 follow immediately to reinforce and complete the instruction. After these basics are internalized by the students, it does not seem to matter whether the other levels are taken more than one per year; this is just significant for the first-to-second portion of the curriculum. We included that information in our school curriculum guide for students to note when registering for classes, and most follow that warning and register for Levels 1 and 2 the same year. For those who do not, however, we have not often seen the dire consequences we were warned about in terms of struggling students. That does not mean that the advice we were given is not true, of course, because very few students take those classes nonconsecutively. I advise you to inform your scheduling personnel—guidance and/or administration—that the Level 1 to Level 2 sequence is crucial, and that students who struggle too hard in Level 2 are very unlikely to proceed to Level 3, which they need to do to become proficient in the language.

> Currently I have some students in Spanish III who have not had Spanish since their Spanish II course ended last year at the end of January. My observation in terms of retention (after such a long period without exposure to the language) agrees with the "studies" that everyone keeps referring to: the longer gap in time doesn't seem to have had any effect on the students. What I see is that the strong and/or motivated students, as well as the strugglers and less motivated students, are performing at the same level as last year!…In my opinion, the gap between Level 1 and Level 2 needs to be removed. By the time the students hit Levels 3, 4, and up, they have chosen to be in the course; therefore, the motivation to succeed is (supposedly) there and they will do what they need to do to achieve their goals.
>
> Beth D. (October 1996, FLTEACH archives)

As class enrollments show across the nation, there is a lot of attrition (thinning) in enrollment between Level 2 and Level 3. Some of it is due to the difficultyof finding room for a foreign language in a standard schedule. (Going to a block schedule helps alleviate this!) Some of it is due to the fact that in some states, such as Texas, two years are required, but not more. (As long as you make the class stimulating and with more electives possible, the block should assist in maintaining enrollment.) And still more of it is probably due to students falling behind in Level 2 and struggling; when a language is too difficult, learning it is not rewarding to students and they quit. This is where judicious scheduling will help you maintain a contented group of students and, to repeat, this is critical.

CAN I COVER AS MUCH MATERIAL IN AN ACCELERATED BLOCK?

This is the second most important question teachers ask about the 4/4 and trimester schedules. Here is where some good preparation before going to the block pays big dividends: developing a course-pacing guide is necessary to keep you on schedule (see Chapter 2 for a discussion and samples). With a good timetable about what objective you should cover and when, you will be successful. Notice that I did not say, "You will cover just as much," although I actually found myself getting farther in the book than I had ever gotten before. Some teachers I consulted told me that they got through less, but the kids learned it better (less review needed the next year), while others agreed with me in saying we'd never taught as much as we could now with the block.

A pacing guide is also needed in larger schools where several teachers teach the same level class; it is important that they all cover the same material as students may switch from one class to another midway through the course; for example, if they had a "half-year" class and are changing to another during a different block. In a smaller school, pacing is not as great a problem; if you are the only teacher, it is quite easy to remember that you finished one chapter short, and make up the difference the following year. And remember, more of your students are likely to continue taking another level when a block schedule gives them more electives. However, that does not mean you can forgo pacing altogether; finishing three or four chapters short would have horrible consequences for what could be covered the following year!

THE BLOCK MODEL DOES NOT REPLACE "PROCESS" (OR: I CAN'T COVER AS MUCH MATERIAL AS I USED TO)

The block schedule changes what happens when classroom doors are open, with fewer classes per day and so on. However, the key ingredient is what happens when the classroom door is shut. The block is especially suited for individualized instruction with more "quality" assignments. The block provides opportunities for instantaneous feedback; effective evaluation of student achievement; use of a wide variety of teaching methods; and greater accessibility of staff for conferring on pedagogical methods, as well as on projects like interdisciplinary teaching, among other topics listed previously. Only the teacher can decide to take full advantage of all these benefits.

Teachers who use the extra class time as time to do homework, rather than to try something like cooperative learning, are either ignoring or wasting the opportunities offered by the block schedule and are often the ones to complain that the block does not work well. It is not until better effects begin to happen behind the classroom door that the block really begins to work.

The fact remains that there are many foreign language programs where the block is being used successfully. The key is to use this new time strategy more effectively. The rest of this book explains the necessary pieces for success: cooperation in establishing standards for learning and for a well-articulated curriculum, as well as in relying on fellow teachers for support and suggestions (Chapter 2); a willingness to try new ways of structuring a lesson during a class period (Chapter 3) or some teaching strategies with proven success in foreign languages in the block (Chapter 4); and willingness to reevaluate assessment according to your goals and the national standards (Chapter 5). I feel strongly that teachers who complain about not being able to cover enough material need to focus on these strategies:

♦ Setting a pacing guide and sticking to it (Chapter 2)

To stick to a pacing guide, teachers need to reevaluate the assignments they give. If they ask students to do three practice activities because they have always done three and it worked, why not give an assessment after the first one to determine if the second and third are really necessary? One way to survive on the block is to eliminate the "deadwood" from old lesson plans.

◆ Using student-centered learning rather than teacher-centered lecture (Chapter 4)

Many critical teachers refer to these new methods as "playing games" and seem to regard them as a waste of time. Cooperative learning, while more boisterous and noisy than the traditional lecture/individual seatwork, has a firm foundation in educational research and a proven track record. A little training in using it should help, and could shorten the time needed to teach concepts, making it easier to get more material covered.

A teacher wrote me, "I am exhausted with only three classes and fewer students. I attribute the exhaustion to the stress of trying to hold their attention for 85 minutes." This teacher is obviously trying to remain the center of attention in the classroom (and probably using too much lecture). The individual needs to learn more about how to be the "guide on the side." One does not need to hold the class's attention; all that is necessary is to see that they are on-task and learning together.

Educational authority William Glasser, after much research and practice, developed a scale that shows how much learning takes place depending on the strategy employed in teaching and on student behavior during that instruction. It is depicted in Figure 1.6 and I have a large version of it hanging in my classroom. Many other educational strategists recommend informing students of what the objective for each day's activity is, at the beginning and the end of class. I not only inform them of the objective, but I frequently explain the method I have chosen for achieving that objective: I keep Glasser's list up and use it to remind my students that if they just listen, they will only retain 20 percent, but if they discuss it with the other students as I asked them to, they will retain 70 percent. Not only is this true, but it is a great motivator for student cooperation .

It is also a great motivator for better lesson plans. Before you write, "Student will do Activity 3 on page 10," think about how to make that writing exercise move down at least one more step on Glasser's scale for greater learning potential. The more high-retention activities you schedule, the less practice is needed, and the faster you can go through the material in the book.

◆ Keeping students engaged

If coverage of material is desired, it also is important that class time be used as efficiently as possible. The use of sponge activities and other active-learning strategies (see Chapter 4) will mean less wasted time; even the minute or so spent erasing the board can be used more constructively.

Active participation methods are a good solution for those who get out their calculators and say, "No wonder I could not get through as much material; by going to the block, we lose 20 hours/2 weeks/500 minutes (or whatever) of

---

FIGURE 1.6. GLASSER'S LEARNING SCALE

WE LEARN…

10% OF WHAT WE READ

20% OF WHAT WE HEAR

30% OF WHAT WE SEE

50% OF WHAT WE BOTH SEE AND HEAR

70% OF WHAT IS DISCUSSED WITH OTHERS

80% OF WHAT WE EXPERIENCE PERSONALLY

95% OF WHAT WE *TEACH* TO SOMEONE ELSE

William Glasser

---

class time from the traditional schedule." Those people believe in the Carnegie Unit, an educational theory or belief that equates "seat time" with learning. (As a result of the Carnegie study, many states have "seat time" requirements.) The problem with that theory is what any classroom teacher knows: students may be in the classroom physically, but it is what is going on mentally that determines how much learning takes place. Using more strategies to keep more students actively involved is more effective than calculating minutes lost.

Also, remember that two 50-minute classes had an average of 5 minutes of startup time (e.g., taking attendance, catching up absent students, passing back papers) for each period; that is halved automatically by block scheduling, and the same is true for the end-of-class time spent explaining homework. To say that 10 minutes were lost by changing two 50-minute periods for one 90-minute period is not accurate when you adjust for less administrative work. Also subtract the average amount of time spent reviewing for a typical day on a traditional schedule because there will be that much less time needed for review when two periods are combined into one. When those adjustments are made, there is little lost time.

♦ Organizing time more efficiently

Consider something as simple as revising classroom routines. Chapter 4 has some useful suggestions on, for example, teaching students to better handle transitions, setting time limits, and getting students' attention, which also pare wasted time from class, leaving more time for education.

LARGE SCHOOL AND SMALL SCHOOL ISSUES AND CONCERNS

For both large and small schools, problems often are rooted in sequencing difficulties over which, unfortunately, teachers do not have much control. In larger schools, most foreign language teachers who report problems have articulation difficulties due to the time that different sections of the same level were scheduled, and sequencing problems when Level 1 and Level 2 are not offered consecutively. In the "best of all possible worlds," the scheduling personnel would listen to an enumeration of what would be best for students:

♦ In an A/B or Alternate-Day schedule, it is best if all sections of the same level are scheduled on the same day. Then any changes due to weather, or assemblies, or testing would affect them equally, and one would not get far ahead or behind the other.

> It's bad enough having a week when a particular class only meets twice. When mother nature (blizzards) or whimsical administrators preempt one of those meetings, you almost despair of getting anything accomplished. Regarding this problem, we finally (after several years) got all the sections of a particular level of a language scheduled on the same day so that big interruptions would have an equal effect on all of them. I remember one winter when one section of Level 1 had met 20% fewer times than another thanks to Lady Luck.
>
> Jim T. (July 1997, FLTEACH archives)

♦ On a 4/4 or a trimester schedule, Levels 1 and 2 of a language should be scheduled consecutively. This means, generally, that at least one Level 1 should be offered in the fall and at least one Level 2 offered in the spring.

Foreign languages, like mathematics, are a subject area where knowledge is learned and taught sequentially. For example, until the numbers are learned, students cannot go on to telling time or doing calendar work. Although there has not been any major scientific research on this, hundreds of teachers on the block have observed severe retention problems when students have too much time off between Levels 1 and 2 of a language. This is not as critical between Levels 2 and 3, and upper levels, probably due to the fact that by then students are well-grounded in the basics of that particular language and also are comfortable with what demands a particular teacher will make upon them.

> The biggest disadvantage is that most students are not able to take two levels of a language in one school year. In other words, they take French I in the fall and French II in the fall of the following school year (or worse, the following spring!). The effects of any sort of immersion environment that you create during the 90-minute period are completely reversed during those "lost months."
>
> Julie H. (July 1997, FLTEACH archives)

I am always surprised that in larger schools, with more staff available to teach classes, more care is not taken to schedule the different levels of language more logically, especially in a 4/4 or trimester schedule. One of the main desired benefits is the possibility of acceleration but, when classes are not always scheduled to make the progression from level to level consecutive, that benefit is lost. Foreign language teachers MUST communicate with schedulers about how severely poor articulation will hurt the students.

♦ In any size school, care also should be taken that the upper level classes of a language, usually offered in singleton form, are not scheduled opposite a highly desirable singleton, such as an AP class or band, which would, of course, limit students' ability to continue studying a language.

♦ Multilevel classes should be avoided whenever possible.

Because of a lack of teachers, small schools have, ironically, some of the same difficulties as large schools do. If there is only one foreign language teacher for two languages, or for two buildings (commuting between middle school and high school, for example), it can be difficult to schedule Levels 1 and 2 consecutively. Singleton classes also abound at a small school; in fact, foreign language teachers at a small school often have another problem generally not found in a larger school: multilevel classes. When enrollment for an upper-level class is small, smaller schools often combine that class with the closest level: Spanish 3/4, Latin 2/3, French 4/5, for example. Sometimes a foreign language class is scheduled with a class from an unrelated discipline such as history or speech. There are even some high schools where the entire foreign language sequence is taught during one single class period!

Multilevel classes are much more difficult to teach: not only are there two (or more) preparations, but it is impossible to do oral work with one group while another works on a lesson in the same room. As a result, most teachers stress reading and writing at the expense of oral work, a technique that does *not* lead to the proficiency demanded by modern standards and society. Not only do students have only half the contact time with the teacher, but classroom management problems also can result when teachers have to teach and try to monitor another group doing seatwork. And, because students do not view foreign languages as easy classes, some might not enroll rather than have a split class.

Obviously, these problems still exist even in a block schedule; however, the block offers some advantages. I know that since the block began at my school, enrollment in upper level courses increased to such an extent that French 5 has been offered as a separate class, rather than as a combined class, for the last two years. This has happened because of the opportunities for acceleration and the increased elective choices offered by our 4/4 block. The administration has also scheduled that class during the spring rather than opposite most of the AP classes in the fall, so it does not have to compete with as many high-homework classes.

Until enrollment increases, however, the block still has all its basic advantages to offer. With more time, there necessarily will be more teacher contact and more time for oral expression than in a traditional, shorter class period. The "immersion-like" effect of working in the language for longer than an hour still would benefit students, as would the variety of learning strategies that could be employed.

Again, communicating with whoever does the scheduling at your building is of prime importance. Things to mention to the scheduler about multilevel classes are:

♦ Because multilevel classes are more difficult to manage, a lower enrollment cap should be set for them. It is recommended that there be no more than 20 students in a multilevel class.

♦ Students in Levels 1 and 2 require much more direction; therefore, these levels should never be combined; it is preferable to put a lower and an upper level together, if need be.

♦ The most effective multilevel classes are those that combine either Levels 3 and 4, or 4 and 5.

♦ Schedule a multilevel class during the period in which lunch is served, if possible. This not only gives the teacher more flexibility, since that period generally is a bit longer, but it also is less likely to be abridged when the school day is shortened, enabling the teacher to have the most time possible for that difficult class.

♦ If the same teacher teaches two languages, schedule classes in the same language back-to-back, so that the teacher does not become mentally exhausted, switching back and forth from one language to the other.

All the above are not only my recommendations but are the result of a study on multilevel classes as well (Strasheim, 1983).

In addition to scheduling concerns, when faced with the fact that there will be multilevel classes of Levels 3 and 4, or 4 and 5 for at least the next several years, a good teaching strategy is based on careful articulation (see Chapter 2): that is, the teacher or teachers of those levels sit down and set up a two-year rotation of topics that includes the chapters mandatory to cover and the activities, cultural topics, field trips, movies, projects, or simulations that need to be done. (There is an example of this at the end of Chapter 2.) Make sure the more attractive (to students) options are equally split between the two years to maximize enrollment for both years, and teach it as basically one class that takes two years to complete (or two half-years in the accelerated block), instead of teaching it as a multilevel class. Many upper-level textbooks are ideally written for doing this. Because my French series has two chapters on subjunctive, two on *si*-clauses, and so on, it divides quite nicely for use over two years.

NOT ALL PROBLEMS ARE DUE TO THE BLOCK SCHEDULE

> *"It is unfair to 'slam' a sound concept because of poor implementation, complex politics, top-down management, lack of resources, or insufficient training for teachers at one school."*
>
> Hottenstein, 1996

Many of the negative comments from foreign language teachers about the block are not due to the block at all, but to situations such as those described by Hottenstein. Poor implementation, for example, would be a block with severe scheduling problems such as those described in the previous section.

Poor implementation also would include giving a teacher too many preps the first year on the block, and continuing to allow many interruptions to the school schedule. "Although we were promised that interruptions would be minimal, they are just as frequent as before: athletic trips, band and choir trips, field trips, assemblies, etc., etc.," a foreign language teacher wrote on the FLTEACH (Internet) list, pointing out also that, in a block schedule, these represent an even larger percentage of class time than ever before. Missing one block period is roughly equivalent to missing two days under a traditional schedule. Schools on the block should recognize this and severely limit field trips.

I recommend that, for the most part, field trips be limited to those that can be done during one block period. Some schools, like mine, have teacher committees that must approve all interruptions of class time; some even have devised creative arrangements for doing state proficiency testing so as not to disturb each block more than twice, a very good idea!

COUNTERPRODUCTIVE BEHAVIORS

"Complex politics and top-down management" often mean situations in which the block is forced on an unwilling or unready staff. One school I know of was informed by its principal that it was going to the block. The faculty agreed and asked for a year in which to prepare through visitations, workshops, and inservices, but were denied that year. In general, teachers at that school felt angry rather than excited about going to the block, fearful rather than motivated. A fairly common teacher complaint on the Internet is that "out of the blue" the teacher was informed that he or she would be teaching on the block.

Here's an example of complex politics: "Prior to a faculty vote, teachers were told that if the block were not implemented, electives would be eliminated and teachers would be laid off. So, a vote against the block would in fact be a vote against music, art, and foreign language, anything that is not a graduation requirement" (FLTEACH archives). Threats do not make for good staff morale, nor do unwilling teachers make a good transition to the block or even approach it with an open mind to its possibilities.

Lack of resources also can be a severe handicap. Imagine being presented with the block and all the time for doing exciting new projects, only to learn that the school library is woefully inadequate for the research; or that the computer lab is not available for a Web-related project; or that the school only has one video camera; or that it cannot afford a language laboratory just yet. Minimum technology for the block should be a television and VCR for every classroom, and one computer. Foreign language teachers also need a language laboratory for effective listening and speaking practice.

Insufficient training was the last limitation mentioned by Hottenstein. Suggestions on training can be found in Chapter 2. I also suggest that the school library begin building a professional library for use by teachers who would like suggestions for activities for block schedules. At the end of this chapter, is a bibliography (by no means exhaustive) of good books I have come across in my own research; any additions to the list for future revisions of this text are welcome.

Finally, the last words of the quote were "at one school." Be wary of the technique in logic called "glittering generalizations." In this method of faulty reasoning, one case proves the rule: if one school has a less than perfect experience, the block is bad; if one student has low test scores, the whole concept is at fault. Be wary, especially, of the type related to "urban legends," the "I know someone whose aunt's neighbor's daughter was on the block and she didn't like it at all." Try to ignore hearsay. The block cannot cure every problem with modern education.

HOW DO SUBSTITUTE TEACHERS HANDLE THE BLOCK?

Perhaps you are lucky enough to have substitute teachers who have experience with and knowledge of the language you teach; many of us are not so fortunate. If it is difficult to leave lesson plans for a shorter class period, how can it be done on the block? First, remember that statistics show that there are fewer teacher absences on block schedules. This may be due to the more stress-free teaching under the block (no more "illness, I'm sick of school" excuses), and it may be because it is a bit more difficult to have an untrained substitute take over a foreign language class.

Before our school went on the block, we offered training sessions on the block schedule for individuals on the substitute list. Volunteers were paid to attend and their attendance moved them higher on the list of people to call. These sessions included both a description of the block and new school rules such as for attendance and hall passes; but more importantly, the substitutes saw some typical lesson plans and received a little training in cooperative learning. As a follow-up, we offered additional training for substitutes on learning strategies that work well in the block. Several people attended and appreciated the chance to do so. For example, several told me they intend to develop a list of sponge activities (see Chapter 4) for use when a teacher's lesson plan is too short or just not working well.

But not all substitute teachers attend these sessions, so the best insurance for a successful day is to leave good, detailed lesson plans *and* well-trained classes. Just as on a day when you are teaching, the lesson plans should include a variety of activities (with one adjustment: written work should be done in pairs or in groups for more self-checking possibilities and feedback because the teacher is not around to supply that), as well as opportunities for student movement. Also inform the substitute of your expectations (how you have trained your students; e.g., giving them 30 seconds to get in their groups) so that students do not try to take advantage of the substitute. Finally, just as when you are teaching, always have a back up assignment planned in case something does not work or the students complete work faster than expected. Your substitute will thank you for it.

I would add that our substitutes have reacted very favorably to our block schedule, and they are willing to return to substitute a second time after their first experience. Some are parents with children in the system, and they are even more supportive after having spent a day as a teacher in a block schedule.

THE ROLE OF THE BLOCK SCHEDULE IN ENABLING TEACHERS TO MEET THE NEW NATIONAL FOREIGN LANGUAGE STANDARDS

In 1996, the *Standards for Foreign Language Learning: Preparing for the 21st Century* was published. Commonly known as the ACTFL (American Council on the Teaching of Foreign Languages) *Standards for Foreign Language Learning*, they do not attempt to describe the current status of foreign language education; they are a goal to strive for and a gauge against which to measure improvement. Nor are they a curriculum guide. A basic list of these goals and standards is included in Figure 1.7.

The ACTFL *Standards for Foreign Language Learning* suggest types of experiences needed to enable students to meet the standards, as well as support the idea of study over an extended period of time, from elementary through high school and beyond. The bibliography at the end of this chapter contains instructions on how to obtain a complete copy of this document. In addition to the standards, there are sample progress indicators, a rationale for each standard at grades 4, 8, and 12, and learning scenarios.

The key to success in a foreign language is basically learning how to communicate: *knowing how, when, and why to say what to whom.* Those 10 words summarize all the linguistic and social knowledge required for effective human-to-human interaction. Formerly, most foreign language teachers focused on the "how" (grammar) to say "what" (vocabulary); now, the current principles are based on communication proficiency, which also highlights the "why," the "whom," and the "when," the more cultural and sociolinguistic aspects of the language.

UNDERLYING PRINCIPLES

First, the standards include a "Statement of Underlying Principles" that seems to tie in directly with several of the strengths of a block schedule. It says students:

♦ "must have access to language and culture study that is integrated into the entire school experience"

While the block does not automatically do this, it does make interdisciplinary ventures easier to accomplish. Because the content of a foreign language deals with history, geography, social studies, science, math, and the fine arts, it would be easy to get together with some of the staff who have the same prep as you do, and plan some interesting projects together. On the 4/4 block, for example, roughly one-fourth of the faculty should have the same preparation period as you.

FIGURE 1.7. STANDARDS FOR FOREIGN LANGUAGE LEARNING

Goal One: Communicate in Languages Other than English

Standard 1.1 Students engage in conversations, provide and obtain information, express feelings and emotions, and exchange opinions.

Standard 1.2 Students understand and interpret written and spoken language on a variety of topics.

Standard 1.3 Students present information, concepts, and ideas to an audience of listeners or readers on a variety of topics.

Goal Two: Gain Knowledge and Understanding of Other Cultures

Standard 2.1 Students demonstrate knowledge and understanding of the tradition, ideas and perspectives, the literary and artistic expressions, and other components of cultures being studied.

Goal Three: Connect with Other Disciplines and Acquire Information

Standard 3.1 Students reinforce and further their knowledge of other disciplines through the foreign language.

Standard 3.2 Students acquire information and perspectives that are only available through the foreign language and within culture.

Goal Four: Develop Insight into Own Language & Culture

Standard 4.1 Students recognize that different languages use different patterns to communicate and can apply this knowledge to their own language.

Standard 4.2 Students recognize that cultures use different patterns of interaction and can apply this knowledge to their own culture.

Goal Five: Participate in Multilingual Communities & Global Societies

Standard 5.1 Students use the language both within and beyond the school setting.

Standard 5.2 Students use the language for leisure and personal enrichment.

The block also provides many more opportunities for longer simulations and role-playing experiences within the classroom which serve to bring in the "real world" to a greater extent.

 ♦ "will benefit from the development and maintenance of proficiency in more than one language"

As already discussed, any block schedule provides students with more elective choices, enabling more students to continue taking the language longer than before, and thereby maintaining their proficiency. The intensive nature of the 4/4 and trimester blocks enables students to learn language in a way that favors retention, and also makes it possible for students to accelerate their studies, taking more levels of one language, or taking a second foreign language.

◆ "must learn in a variety of ways and settings"

The longer chunks of time found in a block schedule offer more opportunity to experiment with and practice a broad variety of language-learning strategies, appealing to a variety of learning styles: the use of images and items from real life for sharpening perception, a wide variety of physical activities and games, involvement in roleplay and other dramatic activities, the use of music in both receptive and participatory ways, and learning experiences that call for sequencing, memorizing, problem solving and inductive and deductive reasoning.

◆ "will acquire proficiency at varied rates"

The block is specifically designed so that motivated students can accelerate their studies, and less capable students can audit/retake (in the 4/4 block) or opt for an extended learning period (in the trimester schedule) to learn at their own speed.

◆ "can achieve success"

Because more and more students are now being required to take a foreign language, rather than just the top 10 percent as was the case, adaptations like those offered by a block schedule will serve to maximize student success and minimize frustration for both the student and the teacher.

With this philosophy in mind, the ACTFL task force identified five goal areas: *Communication, Cultures, Connections, Comparisons,* and *Communities*, the "five C's" of foreign language education. In the remainder of this section, we discuss these goals, emphasizing how the block will help accomplish each.

FIVE GOAL AREAS

GOAL ONE: COMMUNICATE IN LANGUAGES OTHER THAN ENGLISH

Three modes of communication are presented: the Interpersonal/Negotiated, which uses speaking, listening, reading, and writing skills with the goal of conversing or corresponding in the target language (two-way interaction); the Interpretive, which involves "one-way" reading or listening to texts, movies, radio and TV broadcasts, or speeches; and the Presentational, which involves "one-way" writing or speaking, reports, articles, or speeches. The latter two modes differ significantly from the notion of comprehension defined as "understanding a text with an American mindset," concentrating more on bridging the cultural gap through a knowledge of culture developed over time and through exposure. Obviously, proficiency in all three modes is required in an increasingly global society and would be beneficial in finding a job.

The list of activities that enhance communication includes: games, activities with partners and groups, expressing ideas in more ways than one, having a pen pal (maybe a "keypal" over the Internet), planning events and activities to be carried out in the foreign language, acquiring goods and services through basic, culturally appropriate behavior, exchanging ideas with members of the culture through guest speakers and field trips, comparing current events as covered by local and foreign media, watching authentic presentations and interpreting through verbal and nonverbal cues, performing scenes from plays, reciting poetry, and keeping a diary.

Imagine how much easier it would be to do some of these activities if you could explain the assignment, complete it, and discuss it all in one class period, instead of using two, three, or four separate days. This is a major strength of the block schedule. Simulations, movies, guest speakers, field trips, journal writing, cross-cultural comparison studies, and so on, are easy to do in one block, and still have more time left the same day (if you wish) for other endeavors.

GOAL TWO: GAIN KNOWLEDGE AND UNDERSTANDING OF OTHER CULTURES

Culture, as defined by the ACTFL standards, is more than just looking at authentic objects or studying the history, literature, fine arts, and science of another country. It is the values, common ideas, perspectives, and behavior patterns unique to a group and through which the group views and evaluates other cultures. It is important to provide learning activities that allow students to experience (and, ideally, interact with) the culture(s) associated with the target language, with an emphasis on being sensitive to and understanding the cultural differences of others.

This means teaching gestures, story telling, celebrations such as birthdays, games unique to the culture, popular music/dance, use of color, clothing, sports, or cinematography to identify similarities and differences and to understand the significance of these things in the target culture.

These are exactly the sorts of activities that are almost mandated by a block schedule: to vary the menu of activities from just book-paper-pencil stuff and to provide for student movement during the class period (see Chapter 3 on the requirements for a block lesson plan). Teachers on the block try to include more of these than ever before, and they love the results: "I used to play a game maybe once a week; now we do a short one every day: vocab bee, tres en raza, Simon dice, Concentracion."

GOAL THREE: CONNECT WITH OTHER DISCIPLINES AND ACQUIRE INFORMATION

In this goal, the foreign language classroom serves as an organizer by preparing the student to access information through technology, interviews, newspapers, magazines, and other sources. With this information, students then are able to open doors to experiences that will enrich their education in other classes and spill over into their lives outside school walls. For example, by studying German classical music, students could become aware of some of the composer's contemporaries and begin reading their works (scientific or literary), or recognize the music in its use in a movie, commercial, or to convey mood in a short story. They even might learn to pursue a topic further simply for personal interest, a springboard toward lifelong language use.

The block schedule presents longer periods of time in which teachers can require students to research topics (the Internet, described in Chapter 4, is a wonderful motivator) and explain them to others. In addition, through block scheduling, interdisciplinary units set up by cooperating teachers are also much easier to organize and accomplish: at various stages, a foreign language teacher could teach names and events in history, concepts and processes in science, story problems in math, or structures and genres in English.

GOAL FOUR: DEVELOP INSIGHT INTO THE NATURE OF LANGUAGE AND CULTURE

In this area, students are encouraged to compare, to see themselves as others see them, gaining a deeper understanding of their own language and culture, beliefs, and aspirations. For example, the word "bread" brings up entirely different pictures to an American, a Frenchman, a German, or someone from the Middle East. Concepts such as "cheerleader," "weekend," or "prom" may not even exist in another language and its culture. Learning a foreign language offers an alternative view of the same world.

In a block schedule, issues such as family, income, the environment, wars, and natural disasters can be studied, experienced or simulated, analyzed, and discussed in many different ways. Many of the methods and benefits stated in Goal Two would continue to apply to Goal Four.

GOAL FIVE: PARTICIPATE IN MULTILINGUAL COMMUNITIES AT HOME AND AROUND THE WORLD

Students need to be motivated to learn a language, and the best way to do this is to show them how they personally would benefit from proficiency in another language. In addition to emphasizing language as a good job skill, students should see that another language opens the door to many new leisure activities. Interest in soccer, for example, is increasing—teachers could tap into that interest to motivate students to read articles, watch broadcasts, learn the rules and play (and encourage or even tease each other), all in the target language. Again, the block, presenting a longer time frame for audiovisual resources, including the Internet and guest speakers, is ideal for facilitating this concept.

In conclusion, these goals are achievable by a dedicated teacher in any sort of schedule, but the block schedule can make it easier and more enjoyable. The block schedule provides for less stress for the teacher through less paperwork and more planning time for these new or revised activities. Students also experience less stress when they are able to concentrate more fully on three or four classes and have more options or elective choices, accelerating or lengthening studies to pursue areas of interest to them. More opportunities are available to try activities like cooking, field trips, guest speakers, Internet access, and other options that the teacher never even considered doing before because of time constraints. The block can help you improve the education taking place in your classroom. Just ask yourself, how good is good enough, for you and your students? Then, consider the benefits the block will bring, and give it a chance.

My Favorite Quote, Posted in My Classroom

"While it is possible to change without improving, it is impossible to improve without changing."

Anonymous

AUTHOR'S RECOMMENDATIONS FOR A PROFESSIONAL LIBRARY

ACTFL, *Standards for Foreign Language Learning: Preparing for the 21st Century.* Cost: $20.00 available from the ACTFL, 6 Executive Plaza, Yonkers, NY 10701-6801. Tel: (914) 963-8830; Fax : (914) 963-1275.

Canady, R.L., & Rettig, M.D. (1995). *Block Scheduling: A Catalyst for Change in High Schools.* Eye on Education, 6 Depot Way West, Suite 106, Larchmont, NY 10538. Tel: (914) 833-0551; Fax: (914) 833-0761.

Canady, R.L., & Rettig, M.D. (1996). *Teaching in the Block: Strategies for Engaging Active Learners.* Eye on Education, 6 Depot Way West, Suite 106, Larchmont, NY 10538. Tel: (914) 833-0551; Fax: (914) 833-0761.

NOTE: There are also publications for the block for math, special ed, and other disciplines available from this publisher.

The *4MAT* system is available from Excel, Inc., 200 West Station Street, Barrington, IL 60010. Tel: (708) 382-7272; Fax: (708) 382-4510. My colleagues love this series, which focuses on "why some things work with some learners and other things do not." It provides a variety of different ways to approach a single topic while adapting to different learning styles. Little specifically for foreign languages, though.

Gleason, J.B., ed. *You can take it with you: Helping students maintain foreign language skills beyond the classroom.* Available from Prentice-Hall/Regents, Book Distribution Center, Route 59 at Brook Hill Drive, West Nyack, NY 10094, or call 1-800-223-1360. Has six chapters, each discussing specific strategies or activities.

Johnson, D.W., Johnson, R.T., & Holubec, E.J. (1993). *Cooperation in the classroom.* Available from Interaction Book Co., in Edina, MN.

Joyce, B. & Weil, M. (1996). *Models of teaching.* Needham Heights, MA: Allyn & Bacon.

Kagan, S. (1995). *Cooperative learning: Resources for teachers.* Published by Resources for Teachers, Inc., San Juan Capistrano, CA. Good cooperative learning strategies, although none are for foreign language teachers specifically.

2

Preparing for the Block Schedule: An Action Plan

"For things we have to learn before we do them, we learn by doing them."

Aristotle

Imagine getting ready to take a group overseas. First, you decide on a destination. Next, you choose the specific monuments, museums, and other cultural attractions to visit. At that point, after determining how long you will need to spend at each place to see it well, you also decide in what order to visit them. After writing this planned itinerary, you will need to familiarize yourself with the history, culture, and vocabulary needed for the trip, and, of course, sign up the people you'll travel with.

Setting Goals

Preparing for a block schedule requires exactly the same sort of preparation, with the same decisions and steps in identical order, beginning with the broadest "destination" level: setting goals. Goals should be familiar to all of us since they are an integral part of curriculum writing. We look at the state and national standards as well as exercise our own judgment as to our students' educational needs and abilities, and then decide what it is we wish to accomplish. Goals generally are vague statements such as, "Students understand and interpret written and spoken language on a variety of topics." They are written by lifting the focus from the classroom and the text, and looking at the Big Picture: what skills must a first/second/third-year student have?

When considering a block schedule, review these goals you have set, or those which have been set for you, and, with this "destination" in mind, begin to plan your "itinerary," using the text and other classroom materials. What portion(s) of the text fulfill these goals? What outside readings, reports, simulations, or other projects will be necessary? When that list is complete, it is time to write your pacing guides. This process is called articulation, and is very necessary for a successful foreign language program.

ARTICULATION

There are several different types of articulation. The first one to prepare is a vertical pacing guide, which displays the continuity of instruction throughout all levels offered at your institution. In some schools this is called a "taxonomy" or a "scope and sequence." A vertical pacing guide lists, for each level, what new grammar concepts, vocabulary units, conversational skills or situations, cultural topics, works of literature, and philosophical issues will be covered, from the lowest level of language offered to the most advanced level. Any outsider to the school could see, upon looking at this guide, what verb tenses, for example, are taught at which level of study. This vertical pacing guide has many uses besides that, however. A vertical pacing guide is an invaluable tool for new staff members because they can see what their students could be expected to know and exactly which topics they must cover during their class. A vertical pacing guide eliminates overlapping in stories read, movies shown, types of activities between levels and/or teachers and, hopefully, also eliminates unnecessary review of topics the students had already mastered at an earlier level. A vertical guide also provides information for guidance counselors wishing to know in what level class to place a new student, especially an exchange student or one arriving in midsemester from a non-block-scheduled school.

When it is time to rewrite or review curriculum, a vertical guide will clearly delineate your goals for you. And, finally, when cross-referenced with the national and state standards, your vertical pacing guide is visible proof of your efforts to familiarize yourself with, integrate, and attain the national and state standards.

To write a vertical pacing schedule, find answers to these questions:

♦ What concepts and skills are critical for this level?

♦ What activities are essential?

♦ Are there any topics I can combine to save time? Can I rearrange units to cover similar topics together?

♦ What are some of the things I've always wanted to try but didn't have enough time?

With a year's warning that we were going to block, I surveyed my students on the optional activities we did. I was stunned to find that several activities they had done quite willingly rated very low when I asked if they liked them and if they found them useful. I have now eliminated those activities from my curriculum!

If you and your colleagues can easily agree upon the sequencing of projects, movies, and literature, and on how to coordinate the content and culture for each level, a vertical plan can be written in less than an hour. Figure 2.1 is an example of a vertical pacing guide.

The second type of pacing guide you will want is a *horizontal* pacing guide. Horizontal pacing coordinates each level of language between the many or several classes of the same level that are offered at your school. This is especially important in a school in which students' schedules may move them from one teacher's class to another midway through a course, or from one block to another. But, more importantly, items in the horizontal guide will serve as the building blocks of your lesson plans and, therefore, it is invaluable to write. (See Figure 2.2.)

To write a horizontal pacing guide, look at the vertical guide, one level at a time, and compare those concepts with your list of chapters, projects, and cultural events. Next, sequence them, guesstimating for each chapter and project how much time you think it will take to accomplish. Then, look at your sequenced items to see where the end of the grading periods fall, and adjust the projects, movies, extension activities, or shorter units so that semester exams fall at a logical point rather than midway through a difficult grammatical concept.

ADJUSTING PACING FOR THE BLOCK

If you are going to a Copernican or 4/4 block and have taught these classes before, a good rule is to halve the time: if a chapter formerly took two weeks, give it one. In actuality, halving the time is only a rough estimate. One of the benefits I have found in the block schedule is that *less* review is needed. Many foreign language texts alternate a grammatically dense unit with a vocabulary-rich one. However, before the block schedule, I often experienced the following: students would learn a new verb tense, perhaps the preterite (or passé composé) and then they would hardly see it again. They would not be required by the text to even write it until two or three units later, after a unit on something such as foods or clothing or something similarly vocabulary-driven, followed by a lightly grammatical unit on possessives or pronouns. When their text finally called upon students to use the verb tense again, the text supplied a built-in (and much needed) review section. This is *not* needed in a block schedule, because, instead of having covered that topic months ago, it has only been weeks. The students have forgotten less, because less time has passed since it was first learned, *and* because when it was first learned, it was learned so intensively. You will love this aspect of the block.

FIGURE 2.1. VERTICAL ARTICULATION—FRENCH

STANDARD	FRENCH I	FRENCH II	FRENCH III	FRENCH IV
1.1 COMMUNICATION	intro self survival vocab	ordering food talking about week-end activities	trip simulations: customs, hotel, café, shopping	introductions descriptions
1.2 UNDERSTANDING WRITTEN/SPOKEN LANGUAGE	numbers family classroom objects questions time expressions weather places clothing	nationalities food professions	sports and health daily routine home and rooms school subjects	travel arrangements self-description movies domestic chores
1.3 PRESENT INFO TO AUDIENCE	intro self	talk about food	Murder Mystery	Action Adventure
2.1 UNDERSTAND CULTURE: PRACTICES 5.2 USING THE LANGUAGE FOR ENJOYMENT AND ENRICHMENT	Francophone countries holidays	French provinces cooking	trip to France conversation	fashion current events
2.1 CULTURE: PRODUCTS	Paris sights	famous French people	history BC through Revolution	history 1794 to present cinematography
3.1 and 3.2 INTERDISCIPLINARY		French artists	French architecture	French stereotypes and attitudes

4.1 DEMONSTRATE UNDERSTANDING OF THE NATURE OF LANGUAGE BY COMPARISON TO THEIR OWN	present tense subject pronouns stress pronouns possessives	passé composé direct and indirect object pronouns	reflexives future imperfect *y, en*	conditional subjunctive pronoun order
4.2 DEMONSTRATE UNDERSTANDING OF CULTURE THROUGH COMPARISON TO THEIR OWN	*Man in the Iron Mask Hunchback of Notre Dame*	*Les Misérables Le Bourgeois Gentilhomme*	*The Imaginary Invalid* selections in the history text	*Cyrano de Bergerac Le Petit Prince*
5.1 USE THE LANGUAGE WITHIN AND BEYOND THE SCHOOL SETTING	FR IV: Careers unit	All levels use daily classroom activities, as well as holiday celebrations in school. French Club maintains use of the language through an active pétanque team.		

FIGURE 2.2 HORIZONTAL ARTICULATION PLAN

Grading Period	French I	French II	French III	French IV	French V
1st	Ch. 6 Research on Franco-phone countries	Ch. 3 Food unit	Ch. 23 Trip: cus-toms, ho-tel, café	Unit 1 Careers unit	Units 5, 8 First half of *Candide*
2nd (semes-ter exam)	Ch. 12 Reports on countries	Ch. 5 Reports on famous French people	Ch. 27 Trip: tours, shopping, and tickets	Unit 4 Situations unit	Unit 9 Finish *Candide*
3rd	Ch. 19 Paris sights	Ch. 12 Read play	Ch. 31 History text: through Ch. 4	Units 2, 6 Cinema	Unit 10 Poetry unit Begin *Les Jeux Sont Faits*
4th	Ch. 28 *Hunchback of Notre Dame*	Ch. 19 *Les Misérables*	Ch. 35 History to ch. 9 Murder Mystery	Unit 7 Action Adventure	College/AP practice and remedia-tion Soap Opera

For now, though, you have estimated what activities you need to do and how long they will take. Now is the time to purchase a good supply of self-sticking notes, and then, write one element from your horizontal pacing guide on each. A note would say something like "Begin Chapter 3," or "Start reports on cities," or "Bulletin board on clothing," or whatever. Take your plan book and place the activities according to your time estimates. I advise self-sticking notes because these are very adjustable. School convocations, snow or weather delays, and the revelations of that first year on a block schedule will necessitate alterations in your plans. If, after one day on a topic, the students have mastered a concept you had planned to do for three days, don't spend another day just because of lesson plans. Move your notes!

Not only does this keep your plan book neater, but these notes will keep you on schedule. A block schedule offers so much time that it is quite easy to plunge off track, convinced you have so much time that you can waste a day on some-thing that has come up. Your stick-on notes should remind you that you *have* to be on another chapter and may not have time for that digression, or that you could make it homework, or a project for your language club to enjoy.

PRE-BLOCK TRAINING

Now, on our block schedule excursion, armed with your itinerary and maps, it is time to study the area you will be visiting. This means familiarizing yourself with the new bits of language and the new techniques necessary: pre-block training. As we all know, reinventing the wheel is a waste of time, and reading/seeing/borrowing ideas is what foreign language teachers do best; ours is one of the most innovative fields in secondary teaching, with new realia available daily.

First, familiarize yourself with the surroundings you will experience. Observe other teachers' classrooms. Going to a school on the block schedule for a day is a good idea, but here's one that is even more useful: This may shock you, but one of the best suggestions I ever got was to observe a lower-level elementary school class. Watch the teacher's classroom management strategies: children in the first, second, and other elementary grades are in the same room all day and are trained by the teacher to keep busy. They are given opportunities to leave their seats fairly often, but with a planned purpose and in an orderly fashion. More about these strategies can be found in Chapter 3, but seeing how others deal with the extended time period is of invaluable assistance.

There is a whole new language, so you must familiarize yourself with the local usages just as when visiting a new country. When I read the first book of the Canady series, there was a page of strategies to use when developing lesson plans for the block, and I was unaware of what over half of them meant—Socratic seminar, jigsaw, TPS, synectics, concept development—a whole new language. However, in studying them, quite a few were strategies I have used, but never knew their names. Others were valuable new additions to my educational repertoire. Chapter 4 of this book explains and gives examples of all these and more.

The other part of pre-block training is just that: training sessions, both in-school ones arranged by an administrator and others offered by colleges; traveling seminars; and those offered at area foreign language association conventions, such as the ACTFL one, or your state conference. Here are my recommendations:

♦ Get some training in cooperative learning.

As the research in Chapter 1 shows, students learn best when they teach each other. Learn the many cooperative learning strategies and how to avoid pitfalls (such as losing control or becoming a competitive activity rather than a team-oriented one) from someone who has researched them, done them, been there. Even if you already are using some cooperative learning in your classroom, additional training would either reinforce that you are doing the right thing (sort of a pat on the back), or, even more likely, give you a new viewpoint or a totally new activity to use in your classroom. If speakers on this topic are not available, I recommend the books I found most helpful: the Canady books mentioned previously, and a book on cooperative learning by Spencer Kagan. (Both can be found in the bibliography). Chapter 4 of this book presents a variety of cooperative learning strategies that I found or learned and adapted for my classroom.

- ♦ Other really useful workshop topics are:

  - strategies to promote active participation (for suggestions on active vs. passive learners, see Chapter 4)

  - learning about multiple intelligences or learning styles (techniques such as 4MAT)

  - performance-based learning strategies

  - alternative assessment methods such as portfolio development, rubrics, and other performance tasks.

Of course, you don't have to learn all these before going to the block, but if you have the opportunity to familiarize yourself with any of these, take it!

PEER SUPPORT GROUPS

Leading an adventure trip like the one to a block schedule, you must finally recruit participants who want to go to the same places you do. Just knowing a teaching strategy is not enough, for, as we see every day in our classrooms, knowing and using are different, and using takes practice and reinforcement. This means, for the block, that peer support groups are very necessary. Two of the inservice speakers we have had at our school asked us to guess how many people at a typical inservice training session went back to their classroom the next day or the next week and tried out what they had learned. Half? No, only 5 to 10 percent, we were told, transfer learning into classroom practice. But even more disheartening was the follow-up question: How many teachers continued to use those techniques? Only two percent. I'm not sure where those statistics came from, but they were probably close to the truth. I know I've tried something I heard about and it didn't work well; perhaps I felt too awkward using it, or failed to communicate adequately what my expectations were, and because it was easier to fall back on what I was already proficient with, I dropped the new method forever after the first try.

Most schools expect teachers to work alone, in their own room, with their own set of students and their own curriculum materials, competing with each other to see who is best. Teaching is the only profession where this is common; doctors, lawyers, and engineers, for example, all have frequent meetings to learn new techniques, discuss issues and problems, and brainstorm solutions.

Teachers, also, need to form teams. Johnson and Johnson (1993) suggest forming teams of two to five members, with the purpose of increasing instructional expertise and success. Peer support research recommends strongly that you PAIR UP with someone else, someone willing to try the same things, and to whom you don't mind confessing the less-than-perfect results in your classroom. Both of you then pick a new method or approach and help each other devise lesson plans. After teaching them, you then report back to each other your successes and failures; what you had to (or need to) change; brainstorm solutions to polish the rough edges; and try again.

According to Rieken, Kerby, and Mulhern (1996), foreign language programs that are successful use one or more of these techniques: developing a common approach or philosophy about learning, holding frequent teacher meetings, and communicating with other school personnel, especially administrators and guidance personnel. The Collaboration Articulation and Assessment Project (CAAP) also has a model for articulation between secondary and postsecondary programs to ensure more success for students after high school. Their model also has frequent meetings with shared readings and discussion, and results in an ongoing teacher-driven inservice training process and an increased sense of camaraderie (Birckbichler, Robison, & Robinson, 1995). Another recommended strategy, therefore, for learning all these new methods is to get a large group of interested staff together, and, in groups of two to five, select a strategy such as synectics, concept attainment, or Socratic seminar, and then research it, try it, and present it to the whole group. If the oral report format is too stilted for staff, organize activities after the research-and-practice phase such as:

- a "Bring and Brag" session which highlights successes. I got a really good idea on how to introduce the French Revolution from a social studies colleague and some art unit assistance from a fine arts lesson.

- a "Bloopers" session to share mistakes, so others don't follow in suit like lemmings. I heard a comment about a Socratic session that got out of hand, which helped me avoid the same.

- a journal-writing week, with a sharing session to read each other's experiences and reactions.

- a visit to each other's classrooms to observe once someone is comfortable with a new method.

Teachers so often are expected to be self-reliant, compartmented workers that it is quite wonderful to have time set aside to share and collaborate. I have a poster that says, "We all came on different ships, but we're all in the same boat now," that seems especially true when applied to the block schedule. And, because we're all in the same boat, survival means banding together to face the unknown. Johnson, Johnson, and Holubec (1993) itemized the benefits to be derived from working together: First, a team effort provides assistance, support, and encouragement. Second, by helping one's colleagues, your own expertise is enhanced. Third, this process must and should continue for years; don't try to do it all at once or it will be overwhelming. Fourth, the most important effect of working together is transfer (you actually are using these techniques in your classroom) and maintenance (long-term use).

WRITING RUBRICS

Finally, with your trip all organized and the preparations well under way, a final step, if you have time, is to select a good guide book, complete with a good set of maps. In the block, a good time-and-trouble-saving strategy is to write rubrics. A rubric is a clearly written description of an assignment that states what should be done by the student and how the product will be evaluated by you.

To write a rubric, list the steps that must be taken, in order and in great detail, and with examples, if possible. Assign each step a value and a deadline. Students reading your rubric will be able to see clearly the effort level you regard as minimum. These then can be filed and easily copied and handed out, so that students who are absent or who have poor listening skills, and/or substitute teachers accomplish the task you have chosen. A well-written rubric also can turn an in-class assignment that you had to closely supervise in the past into a take-home assignment that can be successfully completed, or which needs only a little polishing the next day; this is another good way to save instructional time and accomplish more on a block schedule.

To return to the topic of peer support, I recently attended an inservice at our school during which we wrote rubrics for a half-day with teachers from content areas other than our own. Showing my rubrics to them helped me to clear up some vague areas in my descriptions, *and* the other people suggested some additions that made the assignment even better. On the next page is a sample rubric on the family tree. This rubric, if used in my class, would have examples added in the target language; I have omitted them so it would be applicable to any language.

The finished product can be shown by the student to the whole class, to a smaller group, or to a partner. Students can exchange these and either talk about the one they got, or ask each other questions about the people on the tree, such as, "How old is Paco/Pierre/Peter? When is his birthday? Does he like to play football?"

FAMILY TREE

The "perfect" family tree includes:

> at least three generations	5 pt, divided as follows:
> at least one aunt and uncle (make them up if you need to)	1 pt.
> at least one cousin of each gender (make them up if needed)	1 pt.
> at least one brother or sister (same)	2 pt.
> two parents	1 pt.
> NO ENGLISH	PASS/FAIL
> labels which can be read across the room	1 pt.
> possessive adjectives in the correct gender	4 pt., ½ pt per person
> a photo, drawing or magazine picture for each family member	4 pt., ½ pt per person
> a first and last name for each family member	1 pt.

TOTAL PTS. 15 points

An "A" tree is complete and neatly drawn, with few spelling errors.

A "B" tree is complete and neatly drawn, with a few mistakes, but still understandable.

A "C" tree may be neat, but is missing an item or two, and has many spelling or grammar errors.

A "D" tree is quite incomplete and messy to look at, and has many errors.

An "F" has half the items either missing, illegible, and/or misspelled.

For my third-year students, I devised the following rubric to use for a conversational unit to make things a bit more interesting:

UNIT ONE: Identity

We are doing a Murder Mystery!

In the next _____ days, you will be asked to introduce yourself to the class. You will give us the following information:

Name

Age

Profession

2 adjectives that describe you, OR

2 things you either like or hate   5 pts., 1 pt each

These five things must be:

in complete sentences

using correct grammar

pronounced correctly   5 pts., 1 pt. each

You must also listen attentively to others   2 pts.

TOTAL   12 pts.

Extra credit points may be given by the teacher for volunteering to go first, and for creativity "above and beyond the call of duty."

THIS PRESENTATION WILL BE MEMORIZED, NOT READ ALOUD

You may be yourself, OR you may invent a persona. You may be anyone, living (e.g., Michael Jordan) or dead (e.g., Albert Einstein), imaginary (e.g., Jack Frost or Santa Claus) or any talking being (e.g., See Threepio the robot, Mr. Ed, Big Bird). If you are unsure if your selection is in good taste, ask the teacher.

I strongly advise writing rubrics to save instructional time in other ways: As students turn in a test or a similar written assignment, a rubric could be available for them to pick up, read, and begin quietly while others are finishing their work. Then, all you need to do is ask if there are any questions about the rubric and let them proceed, or assign it as homework and go on to another activity knowing that they understand exactly what you want *and* have a visual reminder of the assignment. The rubric serves as their map, and they are ready to go. Rubrics are also useful for emergency lesson plans that any substitute could handle easily.

3

LESSON PLANS FOR BLOCK SCHEDULES

"Time is finite; spend it carefully."

Anonymous

Foreign language texts are perfect for adapting to the block. They have lots of short written, spoken, and listening activities in addition to a wide smorgasbord of materials. Students have a text and a workbook, and teachers have audio and videotapes, overheads, CD-ROMs, and so forth. A logical assumption is, therefore, that you can use your old lesson plans and just add a few more exercises. The answer to that assumption is yes and no.

Yes, you do *not* have to write all new activities or extensively supplement the text. But, no, you cannot just haphazardly tack on a few more activities. Above all, you may *not* just paste together two days' worth of lessons. The Wisconsin Association of Foreign Language Teachers Task Force on the Block Schedule surveyed its foreign language teachers on block schedules. The teachers listed as "negative" aspects the need to alter the way they plan instruction and present lessons. Whereas 3 or 4 activities used to be enough, they now found they needed 6 to 10 to fill the longer time. The teachers found this to be "negative" because it does involve reviewing and rethinking old lessons. However, it does not involve inordinate amounts of time or work; you simply must be more intentional than before. You must write lessons to include as much variety as possible. One of the teachers at my school called this process "invigorating," and most teachers posting messages on FLTEACH (an Internet site I highly recommend) listed the opportunity to use variety as one of the most "positive" aspects of the block.

THREE-PART DESIGN

On a block schedule, the key to making a longer time span work is simple: VARIETY. You must write lesson plans with just that goal in mind. This means, first, that you must not think of the block as one big chunk, but as several smaller pieces.

Block schedule experts Robert Lynn Canady and Michael D. Rettig (1995) suggest thinking of a block lesson as having three parts: first, a 25- to 35-minute "explanation" portion (homework review, followed by a minilecture or presentation), followed by an equal amount of time spent in "application," or practice, and ending with a "synthesis" segment, which would involve strategies such as reflection on what was learned, reteaching a portion that was difficult, and an assessment activity. This 30/30/30 format works very well for planning purposes. The essential idea is that you *must* think and plan for smaller portions at a time; thus, you are less likely to waste time. The longer block period is seductive. It is tempting to take an old lesson and supplement it with two or three more activities that were skipped before. More likely, because you believe there will be plenty of time left, you might go off on a tangent raised by a student's question that you normally wouldn't answer during class time, only to discover a week or more later, that you are running behind schedule and cannot possibly cover everything you had planned to cover! Planning for a smaller period of time reduces the feeling that wasting a little time every day is acceptable.

SIX-STAGE INSTRUCTIONAL STRATEGY

There are several other approaches to planning for a block schedule. In Canady and Rettig's (1995) book, an alternative organizational strategy is offered by Phyllis Hotchkiss (Figure 3.1), which suggests writing every lesson plan to include these stages:

- ◆ Review homework

- ◆ Present new material

- ◆ Follow with an appropriate activity

- ◆ Offer guided practice

- ◆ Reteach if necessary

- ◆ Provide closure for the lesson

I find this method to be analogous to the 30/30/30 plan. Canady and Rettig's explanation phase included homework review and the presentation of new material. The application portion resembled Hotchkiss' third and fourth strategies, but listing six different steps in this manner emphasizes the need for a variety of strategies and confirms the Wisconsin study group's findings that at least six different activities are normal for the block.

FIGURE 3.1. DESIGNING LESSONS FOR THE BLOCK SCHEDULE WITH ACTIVE LEARNING STRATEGIES

Homework Review (10–15 Minutes)

Inside-Outside Circles (Kagan, 1990)

Pairs-Check (Kagan, 1990)

Team Interview (Kagan, 1990)

Graffiti (Kagan, 1990)

Roundtable (Ch. 3)

Think-Pair-Share (Ch. 3)

Mix-Freeze-Group (Kagan, 1990)

Send a Problem (Ch. 9)

Presentation (20–25 Minutes)

Interactive Lecture (Ch. 3)

CD-ROM (Ch. 7)

Video Disc (Ch. 7)

Videotape (Ch. 7)

Socratic Seminars (Ch. 2)

Inquiry (Gunter et al., 1995)

Direct Instruction (Ch. 9)

Demonstration

Inductive Thinking (Ch. 4)

Directed Reading/Thinking Activity (Ch. 8)

Concept Attainment (Ch. 4)

Concept Formation (Ch. 4)

Synectics (Ch. 4)

Memory Model (Ch. 4)

Activity (30–35 Minutes)

Role Play (Gunter et al., 1995)

Simulation (Ch. 5)

Synectics (Ch. 4)

Science Laboratory

Computer Reinforcement

Mix-Freeze-Group (Kagan, 1990)

Writing Lab (Ch. 8)

Teams Games Tournaments (TGT) (Slavin, 1986)

Student Teams Achievement Divisions (STAD) (Slavin, 1986; Ch. 3)

Team Review

  Graffiti (Kagan, 1990)

  Roundtable (Ch. 3)

  Pair-Share (Ch. 2)

  Learning Centers (Ch. 6)

  Send a Problem (Ch. 9)

  Pairs-Check (Kagan, 1990)

  Jigsaw (Slavin, 1986)

Guided Practice (10–15 Minutes)

Reteach (10–15 Minutes)

Closure (5–10 Minutes)

Adapted from: Phyllis R. Hotchkiss, Hotchkiss Educational Consulting Services, Richmond, Virginia. (Reproduced by permission from Canady & Rettig, 1996, p. 24.)

DIRECT INSTRUCTION

A third method of organizing a lesson, called Direct Instruction, was devised by Gunter et al. (1995), and is very competently explained by David Vawter in Chapter 9 of *Teaching in the Block* (Canady & Rettig, 1996):

♦ Review previously learned material

♦ State lesson objectives

♦ Present new material

♦ Provide guided practice with corrective feedback

♦ Assign in-depth practice with corrective feedback

♦ Review both during and at the end of the lesson

This method emphasizes the idea that students should be made aware from the outset of the lesson what it is they are trying to learn, and they also should have many opportunities to receive feedback on how they are doing. Here is an example of Vawter's lesson plan form, as adapted by Dave Snyder, one of my colleagues (Figure 3.2).

PLANNING FOR VARIETY

No matter which organizational style you choose for your lesson planning, there will be three or more activities used in each block. The next step is to consider whether there will be one or several objectives for this block. Visualize each objective as a strand or a thread. On some days, you could choose to devote the entire day to a single strand, such as teaching a challenging new verb tense. You also could choose to do three, four, or five different strands. Choose a strand style, and then list the sub- or mini-objectives or tasks for each strand, for example:

> Practice greetings.
> Examine and practice a new conversation.
> Learn about a new holiday and its culture and specialized vocabulary.
> Watch a video.
> Translate a passage into English.

If the above is done as a single strand, for example a particular holiday, then the conversation should contain references to activities involved in the holiday, and the video and passage translated would be about the holiday. If this were a multiple-strand lesson, the holiday portion in the middle would be a change-of-

FIGURE 3.2. EXAMPLE OF A DIRECT INSTRUCTION LESSON PLAN FORM

MUST DO!

Provide "hands on" active learning strategies
during the application/activity period of time
each day.

LESSON DESIGNS

Explanation 15 minutes	Homework Review 10–15 minutes
Application 60 minutes	Presentation 10–20 minutes Activity/Laboratory 30–60 minutes
Synthesis 15 minutes	Guided Practice & Reteach if necessary 5–15 minutes Closure 5–10 minutes

Explanation 15 minutes	
Application 60 minutes	
Synthesis 15 minutes	

pace activity to allow time for assimilation of the previous instruction; and then the translation at the end would review the skills practiced in the first third of the lesson, reteaching and reviewing, as several of the organizational methods and educational research recommend.

An assessment step is critical. It does not have to be a test or a quiz. Consider alternate forms of assessment, such as a paper to be graded, a skit, a creative project, a written or oral response to a question; but whatever you use will provide closure, as well as a measure of how much learning occurred and an easy method for brief review the following day—either reviewing common errors or complimenting everyone on things they did well. (Remember, it is important that papers be returned punctually.)

USING MULTIPLE STRATEGIES

LISTING TASKS

In the days before the block schedule, the above steps were the only things I did. I considered my lesson totally planned when I had a beginning, a middle, and an end, with my objectives clearly in mind. Lesson plans were simply a list such as practice greetings, do workbook page, and read story, written in my own personal shorthand, which any other person would have had difficulty deciphering! This, however, is where lesson plans for the block begin to differ from plans for a shorter time period. To remind myself of the steps I should take, I devised my own lesson plan form, which is included here as Figure 3.3.

FIGURE 3.3. AUTHOR'S LESSON PLAN FORM

Block Lesson Segments

TASKS	TEACHER WILL...	STUDENT WILL...	TIME (approx.)
1.			
2.			
3.			
4.			
5.			

TEACHER ACTIVITIES

Your next step should be, beside each task, to list what your (the teacher's) activities will be for each segment. Words such as lecture, facilitate, model behavior, give direction, MBWA (monitor by walking around), and show video should be used. Figure 3.4 (p. 62) is a list of suggestions.

Make sure you have not scheduled yourself for the same activity for two consecutive segments. Also, be sure that "lecture" is not listed more than once; you should not be the "sage on the stage" for an entire objective. Research shows that even the brightest, most motivated student has about a 10-minute attention span as information is poured in. After 10 minutes, the cup overflows and the lecture becomes a sort of "spray and pray": lots of data is provided and you hope that some or most of it "sticks." I was guilty, before the block, of being at the board talking for 40 minutes or more of a 50-minute period and, at the end of a seven-period day, I was exhausted. In a block schedule, if you schedule yourself as the "sage," not only will you be exhausted, but your students will not be as actively involved in learning. (Active learning strategies are discussed in Chapter 4 of this book.)

"STUDENT AS WORKER"

The Coalition of Essential Schools prefers instruction where the concept of the "Student as Worker" dominates. The National Association of District Supervisors of Foreign Languages has included these similar concepts as some of the characteristics of effective foreign language teaching (a complete list of their recommendations is in Figure 3.5, p. 63):

- Providing opportunities to communicate through activities simulating real-life situations

- Employing mostly skill-using activities rather than lecture

- Using mostly student-centered activities

- Addressing a variety of different student learning styles

This recognition of the need for VARIETY should be reflected in your choice of expected student behaviors. If the students are expected to do the same thing for two segments in a row, either move the segment, or back up a step and rethink your teaching strategy. Instead of lecturing or demonstrating, why not consider concept attainment or induction? Figure 3.6 (p. 64) lists alternative strategies for common forms of instruction. These alternatives are explained in detail in Chapter 4.

After listing objectives and teacher strategies, list the student behaviors you wish to schedule, making sure there is a variety. Information on learning shows that students need short breaks built in to process new information, so be sure to schedule short, frequent practice or evaluation moments in your lesson. Make sure at least every other activity offers a small opportunity for feedback

(Text continues on p. 65.)

FIGURE 3.4. ACTIVITIES FOR LESSON PLANS

TEACHER	EITHER	STUDENT	
lecture	brainstorm	draw	act
show and tell	converse	copy	read
model	tell story	take notes	reread
test	display	research	point
correct test	rehearse	hunt	experiment
feedback	write on board	debate	outline
question and	compare	dance	chart
answer	contrast	sing	rap
show video	paraphrase	repeat	discover
MBWA (monitor by	demonstrate	solve	Jigsaw
walking around)	critique	define	memorize
tell	analyze	describe	cartoon
supervise	videotape	match	reflect
teach acronyms	listen	name	pantomime
philosophize	speak	combine	interview
guide	command	compile	survey
facilitate	discuss	take test	read maps
hand out	correct	practice test	draw maps
use overhead	observe	write journal	make poster
make bulletin board	review	do puzzle	do collage
use bulletin board	teach	act	do diorama
intervene	simulate	categorize	do teaming
assess	improvise	hypothesize	play Bingo
arrange room	evaluate	visualize	play Jeopardy
assign groups	summarize	role play	play Hangman
assign roles	create a product	tell a neighbor	play Pictionary
explain task	list	say forward and	play Scattergories
explain evaluation	Socratic seminar	backward	do homework
criteria	write test	peer tutor	play Baseball
provide closure	write quiz	prioritize	explore Internet
		self-evaluate	do family tree
MISCELLANEOUS:		watch slides	do choral reading
guest speaker		play games	partners discuss
field trip		panel discussion	use dictionary
contest		book report	draw time line
project		think/pair/share	write poem
portfolio		win, lose, or draw	recall
		word search	write story

YOU CAN PROBABLY THINK OF A LOT MORE!

FIGURE 3.5. CHARACTERISTICS OF EFFECTIVE
FOREIGN LANGUAGE INSTRUCTION

The National Association of District Supervisors of Foreign Languages published these characteristics of effective foreign language instruction:

- The teacher uses the target language extensively, encouraging the students to do so, too.

- The teacher provides opportunities to communicate in the target language in meaningful, purposeful activities that simulate real-life situations.

- Skill-getting activities enable students to participate successfully in skill-using activities. Skill-using activities predominate.

- Time devoted to listening, speaking, reading, and writing is appropriate to course objectives and to the language skills of students.

- Culture is systematically incorporated into instruction.

- The teacher uses a variety of student groupings.

- Most activities are student-centered.

- The teacher uses explicit error correction in activities that focus on accuracy and implicit or no error correction in activities that focus on communication.

- Assessment, both formal and informal, reflects the way students are taught.

- Student tasks and teacher questions reflect a range of thinking skills.

- Instruction addresses student learning styles.

- Students are explicitly taught foreign-language learning strategies and are encouraged to assess their own progress.

- The teacher enables all students to be successful.

- The teacher establishes a nurturing climate in which students feel comfortable taking risks.

- Students are enabled to develop positive attitudes toward cultural diversity.

- The physical environment reflects the target language and culture.

- The teacher uses the textbook as a tool, not as the sole curriculum.

- The teacher uses a variety of print and nonprint materials, including authentic materials.

- Technology, as available, is used to facilitate teaching and learning.

- The teacher engages in continued professional development in the areas of language skills, cultural knowledge, and current methodology.

Source: *NASSP Curriculum Report*, Vol. 26, No. 5, May 1997.

FIGURE 3.6. EASY ALTERNATIVES TO STANDARD TEACHING PRACTICES

STANDARD PRACTICE	ALTERNATIVES (See Chapter 4 for details)
Teacher-driven Lecture	Socratic Seminar Inquiry Concept Development Concept Attainment Inductive Thinking Jigsaw Learning Together Synectics Memory Model Learning centers Audio Video Demonstration
Individual Practice, i.e., workbooks	Role play Memory Model Pair-Share Pairs-Check and other paired activities Inside-Outside Circle Numbered Heads Roundtable Interviews Simulation Synectics Learning centers Computer reinforcement
Teacher-driven Review	Graffiti Team Test-taking Send a Problem Team Interview Roundtable Pair/Drill Think/Pair/Team/Share (1-2-4) Student Team Achievement Divisions (STAD) Teams-Games-Tournament (TGT) Four Corners Line-ups Flyswatter

or assessment, either from classmates or from you. Also, keep in mind my favorite quotation from Glasser on how learning takes place (see Figure 1.6, p. 29), and schedule as many opportunities as possible for student-centered activities that will use the higher end of that scale. Furthermore, advice from fellow teachers indicates that for lower-ability classes, more activities are better (Schoenstein, 1995).

STUDENT MOVEMENT

Another student activity you must include is movement. As stated earlier, one of the best lesson-planning strategies I was ever told to use was to observe in an elementary classroom for part of a day. Those students are in the same room all morning; what does the teacher do to enable them to get out of their seats with a purpose? Here are some suggestions based on what I observed and put into practice in my own classroom. These all work well to incorporate movement:

- Instead of having them pass their papers forward, have them put them somewhere in the classroom, or bring them to you.

- Have them pick up handouts instead of you passing them out.

- Have the classroom arranged so they have to shift their chairs or desks to watch a video or do a listening activity. I put my TV in the back of the room for that reason.

- Put workbooks on a shelf for them to pick up.

- Move students in and out of cooperative learning groups.

- Don't forget those old standbys such as writing on the board, or any action songs, dances, or activities you already do. Singing "Head, Shoulders, Knees and Toes" in any language will get them going any time!

Planning for student movement is critical. Educationally, it does *not* waste time because there is no need for any sort of formal break during the block, if students are allowed to move from activity to activity.

ADJUSTING FOR TIME

The final part of writing a lesson plan is, at this point, to estimate the amount of time needed for each activity. These should add up to the length of your block period. If you don't have enough, go back to one of the lists in this chapter (one of the planning methods, or the list of behaviors, Glasser's hierarchy of learning from Chapter 1, etc.), look at the strategies in Chapter 4, consult a teacher-partner as suggested in Chapter 2, or go back to your old lesson plans and look for something to add. Just make sure it is not filling the time with another redundant or empty activity. Activities that basically fill time unnecessarily slow your progress, and 10 minutes of that per day becomes close to an hour wasted in just 1 week.

If your plans are too long, is there an activity which, although fun, is not really needed, or which would be good as a review tomorrow, or which could be shortened or altered in some way to fit? We all did this before the block schedule, so this is not a new strategy. Neither is my next suggestion: always have at least one extra activity ready just in case you have incorrectly estimated how long your plans will take. Some of the new student-centered activities are so effective that you may discover that you need fewer practice activities; having something else ready will save you in these situations. Once again, if you often run out of lessons with 10 minutes or so to spare, that winds up wasting serious amounts of instructional time over a grading period.

MAKE NOTES AFTERWARD

Finally, *after* teaching that lesson, take time to make notes: what worked or didn't, what took too long, or ran shorter/longer than your estimate, what would you do differently next time. Don't trust yourself to remember those things; the fast-paced block will quickly erase the details from your memory until the next time, if you don't write them down.

Also, everyone I have spoken with who has been teaching on the block agrees that it is futile to design daily lesson plans more than a week in advance. You should, of course, have a calendar with your pacing schedule penciled in, or your self-sticking note reminders in your plan book to keep you on schedule. But for actual lesson plans, the first year on the block will hold many pleasant surprises for you. To give yourself room to adapt and not waste time writing plans that will be totally changed, a one-week-at-a-time effort is best.

CLASSROOM MANAGEMENT STRATEGIES

One of the most important items to complement your lesson plans is to design a good method for handling the many daily classroom routines you must engage in. A good foreign language teacher wants to establish a climate conducive to learning. Anyone with a calculator can easily add the number of in-class minutes students had on a nonblock schedule and those on a block, and they will come to the conclusion that they will have much less time to teach. That is true, at least on paper, but they often forget that for two sessions there were two attendance-taking, handing-back-papers, and giving-homework time periods where little was being accomplished, and that this wasted time is now cut in half. Having a good method for handling these daily necessities quickly and efficiently will enable you and your students to use time more constructively. Use this list to see what you need to establish.

```
Ask yourself, do I have a good method for:
        beginning class?
        getting students' attention?
        handling absences?
        setting time limits?
        finishing work early?
        handling transitions between the different activities?
        taking breaks?
```

These are good topics to discuss with colleagues; someone else may have a wonderful method that you could borrow for your classroom.

STARTING CLASS

Let's begin with starting the class. Train your students from day one that when they enter your room they have a task to begin. It may be to get their folder and begin review of whatever is in it, or perhaps a Question of the Day on the overhead or the blackboard. There may be a short poem to memorize on the board, or any other activity you choose to designate. Some teachers have a spot on their desk that is designated for beginning activities, and students know that if something is there, they are to pick it up when they enter the room and begin. There are many different activities you can do of this sort (see Sponge Activities in Chapter 4) but they all send a clear message: in this class, time is not to waste! They are also invaluable for times when, for example, you need to talk to an individual before you can begin leading discussion. Your well-trained students will be working and thinking in the language even before you take over.

SIGNALS

When you are ready to begin the review or instruction portion, do you have a signal that you are ready? I always greet the class with a cheery hello and a "how are you?" The students respond by stopping what they are doing, making eye contact, and answering me. Some teachers raise their hand and have students follow suit. Others use colored cards on each desk, which the students raise or flip over to indicate readiness or that they need help. Several teachers use the colored cards to send these signals: holding up a red light for the whole class to stop, or putting the red light card on the desks of a group who need to stop and think or lessen their volume. My mother always played a little piece of music as her signal for attention. One teacher I observed had some old red and green ping-pong paddles purchased at a garage sale, with "Stop" and "Go" on them in the target language, which she held up to get their attention and cooperation.

Still others just have a certain spot they stand in or a gesture they make to indicate they are ready to begin. Here's a surefire one: go to a specifically chosen place in the room and take the stance of a traffic cop, weight equally on both feet, hands comfortably in front at around waist level, and freeze in that position. (Never try to get students' attention while you are moving toward the front of the room, looking for things at your desk, etc., because what you are asking them to do and what you are modeling are contradictory.) Wait in this spot, in position, until you have the class's attention. Then, calling the group at a volume just above the noise level of the class, use whatever phrase you usually use to get their attention, for example, "Class," then wait. When they are with you, start the directions in close to a whisper, and shift your body out of the traffic cop position. If you don't overuse this, it works well.

It is easy to train students the first day as to what your expectations will be. Develop a clear signal that you wish to begin class, and teach your students what that signal is. Students LOVE predictability; you will love how much time is saved as most of the students react to your cue and help you police/remind the others who do not.

HANDLING ABSENCES

There are many different ways to handle absences. Some teachers use the time-consuming method of stopping the students when they return and informing them what has happened. Block teachers should find something more efficient. One teacher I met has a special form he fills out and hands students when they return (but that seems like a lot of work to me). Most others have a place where assignments are posted, either on the board, on a laminated, erasable poster, in a special folder, or in a second plan book (filled in after class) that is left available for the students to check as they return.

At a seminar I attended, teachers suggested other ideas. One is to assign each student a "Study Buddy" who will take notes for the absent student. Another idea is to assign, on a rotating basis, one student in the class to take notes for one week, for example. Those notes are copied and made available for absent students or any others who request them. Some schools also are lucky enough to have a Hot Line system, where a teacher may leave voice mail for students to check when they are absent. One high school on the block schedule has homework assignments available on the school Internet site.

Yet another method I use and like is to have a checklist on the back wall listing all graded activities, with a check mark when each is accomplished. Any student can walk past that list and see whether he or she has done all the necessary work. This list must be frequently updated.

Any of these methods make students responsible for getting caught up, freeing the teacher to begin class and even, in the last case, freeing the teacher from reminding them (nagging) they have work still to be made up.

TIME LIMITS

Time limits are important, too. When giving an assignment, do not just instruct the students to do workbook page 21 without telling them how long they have to do it. Especially, never use a time limit that is a multiple of five. Five minutes or 10 minutes are not "real" to students; telling them that you expect this page to take them 7 minutes, for example, makes them think that they should get right to it, because they have a limit, and also that you, a master teacher, already know exactly how much time this should take and will not be pleased if it takes more time than you have allotted. Of course, you may allow them more time if they need it, but they will be hard at work, of course, and will not notice that the seven minutes stretched to eight or nine.

FINISHING EARLY

What do you have for those students who finish ahead of everyone else? Several teachers I know have a folder full of extra credit activities for those students. Some pair the stronger students with a student who is weaker or who has been absent, and have them compare papers or tutor a bit. Some have pleasure reading (or listening) materials or computer games in the target language, which can only be used by students who finish early. Use your imagination to see what strategies you can apply.

TRANSITIONS

Transitions between activities are another situation where you can quickly train your students to make swift, orderly changes. Most block teachers have at least one cooperative learning activity per block, and it is important not to lose a lot of time moving to sit near a partner or getting into groups. Set a time limit such as 30 seconds, and rehearse and rehearse until they can move efficiently to their places with a minimum of hubbub. This may take a bit of time the first time, but it saves a lot of time in the long run.

A wonderful way of partnering students for the many paired activities found in modern textbooks is to have an appointment clock page (Figure 3.7). Tell the students that they have to find another student who has an opening (in French it is fun to call these "Rendezvous"), exchange papers, and each write their name at that time on the clock. For classes beyond Level 1, of course, this is all done in the target language. Use only four clock times: 12, 3, 6, and 9. They may only have an appointment with the same partner once, and be sure to give them a time limit for pairing up, usually 3 minutes for a class of 20 to 25. At the end of that time, have them sit and you help pair those who haven't filled their clocks yet. Of course, if the class has an odd number of students, it is likely that someone will always be left unpaired; just tell them not to worry as whenever someone is absent they will take the absent student's partner, or you can form a group of three (or, perhaps, the student can work with you or one of your student aides). Then, when they need a partner, you can just say, "Get out your clocks and find your B-3 partner." It works like a charm. They get a wide variety of partners rather than just those sitting nearby or the same friends over and over, and there is a lot of time saved when no one needs to wait to be asked, or to ask. Several suggestions:

FIGURE 3.7. APPOINTMENT CLOCK PAGE

MY PARTNER LIST

DO NOT FILL IN THREE O'CLOCK; IT IS RESERVED FOR MY SELECTION

♦ Have fewer appointments than there are students. Not everyone wants to work with everyone else in the class. In a class of about 20 students, for example, I would only use 4 of the clocks, or 16 appointments.

♦ If you are partnering for a more difficult activity, do not call a partner from the "A" clock. Students will have obtained "A" appointments with the others in the class with whom they are most likely to get into/make trouble. Use the "A" clock only when they are behaving well or when the assignment is a short, simple one.

♦ Do periodic clock checks; some students will cheat and pretend they have appointments they do not have, just to be with friends.

♦ Make it in their best interest *not* to lose the clock. Perhaps on the periodic clock checks, everyone with theirs gets an extra point, or whatever you use for classroom rewards. I promise my students they can staple theirs to their final exam for an extra point; I can assure you that very few lose them.

♦ One of my colleagues, always reserves the 9 o'clock appointment as "teacher's choice." On those days she identifies whom she has chosen as their partners, either by orally assigning them or by writing group numbers on an assignment that she returns to them. She uses the teacher's choice usually when she wants groups of mixed abilities: one strong student with one weak and one average, for example.

Much more on cooperative learning groups can be found in Chapter 4 of this book.

BREAKS

With a variety of activities and by paying special attention to arranging opportunities for students to move about the room, a formal break is not necessary at all. However, there are still times when students need to get a drink of water, blow their noses, use the restroom, and so on. How do you handle those times? First, teach students how to request those breaks in the target language and require that they do so. Start this the very first day of class. A teacher at a workshop I hosted had the brilliant idea of having the students make passports. Each time a student leaves, the passport is punched. When the spaces are used up or if students have forgotten or lost their passport, they must "take a tardy" if they wish to leave the room. Her students must then evaluate how urgently they need to leave, because tardies accumulate to absences and truancies at her school. Another person at the workshop also volunteered that she does a similar thing, with each pass being worth five points on their final exam, and each punch subtracting a point from the value of the pass. After checking your school's policies, try to develop some similar method for limiting students' breaks. A passport seems like a wonderfully appropriate idea for a foreign language class!

SUPPLEMENTING THE TEXT

Your text is rich in activities, I am sure, but students will appreciate a change of pace from time to time. Most educational groups state clearly that a text should not be the sole resource used (see Figure 3.5, p. 63). Using supplementary materials also will enable you to program student movement into your lesson plans more easily as they go to get the reader from the shelf or to pick up a current events handout from the file cabinet, and so on. The block schedule not only gives you time for such activities, it almost demands them.

The easiest way to supplement a text is to purchase the supplementary materials offered by the publisher. Most foreign language publishers have a reader available; see if you can get a classroom set. There also are several companies that publish weekly magazines to which your students could subscribe, and which afford up-to-date topics, vocabulary, and conjugation practice. I found a book on conversation, complete with a bit of slang, and a chapter on common gestures, which the students appreciate highly; for instance, it is nice to teach them that there are many more ways to agree with someone than just to say "Yes" ("yeah," "of course," "great," "sure," "wonderful," "if you say so," "why not," "good idea"...the list goes on and on).

However, educational research groups firmly state that resources other than print sources must be used (see Figure 3.5, p. 63). Another wonderful way to supplement the text is to use real-life simulations. On some days my students must go through customs, check into a hotel, buy a subway or a theater ticket, order a beverage, tell a doctor where it hurts, and so forth, to simply enter my classroom. There are many suggestions for simulations in Chapter 4 of this book.

You also might already have some ideas of things you have always wanted to do and haven't had time to try yet. In an effort to stimulate conversational skills, I created a series of adventures for each level, refining them over the years. For example, my third-year students have a Murder Mystery that we do periodically for a break and that they enjoy. First, they create a character and introduce themselves to the class. Then they describe a site for the adventure, and we vote to choose our favorite. (Both use the present tense and review things like adjective agreement, time and weather expressions, etc.) Third, they find a message that describes an event in the future tense. Next, they find a dead body, telling us all how the death occurred and their hypothesis on why the victim died (past tenses). After several more steps, they make an arrest, and we have an hour-long trial. This also greatly improves their dictionary-using skills; for example, if they look up "gun" and don't double-check the word's usage, they may have someone pulling a cannon out of their pocket and shooting someone with it! This unit is always one of the top activities the students list on my end-of-the-year feedback survey in both the "most useful" and "most enjoyable" categories. My second-year students take a highly fanciful yet informative trip to France, my fourth-year students do an Indiana Jones-style action adventure, complete with a scavenger hunt, and my fifth-level students have a soap opera activity. Because I have more planning time than I did before and am only preparing for three classes instead of six, I have more time to plan and to prepare for this type of exercise, and I enjoy it as much as the students do.

Of course, the block schedule is wonderful for videos. Consider showing a featurelength movie once a semester, either in class or after school. A German teacher I observed had the students earn "money" to purchase a movie ticket through various devices such as a perfect test/quiz score or skit, speaking in the target language to her in the halls and during lunch, sharing extra credit research with the class, and so on, with leftover cash to purchase popcorn and drinks. Music videos are also great if you can afford them; many companies offer them for purchase. Just check all those catalogs you get in the mail and develop a wish list or organize a fund-raiser to buy some.

THINK INTERNATIONAL

Join a new group! My students and I discovered and joined Pétanque-USA, a group dedicated to teaching and playing pétanque (also called bocci or lawn bowling), a common sport around the Mediterranean. Our grounds staff constructed a regulation court for us, we purchased the balls needed to play, and have since hosted and attended several meets, outside school hours, of course. Through AATF (the American Association of Teachers of French) I discovered the possibility of establishing a video-penpal relationship with a French teacher of English, and, for several years now, we have been having a yearly exchange of videos that are great additions to my curriculum. Amnesty International, a Nobel Prize-winning international organization, has high school groups "adopt" a student their age in another country, who speaks the language you teach, and who is being persecuted for nonpolitical reasons, and write on his/her behalf. I am sure that foreign language students also could find multilingual opportunities and materials from other international organizations such as Médecins Sans Frontières/Doctors Without Borders, the Red Cross, UNICEF, Oxfam, and other international relief organizations.

The Internet is also a rich source of current events-type materials for occasional use. Chapter 4 has long lists of addresses for you to consult to find news items, poetry, music lyrics, and other realia to print and share as high-interest supplements for your classroom, and Chapter 6 has sample lesson plans using Internet sources.

I am a very experienced teacher, but to "cover the material" I have had to rethink everything I do. I try to get the students out of their desks at least once during the class. Believe me, over the years, I have come up with lots of fun and creative ways for the students to learn and use the language, but the block period and the desire to teach more or less the same material has forced me to think again. I have succeeded and my students are flourishing. I am really excited. Everyone tells me after the first semester, block is easy to plan for. I am not discouraged.

Anne M. (September 1996, FLTEACH Archives)

Adjustment to a block schedule lies mostly with the individual. If you are a chalk and talk type, and always want to dominate, then you will get tired. I have been teaching languages for 34 years. If I can adjust, then anyone can! Devote more time in class to cooperative learning. In other words, don't spoon-feed the material, make the students more responsible for their own learning , and make the process part of students' grades.

Cliff K. (February 1996, FLTEACH Archives)

4

QUALITY AND QUANTITY: INSTRUCTIONAL STRATEGIES THAT WORK

"If you think you can, you're right, and if you think you can't, you're right."
Henry Ford

This quotation sums up the most important aspect of teaching in the block schedule: attitude. You must be willing to be a little adventurous. A large block of time could totally rejuvenate and refresh your teaching: 30-year veterans at my school say the block has made a big difference in their job satisfaction, mostly because they are able to try new teaching methods—an old dog *can* learn new tricks! Young teachers at my school, who were overwhelmed and thinking of leaving the teaching profession, have given testimonials at meetings that if it were not for the block, they would not be teaching. The block offers many opportunities to stretch, experiment and add to your repertoire of teaching strategies. This chapter shows you many of the wonderful or useful methods you can try to adapt for your classroom and teaching style.

Don't attempt these all at once. Start a Structure-A-Month group (see peer support recommendations in Chapter 2), or focus on just one for an entire year or until you feel comfortable using the technique. The following classroom activities are all ones that I have attempted, but I am not going to claim that I have mastered them. I will, however, pass along recommendations to you about what worked really well for me. The majority of the educational practices (the how-to instructions), unless someone else is credited in the individual section, were gleaned and/or adapted either from Canady and Rettig's two books on teaching in the block or Spenser Kagan's book on cooperative learning. Other bits and pieces come, like most teachers' classroom practices, from over 20 years of observations, sharing with colleagues, inservices, student-suggested changes, and a variety of other places that I have borrowed from, often so long ago that I no longer remember whom to credit for these ideas. I hope each and every one will find a place in your curriculum.

SPONGE ACTIVITIES

At the beginning of every block and at various times during the block, even in the best planned lessons, there are times when students are sitting and waiting to learn, times, for example, when the teacher is occupied with: passing back homework or tests; passing out worksheets; taking attendance; catching a student up on missed assignments; talking to the principal, another teacher, or a parent; finding a spot on a tape or a video; or writing a pass. According to Elaine and Tom Lubiner (1990), studies have found that as many as 60 instructional minutes *per day* are lost during such times!

Madeline Hunter, at the UCLA Lab School, designed a series of activities called SPONGE activities, which keep students focused and on-task during these formerly idle moments of class. They also minimize the need to discipline students by keeping them busy and focusing them on learning and using the language in many different ways, adaptable to their many different learning styles.

SPONGE is an acronym for:

SHORT, intense, vivid activities, which provide
PRACTICE of learned material, which students can do
ON THEIR OWN, and which will also include
NEW arrivals or those finishing an assignment early, by
    keeping the
GROUP involved, and designed to
ELICIT an immediate response.

Sponge is a good name for these activities, because they do "soak up" the unused little bits of time during any class. They also are very useful for a short break in a lecture or a change of pace when students' eyes are glazing over. Well-designed sponges also appeal to a large variety of student learning styles and reinforce your curriculum quite nicely. The following pages will show how I adapted her ideas for my foreign language classroom.

A sponge should first of all be *short*, taking from 15 seconds to several minutes to complete. It should also *practice* previously learned material, so that students can do these without your help, as the primary purpose of a sponge is to keep students occupied when you are not available. These activities are easy for students arriving late to class to join without needing any explanation from you, or for students who finish an assignment or a test early to begin without needing your assistance. Some are done on an individual basis, but many are designed for groups and all get students involved immediately.

I have adopted and adapted Dr. Hunter's idea about creating sponge activities, and keep lists of them in each chapter folder, both written on an overhead sheet, and on paper, for easy reference when, for example, class is interrupted by someone needing to see me. To write sponges, just think of the chapter in all four of its aspects: grammar, vocabulary, culture, and literature. Then, consider the five different types of sponge:

- Say to yourself

- Say to another

- Say in chorus

- Write a response

- Signal

Try to write as many of each type for that chapter as possible. After these are written on scrap paper, I also like to group them by how long they take to do, so if I need a really short one, or a one-minute, or a three-minute one, I can go to the list and find it more easily.

SAY TO YOURSELF

In this type of sponge, you ask the student to tell themselves something. This type of quiet activity is good for settling things down at the beginning of class, after a fire drill or an announcement, while you are erasing the board, while they are moving into their groups, or after a test while a few slower students are still finishing. Here are some examples of this type of sponge:

- Describe to yourself what you see in this picture/poster/video with the sound OFF.

- Tell yourself all the different uses of the subjunctive mood.

- Think of at least three characteristics of existentialism/the main character of a story or book or poem or video (the Little Prince, La Caterina, Don Quixote, or Madame Bovary, for example)

- Picture to yourself a typical American table setting/class schedule/house/ farm, etc.

- Read the poem/next paragraph/next page and locate the main idea.

- Read the paragraph/dialogue. Look at the illustration, and decide which of the following is the most appropriate title: (a) In a clothing store (b) Clothes do not make the man or (c) T-shirts are in style.

♦ Read the story/dialogue/paragraph and make up an appropriate title for it (or two titles, or three titles).

Notice that all sponges use action verbs in the command form.

SAY TO OTHERS

These sponges ask a student to do a short activity with a partner, such as:

♦ Alternate naming objects you see in the classroom.

♦ Take turns describing each other's clothing/accessories.

♦ Practice the dialogue. Then switch roles.

♦ Tell each other the most important thing you learned in this class yesterday/today (very useful, especially if there were several on a field trip or testing the day before).

♦ One of you name a room. The other name as many items of furniture as possible to be found in that room.

♦ Ask your partner a question about the paragraph you just read.

♦ Ask your partner what he or she did last weekend/will do this weekend.

♦ Taking turns, one of you name a verb, and the other conjugate it in the _____ tense. Then switch.

♦ Each of you take a card. On it is a vocabulary word. Play pictionary/hangman.

♦ Show your partner an object you brought to class/wore to class, and describe its color, size, and so on, also tell your partner how you feel about that object.

♦ Using your family tree drawing, take turns asking questions about the people: how they look, what their profession is, if you like them. Are they pretty, stupid, old?

♦ Describe a snapshot you brought to your partner. When was it taken? How old were you? Who are the other people in it?

♦ Draw a picture of your favorite meal. Then describe it to your partner.

♦ Trade pictures and order a meal just like the one in the picture.

♦ Tell your partner three things that can be opened/closed/put on/taken off.

♦ Ask your partner what makes him or her happy/sad/angry.

♦ Tell your partner a (clean) joke, in *(language)*, of course!

♦ Say something complimentary/insulting to your partner.

♦ Tell your partner six things you used to do that annoyed various members of your family.

Toward the end of a "say to another," walk around and monitor how they are doing, and perhaps ask a few to do theirs for the class. This small-group type of activity is a lot less stressful, however, than speaking to the entire class, and will involve the students in teaching/correcting each other which, according to the Glasser scale, is quite beneficial.

SAY IN CHORUS

This takes a bit more supervision, but students like to say things together: the alphabet, days of the week, months, numbers counting by 5's, 3's, or 10's, and the parts of an irregular verb. But to make it longer *and* better, add the words "forward AND backward!" This makes it less likely that the student will learn only the correct sounds to produce, forcing the student to connect the sounds and what they represent in order to produce them in reverse order.

WRITTEN RESPONSE

This is exactly how it sounds: your instructions would be written on the board, on an overhead, or on cards on each student's desk, asking the student to write something similar to the following:

♦ List the four seasons, and the typical weather for each one.

♦ Write what you want your friends/teacher/parents to do for you.

♦ Make a list of foods that are served (or never served) at the school cafeteria.

♦ Write a five-word description of the story/poem we read yesterday.

♦ Write a five-word description of your favorite place to visit/favorite sandwich/favorite class.

♦ Complete this sentence: The teacher is …

♦ Use the same noun in the nominative, accusative and genitive cases.

♦ List at least five Spanish/French-speaking countries and their capitals.

- ◆ Make a list of famous people and tell where they are from (e.g., Charo es de España..., but they do not have to be from Spanish-speaking countries).

- ◆ List four famous people and adjectives to describe them.

- ◆ List four famous people and what clothes they would wear.

- ◆ Write eight commands that your father or mother often gives to you.

- ◆ Write down three things you ought to do sometime soon.

- ◆ Using *puedo* (*I can, I am able*), list five things you can do well. Then compare your list with a partner.

- ◆ Write a question I could ask on tomorrow's test/could have asked on yesterday's test but didn't.

- ◆ Write a two-sentence description of the poster/photo you see on the front board.

- ◆ List three different uses for the object on the front table (objects such as scissors, a plant, a ruler, etc.).

- ◆ Using adjectives, make up compliments you might give to other students in the class. Examples: *Roger, tu es très amusant. Lynne, tu es très gentille. Annette et Paul, vous êtes charmants.*

In every instance of this type of sponge, these responses might be collected and graded. The students also could take them, get together with a partner, and read them to each other, while you monitor the students by walking around.

A Japanese teacher I observed in Missouri had students' names written on three-by-five cards, and after the student was called on, his/her card was placed at the bottom of the pile, so everyone had a chance to speak; when she got back to the beginning, she shuffled them before using the stack again. This would be a good method if your intent is to grade their oral responses and you need to make sure everyone has a turn, but it does not encourage active participation by all students all the time, unless the topic is of VERY high interest to them; so you would need another assignment or sponge for the class when their turn is over, or have them fill out a feedback page for their folder (see Figure 4.1).

I prefer to keep a container for each class (mine is a decorative tin, but a goldfish bowl or a similar object would also work) with every student's name on strips of paper inside. I draw several names at first, have them read theirs, and

FIGURE 4.1. FEEDBACK PAGE

SKITS: Ordering at a café

THINGS I WOULD MOST LIKE TO ORDER:

1. _____   Who ordered them:_____

2. _____   _____

3. _____   _____

4. _____   _____

5. _____   _____

THINGS I WOULD LEAST LIKE TO ORDER:

1. _____   Who ordered them:_____

2. _____   _____

3. _____   _____

4. _____   _____

TELL TWO THINGS YOU SHOULD DO WHEN ORDERING:

1.

2.

TELL TWO THINGS A WAITER WOULD DO AT A CAFÉ

1.

2.

Which group did the best on their skit and why do you think so?

---

use those to comment on corrections or adjustments needed. After calling on a student, the paper strip is replaced in the jar. Because all students have the potential to be called on, this maintains their attention. (More on active and passive learning in the next part of this chapter.)

A fun variation on this is the M & M game. Bring a bag of M & M's and pass it around the class, telling students that they may take as many as they want with one hand, but, first, they must count them and report the number of M & M's to you. Once you have everyone's totals, you tell them that they owe you a sentence (written *or* oral) for every M & M they have taken. Give them a topic such as their summer, or vacation, or a specific tense they must use. If this is done orally, keep all students actively involved by stipulating that no one may repeat a sentence that another has already used.

SIGNALING

The final sponge method is having the students signal their response. It is especially good because it appeals to almost any student learning style (oral, visual, kinetic, etc.). Examples of this type would be to say or write something such as: "Hold up your fingers to show me how many _____ you know." In the blank would go such things as how many answers to *ça va?*, uses for the verb *ser*, items to order at a (name type of store), classroom items, characteristics of an epic poem/gothic architecture/street scene, and so forth.

Then call first on a student who has a small number of fingers raised; that student can be successful in naming the more obvious answers correctly while the students with a large number of fingers can name the more exotic ones. This is great for involving all students because they *must* listen so as not to repeat what anyone has previously said. Yet, once they are done with their contribution, they are still curious to learn which items they forgot and will remain active listeners.

Another, briefer type of signaling sponge activity is to have students signal by hitting their desk, stomping their feet, standing up, lifting a piece of paper, or some other sort of physical demonstration to indicate if:

◆ a word is masculine or feminine, singular or plural, nominative or genitive, and so on.

◆ a sentence (either written or spoken) is true or false.

◆ a verb is in the past or present, future or conditional, indicative or subjunctive (to differentiate tenses).

◆ a given situation requires *saber* or *conocer* (*savoir* or *connaître*, in French)

◆ a given situation requires the passé composé/preterite or the imperfect

In this type of sponge, however, you must supply the cues, either on an overhead projection, a handout, or orally, so you must be available during the signaling to monitor the correctness of the answers. This is a really good thing to do while erasing the board, quickly cueing a tape, or some other short activity.

In summary, sponge activities keep you from wasting valuable class time and help minimize discipline problems, because students are kept busy all the time, thinking and performing in the language rather than remaining at loose ends. Additional time thinking and performing in the language is exactly what you want. Used with variety, sponge activities make class time pass more quickly, and your students happier. Make every minute count, and test scores should go up, too.

At a recent workshop I hosted, a teacher informed me that she had been doing "sponges" for several years to begin her class, but that when she learned them, they were called "bellringers." Sponges can be bellringers (beginning activities) but I encourage my students to start *before* the bell, and I also use them during other portions of the class, for example, when erasing the board or cueing a tape.

I spent an entire year developing sponge activities as a part of my formative evaluation process, and I continue to work on them. This is not a skill you gain overnight, but don't give up as you will see a big difference in classroom discipline and in learning.

ACTIVE VS. PASSIVE LEARNERS

Too many classroom activities give students free time or let them choose not to participate. I used to ask a question at the beginning of each class, call on students first who raised their hands to answer, and then on the others; that is what my teachers had done. But many times I found myself with no one willing to answer, so I answered myself, or, worse, begged for someone to answer. Also, after the last student had answered, I needed to call back to order/attention those who went first, in order to proceed with the next portion of my lesson. Sound familiar?

An easy way to avoid this situation is NEVER to ask a question of the class, even something such as, "Can you all see/hear this?," or "Do you understand?." It is a difficult habit to break, but worth trying. Instead, phrase everything you say as a command (use imperative forms of verbs):

- ♦ Raise your hand if you can see/hear me OK.

- ♦ Stomp your foot if you understood the directions.

- ♦ Stand up if you know the answer.

- ♦ Hold your thumb up, down, or sideways: up for *yes*/agree, down for *no*/disagree, sideways for *don't know*.

- ♦ Point to the picture of a _____. (An old TPR (Total Physical Response) trick I'm sure you recognize.)

- ♦ Write the word for _____ in the air with your finger.

- ♦ Show me with your face how this character felt.

- ♦ Thump your desk/clap if I make a mistake as I write this sentence/ when you see the mistake in this sentence on the board.

There are many more such active learning strategies: every one listed in the sponge activities section involves students participating actively, rather than passively or not at all.

You can still use questions for the whole class to answer, if you must, but you should approach them differently. If I ask everyone to name a sport, and just go up and down the rows in order, they spend time preparing until it is their turn, respond, and then tune out afterward. If I go one step further and call on them randomly, this is better until they have responded, and then they are free to tune out, write notes, or make noise. If I call on them randomly AND mandate that no one can use an answer that has been used previously, they have to listen to everyone who goes before them, as well as to prepare several answers . Calling on students randomly is better practice, but there is still the problem of being done after their turn has come to speak. Therefore, they should be told that they may be called on more than once: that keeps them involved until you end the activity.

To summarize, the ideal way to conduct questioning activities is to:

♦ call on students in random order (I use names on strips of paper)

♦ mandate a unique response (so they listen to everyone else)

♦ call on people more than once (I put the strips back in the jar or sometimes just pick on those who look as if their attention has strayed).

Several teachers at my school, suggested another easy method to actively involve students: the use of manipulative objects. Students each get three differently colored cards, rods, chips, or whatever you prefer. Let's say one is red, one is green, and the other is yellow. There are many ways to use these. Students could hold them up to signal their opinion; for example, red if it's a regular verb, green if it is irregular, yellow if the student is unsure. They also may use the cards to signal you quietly and unobtrusively for help on an assignment: green card if things are going smoothly, yellow card if help is needed but not urgently, red card if help is needed urgently. This makes it very easy to just survey the classroom and see who is in trouble, and it also makes it easier for shy students to request assistance if they have a question.

A new (to me) technique I began using this year is the occasional use of whiteboards. These can be purchased from foreign language supply catalogs *or* you can go to a building supply store and purchase a 4x6-foot piece of shower-board and have it cut into 24 one-foot squares. Students can use crayons, felt-tip markers, or overhead markers on these. To erase, try old pieces of flannel, old socks, or other similar fabrics. Have students spell a word you say, as you quickly scan the boards for accuracy. Have them draw a face that shows how they would answer the question, "How are you?" and then trade boards and "read" them to each other. Dictate math problems or phone numbers, have them write all the forms of a particular verb, draw a person as you describe him or her, write a synonym or antonym for a word you say, and so on. These are all things that could be done on paper, but the whiteboards are a change of pace that students really seem to enjoy.

Does this mean you cannot lecture any more? No, but you should do it with a different twist: talk in short bursts of under 10 minutes, and then stop for what I call a comprehension break. Gale Elkins, whose workshop I attended, compared a student to a glass of water; you can only pour so much into it and then it overflows. That is a good metaphor to keep in mind as you talk; it will remind you to pause every so often for a brief change of pace. Remember using the TPR (Total Physical Response) method of teaching? One of the main caveats was to teach new vocabulary or grammar in small bursts, specifically in groups of three, give students a chance to practice those three, and then incorporate them with items learned previously before introducing new ones. This technique also applies nicely to a lecture situation.

Research shows that even the best, most motivated students need, every 10 minutes or so, to stop and process what they have learned. Try things such as:

- ◆ Write what I just said on a piece of scrap paper, in your own words.

- ◆ Draw a star next to the most important item in your notes so far (or, on the most important item in your partner's notes so far).

- ◆ Read your neighbor's paper. Do not talk. Put a question mark, a *no*, or a *yes* next to what he or she has written.

- ◆ When I clap my hands, say a new word/verb form/idea you learned today.

- ◆ Write a question I could ask on your next test about what I just said. Then answer the question.

After such pauses, during which students will have reviewed what was taught and highlighted or starred the significant portions for easy review later, you may proceed with either clearing up any uncertainties that arose when they did the pause activity or continue the lecture. These breaks are not a waste of time at all, as they fix information more securely through brief practice and also give you a bit of feedback or assessment of how well things are being processed and absorbed by your students.

How about oral reports or skits? Have the students help you grade or evaluate. For oral reports or skits, either have them take notes to be put in the folder or the journal that you collect periodically, or have them fill out a critique form such as the one in Figure 4.2, and have filling it out be a part of their grade.

FIGURE 4.2. CRITIQUE FORM

CRITIQUE SHEET, Oral Reports, French II

Rate your clssmates' reports on this scale: 5   Excellent
                                               4   Good
                                               3   Average
                                               2   Needs improvement

NAME(s): _____

    Pronunciation   5   4   3   2

Words pronounced incorrectly: _____

    Correct format   5   4   3   2

Comments _____

    Interesting/Creative   5   4   3   2

Comments: _____

    I LIKED MOST: _____

    I LEARNED: _____

Think for a moment about what an active student looks like. Words like eye contact, taking notes, speaking aloud, nodding heads, and asking questions would come to mind. The above strategies will force students to participate more actively in your chosen activities, and these only involve minor adjustments in what you already do in your classroom.

COOPERATIVE LEARNING STRATEGIES

Cooperative learning raises student participation and performance to the bottom portion of Glasser's hierarchy (see Figure 1.6, p. 29), where teachers will be the "guide on the side" and students will work together either in pairs or in groups. Older students prefer to listen to their peers, and they will listen better to a peer "authority." These strategies encourage participation in many different ways.

GROUPING STUDENTS

Cooperative learning is when students work together to maximize their own and each other's learning. Work is done as a group, with individual accountability. Since 1898, more than 700 studies have shown cooperative learning to offer these benefits:

♦ higher achievement and greater productivity,

♦ better and more supportive relationships, both among students and with the instructor, and

♦ greater self-esteem and better social skills on the part of the students.

This has been true in urban, rural, and suburban schools, and with studies involving different ethnic groups, say Johnson, Johnson, and Holubec (1993). Robert E. Slavin (1991) also found these benefits: a greater liking for classmates; more acceptance for mainstreamed students; a development of attitudes such as fondness for school and peer models who favor doing well academically; feelings of individual control over one's fate; and expressions of altruism. Slavin noted that these findings were true for high-, medium- and low-ability students. Kagan (1995) says that cooperative learning works because it fosters peer tutoring, frequent practice, a lot of time on task and, due to peer support, lowered anxiety over performance.

In a foreign language classroom, then, cooperative learning seems ideal. It quickly builds students into a working unit, encouraging them to help each other be successful, at the same time lessening their anxiety over performance (who hasn't had a freshman shaking and near tears during a skit, or freezing up, or even refusing to participate?). In addition to these social benefits, these methods also use Glasser's higher-retention levels of performance and provide more time on task than other types of activities, which makes them definitely worth trying.

Kagan (1995) suggests trying cooperative learning on a very limited basis at first, but with an eventual (and this could be years down the road) goal of using it 60 to 80 percent of the time. There are basically three different types: formal (the group stays together until a project is done), informal (extremely short-term activities such as checking with a partner), and base group (a long-term group whose goal is to provide peer support for each other as well as to be accountable in the long-term for grades and participation/performance).

GROUP SIZE

Opinions vary on how big a cooperative group should be. Johnson, Johnson, and Holubec (1993) say "the smaller, the better," recommending pairs or triads. They remind the reader that the larger the group, the harder it is for each participant to speak extensively, to reach consensus, to keep on task, and to maintain good working relationships. It is also true that, especially if your activity is to last only a short time, a smaller learning group takes less time to organize, gets going faster on task, and has more time to interact with one another.

Kagan (1995) points out that he favors four-person teams. These would still allow pair work, but instead of two possibilities (student A to B, and vice versa), a four-person team would have six different pair possibilities, with the option for the pairs to also operate as a larger team. He rejects the triad set-up, stating that he finds that they usually end up as a pair who work well together with another person who is "odd man out." (We all know several other sayings about threes, such as "Three's a crowd.")

I have had good luck using groups of four. However, classes often are formed of numbers of students not divisible by four. If I have one student left, I make one group of five (usually putting a student who is often absent or who is having difficulties with a strong, supportive group). If I have two left, then I have two groups of three, and, if three, one group of three. If these are formal (long-term) groups, I may even have the fourth persons in the other groups move from group to group, so that each group temporarily has three at some point during the grading period, unless my goal is to have strong group bonding.

CREATING GROUPS

There are also quite a few different ways of grouping students. The first is random grouping; students would, for instance, draw cards. Some would have a country's name and others would have capital cities, and students would find their "match" to pair up. Other pairing possibilities include a sport and its equipment (tennis/racket, baseball/bat), a classroom item with its picture, a clock time with its picture, an adjective with its opposite (rich/poor, tall/short), a color and something that would be that color (sky/blue, banana/yellow), and hundreds of other combinations. Sometimes I simply use an all-purpose set that has a color and a number; students find others with the same color, and each already has a number for his or her role in the activity. Of course, I reuse these, collecting them quietly as the students work and I wander around monitoring their performances.

Another way is called *stratified random*. This method divides students based on their performance on a pretest. The first group is formed by selecting the student with the best and worst scores of the class, and taking the two middle scorers. The second group would have the second best and worst, and the two on either side in the middle, and so on. This is still random, but provides a good mix of low, medium, and high ability students. This can only be done the day after the pretest, however. When I return their tests, I have noted their group and number on the bottom (for example, A1 for the best, A2 for the worst, A3 and A4 for the middle). I like to use this method when we get in groups to go over the test or to preview the next chapter which builds on skills from the previous one. However, I do not completely follow the random portion if that gives me a single-sex group, or if it contains a best-friend or worst-enemy combination (our school does not contain many different ethnic groups, but if it did, I would consider that factor, also).

Another variation on this random-stratified is called *line-up* and is one that students perceive as being very fair. This method is also a teaching strategy described in the "Line-up" section of this chapter.

The third selection method is called *teacher-selected*. Once again, the teacher chooses people while attempting to have as heterogeneous a group as possible, and whom the teacher considers will work well together with a minimum of difficulty. I use this based on willingness to participate, pairing highly motivated students with less motivated ones in the hope that the enthusiasm will "rub off."

One word of caution: do not be tempted to announce the groups orally. This wastes a lot of time, and often at the end of reading each student's assignment individually, several have forgotten theirs, or have questions. Instead, have the groups written on cards at their work stations, or on an overhead or poster, so they may move quickly to their groups. A teacher I observed announcing the group assignments took over 10 minutes before everyone understood where they went; with cards or an overhead the time to assemble is reduced to next to nothing, especially if the class is already trained about your expectations so that they move quickly and quietly to their assigned spots.

Another method suggested by all three books mentioned so far is *support groups* (I am not sure where the method originated). In this, students are given a list of the other students in the classroom, and are asked to mark a plus (+) next to the three with whom they would most like to work, and also to indicate a minus (-) for the three they prefer the least. They are NOT promised to get all their choices but are told that their opinions will be taken into account whenever possible. The teacher then graphs their choices and can easily see who is popular, who is not at all popular, and who is an "isolate," chosen by no one. The teacher then should carefully structure the groups so that these isolates have a good support group to draw them into the class activities. This might be a good method for the beginning of the year, when students and their abilities are not yet known to you. It also has the benefit of making the students feel more comfortable with the group right away, because they had a hand in choosing their partners.

The fifth method of assigning groups, and the least recommended, is *student-selected*. These groups tend to be too homogeneous as students of the same ability level tend to select each other. One way to use this and avoid at least a few problems of that sort is to specify that groups may not be homogeneous, i.e., all football players or all female. I also read of another hybrid variation that sounds quite good: first, after determining the students' ability levels, the teacher meets briefly with the highest-ability students (but without labeling them as such to the class). Presenting these students with a list of the lowest-ability students (but without identifying them as such), the teacher informs the first group that they must decide who from this list will be their partner. The following day, these students will, without prompting, approach their new partners and ask them to be partners, and together they select the other two group members from the remaining members of the class. I particularly like this, because often the lower-ability students are the last chosen and this may be their first time ever to be picked first. In fact, the instructions suggested that there may be a very touching moment from time to time when this happens. I can't wait to try it!

ASSIGNING ROLES

Once the students are divided into groups, by whichever method used, each student in the group must have one (or two) roles assigned to him or her. The usual method is to have students number off from one to four (or the card they had received will already have done this for them). Then, based on these numbers, roles are assigned. Some possible roles are:

- ◆ Task Master—This person is in charge of making sure everyone works. He/she has the instruction sheet but does NOT assign duties; that must be a group decision.

- ◆ Encourager/Praiser—This person encourages everyone to participate.

- ◆ Summarizer—This person restates or summarizes whatever answer the group decides on.

- ◆ Checker—This person makes sure each individual on the team understands the answer, how it was done and that each can do it.

- ◆ Accuracy Coach—This person makes sure that everyone on the team has the answer absolutely correct (corrects minor errors, adjusts minor differences).

- ◆ Researcher/Runner—This person checks the text, dictionary, or other resources for information when the group needs this.

- ◆ Recorder/Secretary—This person puts down on paper the group decision and/ or reports it to the class.

Not all these roles are needed every time. For filling out a worksheet, I would use a Task Master, a Checker, a Researcher, and a Recorder, and would tell the entire group that they all must fulfill the Praiser and Accuracy Coach roles for each other. This is because my primary goal for a worksheet is to have each student know how to conjugate the verb, or to make adjectives agree in gender and number, or to correctly choose and position direct object pronouns (basically factual, one-correct-response situations). However, if I had the group discussing a poem, I would have a Task Master who reads aloud, a Researcher who looks up unfamiliar words, an Encourager to make sure each person contributes and receives praise for doing so, and a Checker to make sure everyone understands and can respond to the questions.

The Checker is the role every group must have. Rosensline and Stevens (1986) found that checking frequently for comprehension was significantly correlated with higher levels of student learning and achievement. The Checker makes sure everyone knows whatever the essential learning is, because to be successful the group must have group goals (e.g., filling out the worksheet) and individual responsibility (each person must know everything).

Kagan (1995) suggests actually giving the students "role cards" stating which role they have and suggestions on how to perform it, at least the first few times you do cooperative activities. An example would be something like this: Task Master, your job is to keep everyone working on the assigned task. If someone distracts the group, you may wish to say something like, " This is an interesting problem," or "Do you think we will finish this activity on time?" to call the group's attention back to the job.

Because students are going to be working together more frequently, I have developed a "Useful Phrases When Working in Groups" list (Figure 4.3.) to give to students. For this book, I have put it in the three foreign languages that I know; you would want these only in the language you teach.

Each type of cooperative activity will have different instructions, purposes, and types of assessment. When planning the activity, the teacher must always decide on these four factors first: type of group, group size, how students are assigned to the group, and student roles. In a cooperative activity, the teacher assumes these duties:

- ◆ Specify the type of activity and its objectives.

- ◆ Make decisions about placing students in groups.

- ◆ Explain the task and goal structure to the students.

- ◆ Monitor student performance and intervene when necessary.

- ◆ Evaluate/assess the learning that took place. (Provide closure.)

The teacher should be careful when explaining the task and goals to highly structure the description. In other words, the teacher should not just say, "Work with your partners and ask each other questions," but, rather, "Everyone ask Student C one question. No one may ask a second question until all the rest of the group has asked C a question."

FIGURE 4.3. USEFUL PHRASES FOR COOPERATIVE LEARNING

FUNCTION	SPANISH	FRENCH	GERMAN
Ask for information	Me gustariá saber… Sabes… Dime…	Je voudrais savoir… Est-ce que tu sais… Dis-moi…	Ich möchte wissen… Weisst du… Sag mir…
Request clarification	Cómo? Porque? No entiendo Repite, por favor Tengo una pregunta Yo pienso que…	Comment? Pourquoi? Je ne comprends pas. Repétéz, s'il vous plait. J'ai une question. Je pense que….	Wie? Warum? Ich verstehe nicht. Noch einmal, bitte. Ich habe eine Frage. Ich glaube dass…
General statements	En general Entonces Normalmente	En général Ensuite/puis D'habitude	Im allgemeinen Denn Gewöhnlich
Check for understanding	Entiendes? Vale?	Tu comprends? Ça va? C'est correct?	Verstehst du? Gut? Richtig?
Show understanding	Sí Tienes razon Vale	Oui/ouais Tu as raison D'accord	Ja (jawohl) Du bist richtig. Gut
Express disbelief	De veras? No me digas	Ce n'est pas vrai! Je ne crois pas.	Das ist unwöhnlich. Unglaublich!
Express approval	Fantastico Que bueno Buena idea Eres inteligente	Fantastique Très bien Bonne idée Tu es intelligent	Fantastisch Prima Gute Idee Du bist klug

GROUP INCENTIVES

Except in cases where the group product is something creative like a video-tape, mural, or group performance, the general rule is that a group grade is never given. Instead, the teacher should provide two things: praise and incentives. As the groups work, find examples of behavior you wish to see, and call them to the entire class's attention, describing in exact terms what they are doing that pleases you. This is particularly effective, for example, if the classroom is getting a bit rowdy and you would prefer more sedate behavior, or if the assignment is quite difficult and one group has found a good method of breaking it into smaller, more manageable units.

Incentives can be in the form of play money, free time, bonus points, or whatever activities the class really likes to do (my students love to play *pétanque*, a game called *bocci* in Italian; they also love music videos and movies, and I may use those as rewards for jobs well done). Incentives should be based on performance and should be announced to the class before the exercise. Perhaps an incentive may be given when everyone in the group scores above 90 percent on the quiz (or a specified criterion), or when all the members improve their scores over those of the pretest, or when everyone gets 100 percent on a set of answers, or when a group's total score is above a certain level. You decide what you would like to see and they will strive to fulfill your expectations.

TYPES OF COOPERATIVE LEARNING ACTIVITIES

This is by far the largest category of activities for foreign language teachers. Because our main focus is on communication, we want our students to listen and speak as often as possible. I divide the activities according to whether they are for pairs or for groups, but you will notice that many paired activities are easily adaptable to working in groups, simply by having the pair join another pair and sharing what they have done; or by forming new pairs with the two new partners.

The clocks discussed in Chapter 3 (see Figure 3.7, p. 70) are the system I use to pair my students quickly and easily the very first day of class. It not only serves as a getting-to-know-each-other activity, it is also an opportunity to build student movement into that day's lesson plans. I also schedule a paired activity for that day, and begin training them to move quickly and quietly together, with a minimum of fuss. One clock page will last an entire grading period.

THINK/PAIR/SHARE (TPS)

This may be the strategy I use most often. It begins as an individual active learning or sponge strategy. The teacher asks the students to think of:

- three words to describe their clothing

- two different ways to greet someone they know

- the most important thing learned yesterday in class

- three uses for the imperfect tense

- all the forms of the verb *to go* in the future

Or the teacher may ask for any similar topic that is in that day's lesson. This strategy may call for a fact or facts, an opinion, a review or an extension of yesterday's lesson, based on something seen, heard, or remembered. Give the students what you judge to be enough time (some exercises will take more thought than others), and then have them find a partner (pair) using the clock page or another method. Then the students will tell their partner what their thoughts were (share).

If you like to use Venn diagrams, this is a good activity to do before completing one. The students will have already thought about the topic and, during the sharing session, it is easy to fill in the diagram: Student A likes soccer, and so does B, so it goes in where the circles interlock (Figure 4.4). This keeps the students talking to each other, sharing likes and dislikes, and writing in the target language, which becomes a good product for assessment purposes, or even to post on the bulletin board if the class is still getting to know one another.

FIGURE 4.4. VENN DIAGRAMS

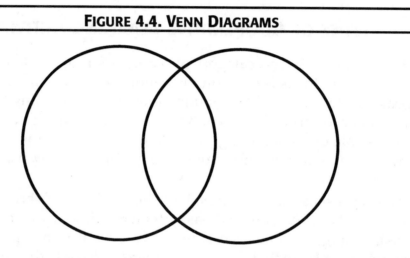

In the target language, students discuss food preferences, sports, or whatever. Student A will record any preferences in the left circle and Student B in the right circle, but preferences they both *share* go into the overlapping area.

Here is a fun activity that uses think/pair/share, as another illustration of this technique. It requires students to use familiar vocabulary and grammar to first make a list, and then share it with a partner:

> Imagine that you are working in a shop that sells T-shirts and blue jeans. Your boss wants you to put sayings on all of the T-shirts. Come up with several different slogans.

Give them, say, seven minutes to come up with at least three slogans. Then, using the clock system, pair them with Partner B6, and have them compare slogans, choosing the two best ones to share with the class or drawing the two best on a piece of paper for posting as a high-interest bulletin board. If you want the paired students then to share their opinions orally with others, there are several options. One is to combine the original set of partners with one other set and have them interact once more. This is really beneficial if the phrase they are practicing, for example, "I play soccer every day, but I do not dance," is a structure or vocabulary that will come up on a test. The more times they must say it, the more firmly it will be embedded in their minds, and the more different versions of it they hear from others, the more likely one will stick in their minds.

Another way to have them share with others is to call on selected students to say their slogan. This could be done randomly by the teacher (or perhaps based on good ones heard while walking around during the sharing sessions); by having each team pick their favorite; or by using the draw-a-name-from-the-jar method. However, my favorite way to have the whole class share is to ask the students to stand up when they have finished sharing with their partner. Not only can the teacher see clearly who is still working (or needs help) and go to that area, but it is one more chance for students to get out of their seats—student movement which is built into the lesson plans. Once everyone is standing, there is another benefit: the teacher can pick one student at random to say the phrase for the class. When the student is done, and sits down, the teacher asks everyone else with that answer to sit also. The whole class will look to see who has the same answer, and a little bit of "bonding" occurs based on similar interests. The teacher will also get a very good idea of how similarly the class feels on that topic, and, by writing on the board what each person/group answers, will have a nice list for review (or for visual learners) by the time everyone is seated.

To practice our newly filled-out clock pages, I use Think/Pair/Share the very first day of class, with the question, "What would you most like to do/learn this year in this class?" for Levels 2 and beyond; and "Why did you take this class?" for my first-year students. After they are all seated, we look at the list on the board and I am able to reassure them that, yes, we will do those things they want to do, and more (last year I had a group who wanted to learn more slang, and I was able to use that as an incentive quite successfully). For the beginners, we had a nice list of reasons to take a foreign language, which we later used to make posters to enter in the annual IFLTA poster contest. It also serves as a nice ice-breaker or class-building activity.

PAIRS/CHECK OR PAIR/SHARE

Pairs/Check is a good method for checking either notes or homework. Students simply trade notes from the previous day and underline or star important points, trade homework papers and check them, or compare papers on the assignment they just did in class. I also use this when I send students to the blackboard: one writes an answer and the partner checks it before they return to their seat.

This does *not* have to involve any talking whatsoever, if you prefer. Students would, in this case, simply write a *Yes*, *No*, or *?* next to the items on their partner's paper or notes, and then when the students return the papers to the owner, he or she could, on an individual basis, check the *No* or *?* answers using the text.

This is a good method to use for activities like changing a story from present to past tense, substituting pronouns for nouns, adding adjectives to a sentence (with attention to gender and number), or for simpler things like matching a picture to a sentence describing it, or writing a sentence to describe it. Culturally themed activities could include drawing a time line for a history unit, locating cities and countries on maps, or identifying famous people with their accomplishments.

This activity is often called Pair/Share if students are allowed to talk, which I recommend if there are several alternative answers; for example, if there are two or more possible ways to translate the word *you*, which there are in most foreign languages. If any changes are made or differences in answers discovered, the partners will discuss why they wrote their answer and reach a consensus on what answer is correct. The partner whose answer is chosen will then check that the other knows how to do that activity or a similar one (remember, checking for knowledge is the MOST important part of any group). Checking is done either by having them say back in their own words how to do the assignment or by asking them to do a similar one proposed by their partner or in their text.

Another slight variation on this is, when practicing a new skill, to check the papers in the following manner: Student A will read his or her answer aloud, also telling why he or she chose that answer (explainer); Student B will either agree with that answer or explain why he or she thinks it is incorrect (checker). When they have gone back to their text and found the correct answer, they switch roles for the next item. Students sometimes will not see the reason to go to all that trouble, wishing to simply copy from each other's paper. Therefore, if using this method, the teacher should plan to announce that the quiz over this skill will be scored in two ways: the individual points earned by the student, *plus* the points earned by their partner. In this way, they will see that it is to their own benefit to make sure their partner is very clear on how to do this new skill.

To increase the benefit from this, the teacher may wish to combine two pairs into a team because, if it is a difficult skill, four heads are better than one when checking. Make it clear to the group that no one is done until everyone is done, and that they are expected to explain the answers to each other, not just check their papers. If all four are stumped by a problem, they should all raise their hands for help from the teacher. If all four agree, a team self-congratulation (special handshake or whatever) is in order!

Think of the advantages of this strategy over the traditional method where individuals fill out workbook pages in isolation and, individually, turn them in.

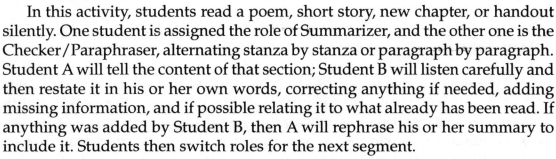

Pairs/Check	Traditional
Immediate feedback on performance	Delayed feedback (next day, at the earliest)
Frequent opportunity for correction	Infrequent (could do entire paper incorrectly)
Receive peer support and praise	Teacher's mark
Value placed on learning	Value placed on grade/points
Value placed on helping others	Value placed on winning (doing better than others)

You may not have thought of this yet, but if you do pick up these papers, you will find you need to make fewer corrections than ever before (papers take less time to grade), a hidden benefit for you.

PAIRS/READ

In this activity, students read a poem, short story, new chapter, or handout silently. One student is assigned the role of Summarizer, and the other one is the Checker/Paraphraser, alternating stanza by stanza or paragraph by paragraph. Student A will tell the content of that section; Student B will listen carefully and then restate it in his or her own words, correcting anything if needed, adding missing information, and if possible relating it to what already has been read. If anything was added by Student B, then A will rephrase his or her summary to include it. Students then switch roles for the next segment.

Obviously, this activity begins on an individual basis, but forces the students to find the essential information and restate it several times, participating actively 100 percent of the time. Compare that to a situation in which a teacher asks one student to read aloud to the class, and you will see the benefits of this method! If you feel you need to check for comprehension, there are several ways. A worksheet that is collected would work; so would a short quiz either immediately after the activity, or the next day.

PAIRS/LISTEN

Pairs/Listen is an adaptation I made for my foreign language classes. Instead of reading something, I have students *listen* to a conversation on the tapes provided by our text. It could be students trying to get a hotel room or a date, looking at a photo album or gossiping about someone with a new boyfriend; but the students must listen individually, and I 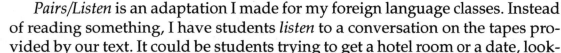stop the tape periodically for them to work with their partner to summarize, correct, or comment on what they have heard to that point, as well as to fill in the workbook. After going completely through the conversation and filling out the activity sheet, I ask them to listen silently to the complete conversation without interruptions, as it is repeated on the audiotape. With long, rapid conversations broken into smaller pieces, and with feedback from another student so that they can "catch up" if they become confused, students with poor listening skills don't just give up; they learn to be better listeners. Scores on the listening portions of our tests soared after we began doing this.

An interesting variation on Pairs/Listen for upper level classes is one I call *Eavesdropping*. Instead of listening to the same conversation, I have all the Student A partners listen to one, and all the Student B's listen to another similar one. Then, as partners, the A's tell the B's what they heard, with the B's asking questions such as, "Who was speaking?," "How old were they?," "Where were they?," "Were they happy or sad?," "How did B react when they said that?," and so on, until the substance of the entire conversation has been related. To assist them in asking questions, I give them a worksheet to fill out (Figure 4.5). Then the B's will relate the conversation they heard in the same manner. Other than the worksheet, this is very close to simulating what might actually occur when gossiping with someone, telling someone about a movie or TV show, etc.

PAIR/DRILL

 Have the two partners drill each other on facts or concepts they need to know: countries, provinces, or Länder and capitals, days of the week, the alphabet, rooms and furniture, family pairs such as uncle/aunt, brother/sister, subject pronouns and their corresponding possessives, and other grammar concepts. This may involve something as easy as providing an A and a B list, each with half the items from the unit being reviewed, and alternately calling out these items to each other, or the use of flashcards, with one quizzing the other all the way through the cards, and then trading roles.

This is good both for daily practice (trying to get the pile of "missed" cards smaller each time) and for test review situations: one might name an artist, and the other answer characteristics, or name a verb and list its forms in a certain tense, a noun and its declensions, a subject pronoun and its corresponding stress, or object pronoun or possessive adjectives, and so on.

FIGURE 4.5. CONVERSATION WORKSHEET

CONVERSATION REPORT: _____

Who was talking first (Speaker A)? _____

To whom (Speaker B)? _____

Where were they? _____

Information on speakers: Approx. age   A _____   B _____

Profession: A _____   B _____

Main topic of conversation: _____

Mental/emotional state during conversation: A: _____

B: _____

End result of conversation: _____

Did the speakers say good-bye? If yes, what words were used?

_____

Your opinion of what happened after this conversation took place: (be brief)

PAIR/INTERVIEW

With this activity, instead of a discussion, one partner merely interviews the other about hobbies and interests, future plans, family size and members, class schedules, or weekend activities, and then they switch roles, with B interviewing A. Each reports on his or her partner to the entire class in either written or oral form. This has an advantage over self-reporting because the students must convert the verb from the "I" form to the "he/she" form, making any other necessary changes. Once again, this simulates a real-life situation that often arises, introducing a friend to someone else.

Interviews also can be done for many other purposes: as an anticipatory set ("What do you want to learn most?," "What sort of experience have you had with____/meeting a stranger/traveling to a foreign country/buying a___?"); as well as for closure ("What did you learn today?," "What did we do that you would like more information/more practice on?," "What was the most interesting thing we did?," "How will you use what we learned today?").

If conversation is your basic goal, as when practicing greetings or basic self-description with first-year students, consider elaborating this to *Team/Interview*: after the pairs initially interview each other as above, put two pairs together. If the students are unusually shy, have them introduce their partner to the other pair (much less stress for the speaker than talking to the whole class). Otherwise, why not get new partners: have A talk to C, and B talk to D, then C talk to B and A talk to D- six different interviews, and much more practice speaking.

PAIR/COMMAND

This is basically a "do what I say" activity, with one person commanding the other as well as being the Checker, and the other obeying the orders. Students love this type of short activity:

- Draw the person I describe: he is tall, with long black hair...big hands...

- Color the table blue...and the desk green...and the teacher purple...

- Put the book on your head....Put your hand on my desk...

- Go to the door and state your name....Go to the blackboard and write your age...

- Draw a square. Put a triangle to the left. Draw a circle inside the triangle. Put a small square over the larger one...

These are more successful if you give students time to work on the commands before beginning. This practices not only the command forms of verbs, but also vocabulary such as classroom objects, colors, body parts, prepositions, or whatever you wish to build into the exercise. Of course, have them switch roles after a suitable amount of time has elapsed.

GET THE PICTURE!

This excellent pair activity format really motivates students. On the first day, the teacher asks students to cut out any photos from color magazines that they find interesting to look at (or, if you wish more structure, ask them to look for good illustrations of a certain vocabulary group such as emotions, foods, furniture, clothes, colors, etc.). These are mounted on paper by the students. The teacher selects and numbers the pictures to be used in a variety of ways by student pairs:

- Student A looks at the picture, but does not show it to Student B, instead describing it to Student B, who attempts to draw it according to the description. Reverse the roles, using a different picture.

- Student A looks at the picture without showing it to Student B, who asks questions to determine what is in the picture (only *yes/no* questions). Set a time limit *and* a limit on the number of questions that can be asked. Then, Student B must write down what he/she has in mind. Collect this description before the picture is revealed. Reverse roles with a different picture.

 ◆ Both students get to see the picture. Student A begins talking about the picture, talking nonstop about it until he/she cannot think of anything more to say. Then Student B must continue the description or story (these can get VERY creative) by either making statements or asking questions. This nonstop conversation continues for a period of time specified by the teacher before the activity began, until the teacher gives the command to stop. Our annual foreign language area competition has Nonstop Conversation as one of the competitions, and this is good practice for that.

COOPERATIVE ACTIVITIES FOR GROUPS

JIGSAW

This is my favorite group activity because I have shared it with so many teachers who have been so delighted when they tried it and were immediately successful *and* impressed by the learning that took place. However, it is not for everyday use, nor is it adaptable to all situations. Used occasionally, it is definitely a valuable addition to your classroom repertoire. This is my adaptation, borrowing a little from what textbooks call Jigsaw I, and rather more from Jigsaw II.

First, divide the class into teams, usually of about six members. Tell them they will all be learning the same unit. Each person on the team gets a different assignment and a different worksheet or activity to do. They all work independently. Then break them apart and reassemble them in Expert Groups, each made up of one person from each team, all of whom did the same assignment. First, they all check "their" section, do any research necessary, discuss the section, and plan how to tutor their teams about this subject. They then return to their original teams (regroup), tutor them, and administer a practice quiz to see if their team has mastered the topic, and do any reteaching necessary. Each member of the group tutors and pretests his or her topics and the whole group does a cooperative review; then the class is tested by the teacher.

Here is a more concrete example. I use Jigsaw as the very first group activity of every year, for the brief review needed before proceeding to new material, replacing the three to six review chapters in my text.

◆ Day One: Set up four teams of six students each. Give each member of the team a different assignment to do for tomorrow. A typical assignment is to read a page or so of one of the review chapters in the book and to do an activity from the text or workbook that tests that skill (takes about 20 minutes).

At the second-year level, I usually have a present tense group, past tense group, agreement of adjectives group, a pronoun and possessives group, a question-writing group, and a noun markers (definite, partitive, demonstrative, etc., articles) group.

♦ Day Two: Arrange students in six "Expert" groups of four each (all of whom have done the same assignment). They check their work, decide how to teach their topic, and write a practice quiz (about 20 minutes).

♦ Days Three, Four, and Five: The teams reform as four groups of six students each with one member only from each Expert group. Each day, two experts teach and pretest their topic, returning the corrected quizzes and reteaching as necessary the next day (25–30 minutes each day).

♦ Day Six: As a group, they complete a practice test over all six areas (25 minutes).

♦ Day Seven: Test is given by the teacher (15–20 minutes). Usually, each student receives a grade only on his or her own performance, so if the tutors don't do their jobs, the others get on their case to do a better job!

Notice that I use less than a third of any class period doing this review and that we have covered 27 pages in very little time. In the meantime, I have begun Unit 1 of the text, as well as a conversation unit. Another advantage of beginning with Jigsaw is that students see how interdependent they are upon each other for learning, and quickly learn to support each other's efforts and work together for future group work situations.

Jigsaw also can be used to introduce new material, such as a poem. Perhaps all the students would receive a poem by the same author, but one expert group would work on rhyme and/or meter, another on symbolism, similes, and metaphors, and yet another on the author's biography and how that might be reflected in the poem. Then, they would reassemble and teach each other what their expert group had discovered, all in about 45 minutes. If it were a new chapter, each expert group would get one portion of the chapter to read, study, analyze, teach, and give a quiz.

Jigsaw also can be used for concept attainment. I have a particularly interesting unit on medieval life, with expert groups on music, art, architecture, warfare, the feudal system, epic poetry, and food/clothing. After watching a video and taking notes on their expert area, each group has some time in the library to research, then class time to regroup, and then they present to their teams. At the end, I ask each team to try to find some common issues or themes that were true for as many of these areas as possible. They arrive, of course, at the important influence of the Church in every aspect of medieval life and make some very interesting observations.

INSIDE-OUTSIDE CIRCLE

This activity can be used almost daily for any type of communicative exercise. First, have the students count off by twos (in the target language, of course). Have all the ones stand and form a circle facing outward. Have the twos stand in an outer circle, each facing one of the inner circle students. Explain the activity as follows: Each student should tell the other his or her favorite sport or greet each other appropriately (Level 1), tell what they were doing at seven o'clock the previous evening, or what they would like their parents to give them for their birthday, or whatever concept the students are working on at the time. After about 30 seconds, the teacher will interrupt, have each make a quarter right turn, move two places, and do the same. Within several minutes, a student will have had four or five different partners, at which point the activity is over, or the teacher assigns a different topic of conversation.

Compare the efficiency of this to the traditional method of questioning each student individually, going up and down rows until each has answered; in Inside-Outside Circle, each student speaks many times (and will be gently corrected by classmates if pronunciation is incorrect, or the student spoke incorrectly or cannot be understood) rather than only once, and it takes much less time. It also requires memorization of the phrase, sentence, or pattern being practiced, as well as actively listening (rather than passively) to partners whose answers may vary.

Here are some other Inside-Outside Circle topics I have used and liked:

♦ The inner student runs into (literally) another, apologizes, and introduces a friend.

♦ The inner student calls the outer to ask about a homework problem. The outer helps and is then thanked politely.

♦ The outer student is walking down the street and meets the inner student, who asks him/her to do something that evening. The outer declines, explaining that he/she has a test, and says good-bye.

♦ The outer student is a salesman selling dictionaries (or whatever). He/she introduces him/herself to the inner student, and tries to sell them something. The inner person doesn't want one, as he/she already has one. They, of course, stay polite and end the conversation.

♦ The inner person calls the home of a friend to tell him or her something important. The outer person answers as a parent, says that the friend is not home, and asks to take a message.

A fun spinoff from Inside-Outside Circle is to break the circle into a game of Linkages. For example, a student will announce that he or she likes baseball. If the student's partner also likes baseball, they link arms and proceed as a team to another student or linked group. Once everyone is linked into a group, survey the groups (choral response) for the sport they like, and have them return to their seats.

Inside-Outside Circle is just great for doing skits. Put the skit pairs facing another pair. Pair A does their skit, then Pair B, then they each rotate one space and repeat. If the teacher stands in one spot, in a class of 24, after six rotations, the teacher has heard every skit; every student has done the skit six times instead of once (more practice speaking *and* receiving gentle peer advice/correction/encouragement). This is much less stressful for shy students *and* it saves a lot of class time:

♦ If each team did a 3-minute skit, plus a minute to get up from and return to seats, and a minute of teacher feedback, that would be 12 skits at 5 minutes each (60 minutes of class-time).

♦ Using Inside-Outside Circle, two 3-minute skits plus feedback times 6 rotations = 42 to 45 minutes, enough time saved to do another activity or two!

And, if the teacher doesn't have to hear every single skit, there is no need for 6 rotations; 2 or 3 are sufficient practice, so this activity now takes 25 minutes—less than half the time—and students were active all the time, either performing or listening, and they have repeated their performance 3 times.

Kagan (1995) says that requiring the students who listened to provide feedback (praise or correction) after each performance is perhaps the most valuable aspect of this activity, so don't skimp on that portion. I have been known to give my whole class grades based on how perfect the skits were. If I heard serious errors that their partners should have caught and corrected, then the whole class lost points on the activity. This is an excellent way to teach and promote social language.

Another variation on Inside-Outside Circle is to use cards. For example, the inside circle receives cards with the name of a room in a house. After stating what room they are in, the outside circle asks if they see a (name of a piece of furniture), to which they answer *yes* or *no*, depending on whether or not it was logical. The students then rotate to the right, but also pass their card to the right, creating many different situations for BOTH circles. In an upper-level class, we practiced the subjunctive tense in this way. The inner circle had a card with a situation on it (sort of a "Dear Abby" type), while the outer circle advised and was required to begin their answer with a phrase such as "I think that you…" or "In my opinion…" (which in French requires the subjunctive). Again, both students and cards rotated. The advice was sometimes silly and sometimes serious, but it was a very high-interest activity.

⭐ GRAFFITI ⭐

This method is what it sounds like. Students are placed in small groups (pairs or teams). Each is given a marker or crayon, and a paper is either placed on the desk top or taped to the wall. An alternate idea, if it is a sufficiently small class, is to situate each group at a different spot at the chalkboard. Give them a topic, and tell them to quickly write or draw a picture of anything they know about this topic, with as little discussion as possible so other teams will not hear. Give them a time limit; two or three minutes if the topic is not something huge like food or school. Pick up the products and go over them, assigning one point for every good, solid fact, and a half-point for every silly or nitpicky one; reward the best product, best drawing, or whatever.

This is an excellent activity for introducing new topics, such as professions. As you go over their work, teach them the word in the target language. It is also a good way to check to see what they already know before beginning a review unit; for example, have them list as many calendar things as they can. It is also good for pretest review. I did this before a test on Charlemagne and test scores were great. The drawings were especially effective in fixing ideas in the students' heads.

An alternate way of scoring these products came to me while I was playing Scattergories with friends: the next time I did Graffiti, I had one student from each pair stay with the group's paper to explain it, and the other students move one paper to the right to correct the next team's paper. I picked one group at random to name an item on the paper they were correcting and, if another group duplicated it, all examples of that fact were crossed out. Rewards were given to the team whose paper had the most original items on it, just like in Scattergories. All students were more actively involved listening and rereading during the correction portion than when I went over the papers one by one; so although it takes a bit longer, it is definitely worth the time. One bit of warning: my students get very enthusiastic, even a bit too lively, during this activity—so schedule an activity right afterward to settle them down a bit, if the quiz doesn't follow immediately.

ROUNDROBIN

The original version of this activity is to place the students in circles of about 10 students each. In this activity, students are given only one paper on which to respond, and pass it around and around the circle until it is completed. Each student, in addition to completing the next item on the paper, is told to read the previous ones, both as examples of how to do the exercise and to correct any errors they may see in the work of others; if an error is detected, it must be presented to the group and a group determination made that it is actually an error, before corrections are made. After any corrections and the addition of the new answer, the paper is passed to the next teammate.

This method is obviously preferable to individuals filling out papers in isolation, but there are a few problems, especially with a group of 10. What do the other nine do while one fills out the paper? This is why I advise smaller groups, to both minimize inactive time (and ensuing discipline problems) and to allow each person to fill out a larger proportion of the worksheet (more written practice). I also like to provide each group with more than one paper to complete; for example, while doing a foods unit, have one paper for each food group, and ask students to list foods from that group on that paper—dairy, meats, vegetables, fruits, sweets. Many papers means that every student is working all the time. If students have two or three versions of the same paper (e.g., a past tense verbs fill-in), they will not be doing the same example when it comes to them, so even that is better than just one paper.

I also like to use Roundrobin for textbook activities where students are asked to do a "timed writing," using a subject from Column A, a verb from Column B, and an object from Column C. I provide a separate sheet for each subject, and require that every sentence be different, as well as that every sentence on the card be correct. We often do this as a race, but I make it clear that quality (every sentence correct) is my most important criterion; groups turning in imperfect papers must wait 30 seconds before resubmitting them. This encourages the group to reread and correct the exercise rather than just speed through it.

Another form of Roundrobin is the old standby, row sentences (it has many other names; in fact, in French it is called, rather gruesomely, *Cadavres*). The object is to form a sentence using the cue word on the slip of paper. The first person takes a strip of paper and writes a noun, folding it over and passing it to the left (or, if seated in rows, to the person behind). The next person writes a verb, the third an adverb, then a preposition, another a noun and an adjective (the latter two are in that order only because in French most adjectives follow the noun: German and Spanish teachers would want to reverse these). Then the sentences are opened up, and shared around the circle, and perhaps even passed from group to group. They are often silly, but students enjoy reading them (especially if students' names are used as the first word—ask them to use their own or their partner's so there is one sentence for everyone in the class), so it is also a high-interest reading activity. There may even be a competition, with another version of this, to see which Roundrobin group can write the longest sentence that still makes sense.

Try using Roundrobin as a brainstorming activity. Give each group a statement, and have them think of as many ways as possible to say the same thing in different words. An example might be: "Ernst is unhappy today," and possible answers would be that he is miserable, he is not happy, he is sad, or he is depressed. Group storywriting for upper-level classes is also a type of Roundrobin. Several groups I know of on the Internet do this, and it is quite interesting to see how your story has evolved when it gets back to you. When I begin this type of activity, I assign the very first part as homework, so that the group does not wait for one person whose inspiration is perhaps lacking that day.

Rallyrobin is the same as Roundrobin, except that students work in pairs rather than individually. This would probably be good for a class with either low self-confidence or low ability; otherwise, I think it should not be necessary to work in pairs, because the peer correction portion of Roundrobin would provide peer support for everyone's effort. An example of Rallyrobin is the following, designed for a beginner-level class: Construct meaningful sentences from these sentence pieces. Pieces include nouns, verbs, and adverbial expressions. Sentences formed might read, "My mother dances in the gym. Your brother sings tonight. The dog eats quickly." After the pairs have formed sentences, they recombine and share their responses. It is good reading practice, and easy for students of even quite low ability. Rallyrobin is probably the same as Pair/Share.

If the Roundrobin effort involves some sort of project, such as a poster, instruct the students on proper behavior, remind them to stay in the target language, and then let the groups briefly do a Roam Around the Room to view each other's products (more student movement). Then tell them to return to their teams to briefly share what they saw and liked before disbanding. Immediate feedback is better than posting the products on the board for viewing the next day. Roam Around the Room is also a good way to conclude the sentence-writing activity in the previous paragraph, with students returning to their groups to add any new sentences they saw to their own list.

TEAMS CONSULT

This activity focuses on group work that does not require consensus, be it the answer to a homework problem or an opinion. The first requirement is that the whole team lay down all pencils and writing instruments, so they can focus on listening. One student reads the problem: "Love is...(fill in the blank)" and then starts the discussion. The student to his or her left is the Checker, and checks the other members for their opinions. Once everyone's opinion has been expressed, students pick up their pencils and write, with no one dictating, the answer they prefer. The students switch roles for the next problem, or, in the case of "Love is…" they might fill out valentines. This is a good activity for students to fill in open-ended statements ("Existentialism is…"), sort of group brainstorming of possible answers for something that has many correct answers. It is also a good anticipatory activity before assigning a project or a paper.

CHORAL RESPONSE

This activity is very effective for memorization: the students together recite or chant a list of information. This may be the days of the week, months, numbers, alphabet, verb endings, noun endings, or declensions. Thirty years after my last Latin class I can still chant "hic, haec, hoc" all the way through. One valuable addition to chanting these in order, however, is to add the words "forward and backward," because it forces students to think of what the word means, rather than just learning a string of "funny sounds" successfully.

A variation I found called "Schreibmaschine" (Typewriter) involves assigning each student in a team or row a certain number of letters of the alphabet. When another team (or the teacher, or a student on the team drawing a slip of paper from a dish) calls out a word, the team must immediately spell it, each student contributing his/her letter when it is needed, but staccato (with no breaks) just like a typewriter: "bleiben!" "B—L—E—I—B—E—N!," "Richtig, naechste Gruppe!," and so on. Of course, this works in any language and covers vocabulary as well as the alphabet.

Occasionally, I have my students play a game we call Beanbag. I have sewn several beanbags. We all form a big circle and toss a beanbag gently from student to student. (One of my colleagues uses an inflatable beach ball.) At first, we say the forms of a verb, or the words to a song, or whatever, all together to the rhythm of the throwing of the beanbag, but then only the student who catches the bag (or was supposed to) says the answer and tosses it to another; this goes quickly enough that the whole class has to be ready to answer the very next one. When we get good at that, we can add a second bean bag, or a third. Again, this is only good for items in order, forward or backward.

There is also the old standby, Flyswatter. The teacher lists either on an overhead or the board, or on large pieces of butcher paper, a list of things studied: vocabulary, verb endings, geographical locations, or whatever needs reviewing. Then divide the class into teams, with a volunteer from each team to receive the flyswatter. Give each participant a flyswatter and then call out a word or concept. The first to swat the correct response gets a point. (If one list is used, the first is the one whose flyswatter is on the bottom. If two lists are used, be sure to NOT write the same word in the same position on both lists because one student could simply check the direction of the other's swatter and copy it.) This can be done from English to target language, or looking for synonyms, antonyms, or, in the case of a verb, the correctly written form. It is swift, high-interest, and enjoyable as an occasional activity.

FOUR CORNERS

In Four Corners, the teacher "labels," either orally or literally, the four corners of the room and instructs the students to get up and move to their preferred corner, where they will have a discussion as directed by the teacher. For lower-level classes, the four corners could represent vocabulary such as the four seasons, four types of buildings (stadium, movie theater, etc.), four colors, four sports, four food groups, or film preferences. Once in their corner, students are instructed to list things to do during that season or the types of weather that occur during that time, activities to do at that type of building, objects that are that color, and so on. More advanced classes could do pantomimes with appropriate dialogue, for example, "Say, Paul, how are the slopes? Great! I'm going back up right now. Is the snow good? Yes, it's deep."

Also, for more advanced classes, corners could represent characters from a novel or from history, professions, types of cars, or even variations of one statement such as "The future is...(bright, scary, what we make it, etc.)." Again, discussion in the target language would take place. At any level, the teacher would assess the success of this discussion by spot-checking various members of each corner for responses.

This activity is brief, and it practices or reviews material previously presented. It has the advantage of getting students out of their seats, and talking to one another. It can also lead to another activity. For example, if you have kids form groups based on movies or television shows, you could have them prepare a scene from the movie/show to act out in the target language.

MIX/FREEZE/GROUP

This is a similar, short activity. Students are told to rise from their seats and circulate about the classroom, and, at the teacher's signal, to group as ordered. For lower-level classes, it is fun for the teacher to do activities such as the following: say "What is (clap hands twice) and (clap hands four times)?" at which point the students should form groups of that number and shout the number in the target language; or say a letter of the alphabet and have students group themselves to shape that letter while saying it in the target language. Other ideas include forming shapes or simple, short two or three letter words.

For middle-level classes, I like to have students pick a character from a story, get up, circulate, and group with others who have chosen the same character to describe that character.

Another activity that I do, I call "Exchange Students." I have them draw a slip of paper with a country's name. Then they mix, freeze, and try to locate others from the same country, without naming the country or their nationality. They may tell what city they are from, what they like to eat, places they like to go, or holidays they celebrate. Once everyone has found a group, they tell the class their nationality. Sometimes I reward the biggest group (determined by fate, since there are more strips of paper than students).

Like Four Corners, Mix/Freeze/Group is brief, active, and allows student movement and discussion.

LINE-UPS

Line-ups is another easy out-of-seat, discussion-generating activity. The teacher asks students to line up according to factors such as height, birthday, first letter of middle name, or similar facts (for a lower-level class) or factors that will generate a lot more discussion, such as who likes chocolate the most, who would most like to be a teacher, or their opinions on issues such as, "parents should never divorce" or "capital punishment should be abolished." For slightly less serious discussions, they could also complete open-ended statements such as, "If I could live anywhere in the world...," "The person I would most like to meet is...," "My idea of a really fun Saturday is...," "If you call me at home I will probably be busy doing... ," "Ten years from now you will find me...."

Sometimes the lining up is the main objective of the activity, but more often this is used to pair students for further discussion. There are two ways to turn a line into pairs. One is to bend it at the middle, so the most opposed ends meet; but then, so that the ambivalent ones in the middle are not paired with two other ambivalent ones, have the two most extreme students promenade to the opposite end of the double-line, and then group students by fours. The second way is to find the middle and have the left half of the line step forward two steps, turn a quarter turn to their right, and walk until the farthest right person of this new line meets the farthest person on the old line; then group by pairs or fours and discuss.

Discussion topics can include matters such as: If height were the characteristic, is that person the tallest/smallest in their family? Who is taller/smaller? Name other people at school who are tall/small, and so forth. If ecological attitudes were surveyed for the line-up, then have them discuss what they do, or would wish to have done, or would not do.

If the line-up topic is one that will be used for several days, consider having students write their name on a clothespin and clip it to a line that can be saved for use on other days, or take a picture of the line-up for future reference or for comparison with how they line up after several days of discussion when some may have changed their minds.

Discussion could be shared with the class or with another team, or become a Roundrobin opinion-writing session, a team research assignment, or any other sort of direction you wish to take. This activity takes a lot of preparation, but is worth it: cut out pictures of recognizable places in the world and glue them onto index cards. On the back, write a brief postcard-style message that gives a clue about what the picture is and where it is, and that also includes a date. Pass out the cards and have the students read them first, then have them circulate and converse in the target language to reconstruct the "traveler's" itinerary, with the goal of lining up in chronological order. Once in line, they could then orally present their destination (place and date). This could be followed up by a quiz, if you wish, to encourage others to pay attention: On what date was this person in Toledo? In what city is the Sagrada Familia cathedral located?

FIND SOMEONE WHO

Find Someone Who is a speaking activity much like mixers you may have played at an adult meeting. First, have students write several things about themselves that no one or few in the class might know. (Reporting on summer experiences is great as a back-to-school activity.) Then choose one thing from each student and type it on a sheet of paper with a line next to it for writing the name. The students are given a chance to read the sentences and then rise from their seats to circulate through the class (be sure to give them a time limit!), questioning each other in the target language to find students who answer that description. If they find that student, they have that person sign his or her name next to that description. This is a good early activity for mid- to upper-level classes, necessitating discussion, and is especially good for shy or less capable students as they can quickly become an "authority" when they fit, or discover a classmate who fits, a hard-to-find item on the list.

For lower-level classes, you list characteristics such as "Has a September birthday" or "Likes hamburgers" or "Hates country music," and then let students circulate, questioning each other, until they locate at least one person for each item. (Don't forget to give them a time limit.)

This activity could easily become a brief writing activity to "publish" as a class newsletter. If you wish to make this a bit more academic, have the students find someone who knows trivia about a book the class is reading, or some highly irregular verb stems, and so on.

NUMBERED HEADS TOGETHER

This is a seated group activity that emphasizes helping from the group, but makes each student individually responsible for learning the material. As the students sit in groups of four, the teacher has them number off: one, two, three, and four. The teacher then gives the class a topic, stating it as a command: "Make sure everyone in the group knows_____," giving them a time limit. Student teams then literally put their heads together and discuss.

When they have an answer, the Checker on the team checks with each team member individually to make sure each member knows it. When time is up, the teacher is supposed to call a number between one and four, and the students having that number must all give the answer together.

This is a good replacement for the traditional whole-class questioning, where the teacher asks a question and usually calls on the high achievers. However, the formula presented above posed a few problems for me, so I changed it. First, calling one number relieved three-fourths of the class from having to answer, so I needed to force them to "stay tuned." I decided that the students whose numbers were called should go to the board and write their answer (conferring, if there were different answers), while the rest of the class must respond with a thumbs up or thumbs down signal if they agree. If your class is using the red/green/yellow response cards, they could use red for *no*, and green for *yes*.

This activity is good for practicing basic facts like noun, adjective, or verb endings, for reviewing anything before a test, or even as an anticipatory set. I love it for review. It can even become a review contest, if each team is allowed to make up questions and submit them. One teacher I know even assigns numbered roles, as teams take turns asking the questions. Student 1 states the team's question, 2 calls time up and what number should respond, 3 evaluates the answer (right/wrong), and 4 adds any additional bits of answer or information if the answer was incomplete. Then another team would ask its question. The object is for every team to have a perfect score, so this is a noncompetitive activity, which I also like.

SEND-A-PROBLEM

A team review activity, Send-a-Problem asks students to write review questions based on whatever material the teacher assigns. If it is a big chapter, every team may have a different section to write questions on. In either case, make sure the teams know that their questions must be based on/findable in the text. I generally use a team composed of four students. Each student on the team, on an individual basis (perhaps even assigned as homework), writes one or more questions. Each question is written on a separate card or piece of paper.

The student then asks his or her question of the team. If the team agrees on the answer, then the student writes the answer on the back. If the team cannot reach consensus, then the student must revise the question. Label the question side with a big Q and the answer side with a big A. The team then passes its stack of questions to another team, Q sides up. When a team receives another team's stack, the first student takes the top question and reads it to the group, which then agrees on an answer. The student turns the card over and the team checks its answer. If the students are right, team congratulations (handshake, cheer, or whatever) are in order. If their answer did not match, they must go to the text and research their answer. If they still think they are right, all eight hands go into the air, and the teacher verifies their answer. If it is correct, the team writes it on the A side as an alternate answer (and congratulate each other). Teams continue to send these questions around until each team gets its original questions back, and the team must reanswer its questions as before, checking to see if alternate answers were added.

I have found that my students were very thorough in covering all the questions I would have asked (sometimes they were too picky), but if it seemed that coverage was incomplete, the teacher could pick up all the cards and look them over before giving the quiz. This activity is good to do right before the quiz, or the day before.

TURN-4-REVIEW

This makes reviewing for a test game-like. The teacher provides each group with five stacks of cards: Question cards, Turn cards, Check cards, Answer cards, and Praise cards. A student begins by reading the top Turn card to the group. It will say something such as, "Student #1, read the question." That student would take the top Question card and read it to the group, which then thinks, silently, of the answer—NO talking. That student then turns over an Answer card, which designates which student of the group should answer. The designated student gives his/her answer, and turns over a Check card, which says something such as, "Student #2, check with each member individually to see if they had the same answer and can explain why that is the answer." After that is done, a Praise card is turned over, and the designated student praises whoever got the answer right, including himself or herself, if the same student is designated twice in one round. I usually appoint someone to be Time Monitor so that things flow smoothly (sometimes I do it myself). Also, make sure students take turns turning over cards.

TEAM TEST

In Team Test, the team literally takes a test together. The suggested method is to give each team the actual test the day before, and have them complete one copy as a group, re-collecting it at the end. It is very important for each team to have only one copy and only one writing instrument so that no one notes the questions and answers.

Another variation is to give them each a section of a quiz or test and tell them to complete their copy with only those answers about which they are completely sure. When they have filled it out to the best of their ability, they pass it (Roundrobin) to the person to their left, who will complete any empty portion he or she is sure of, and so on. When each person has his or her original paper back, then the group quietly discusses answers until they all agree. These are stapled together, and a group grade is given. (Only one paper of each set is graded, because they are all the same.) Dorothy Goff, who has used this, says, "The students think they are really getting away with something, when they're really working together on a goal. It is surprising how they tend to spend more time on a quiz or test. They're more careful about their answers." Note also that you do not give the entire test this way, only part of it.

If the test is so simple that they could simply memorize the answers in order without really comprehending them, or if you feel funny about giving them the actual test, then perhaps the team should be given a practice test which is similar to, but not exactly the same as, the real test. This is what I usually do; the questions are the same type, cover the same material, but differ slightly from the next day's test.

The point is that, if students are still struggling with the material, asking them to review on their own is not at all helpful to them, but teaming them with others who will not only help, but even put peer pressure on them to learn the material, is just what they need to be more successful. In Chapter 5 on Assessment, I discuss several strategies for making the team feel that helping struggling students is something that is to their benefit. I also show how poor students whose grades improve, even though they still receive an F, can be made to feel like useful members of the team rather than a liability.

My favorite way to use Team Test, however, is *after* a test is given. I give students a test individually, and then, first thing the next day, I have them retake the test as a team, using the text to check their answers, with assigned roles. On a rotating basis, one student reads the question, another answers, a third explains the answer (or disagrees), a fourth verifies it in the text and checks with each member of the group to make sure they understand that answer. Retaking the test makes the students responsible for knowing the material more than once, makes the students explain their answers rather than being able to just make a lucky guess, gives them an opportunity to receive praise from the group for being right, and cuts down enormously on students arguing with me (the teacher) about what is or is not the right answer, an added benefit I only discovered when trying this method. I also found that semester exam scores improved when I did this regularly. Dana Paramskas, on the Internet, included this comment about Team/Test: "They write more, but I have many fewer papers to grade. An additional bonus is that errors that survive are significant and common ones; I print them on an overhead for whole class discussion."

TEAM INTERVIEW

This activity is similar to the Pair/Interview, but with more people involved. It is excellent for conversation skills and for shy students. Team Interview begins with one pair interviewing another, and continues with students forming new pairs with others on the team; with a team of four, there are six different pairings possible. *Gossip* is another similar type of interview format my students enjoy. The students on the team would pair first and interview each other about a topic selected by the teacher: what color is their room and what furniture do they have; what family pets do they have; when did they meet their best friend; what are their summer plans; or whatever. Then, choosing a new person in the group, the students "gossip" about the person they just talked to, and ask the new partner about their room/pets/friend/plans/whatever; then they pair with the other person they haven't talked with yet, and "gossip" once more. Even the shyest student is quite willing to gossip!

African Introductions, another form of Team/Interview, is supposedly based on a tradition in which it is considered really bad manners to ask someone direct personal questions. The student are assigned another person in the class and must find out as much as possible about that person by talking to others who know him or her. After some time for investigation in the target language, this student then tells the class everything he or she has found out about the subject.

Another Team/Interview variation is *Deferred Instruction*. In this, one member from each group is sent from the room. The teacher tells a story to the remaining students and then brings the "outstanding" group back into the room. The three other team members must take turns (hint: use a timer and make them switch every 30 seconds or so) retelling the story to the group member who was not there to hear it. Then, the teacher gives a brief quiz taken only by the "outstanding" group, with the team getting either the test-taker's score or a prize based upon that score.

Another interview format we use is called *Hot Seat*. Sometimes the hot seat is a specially decorated seat; other times the hot seat person is designated by a hat, a sticker, or a button to wear. Each person on the team takes a turn in the hot seat (or passes the hat/button to the next), and must answer one question (or two or three- whatever number the teacher chooses) posed by teammates. Usually the students write the questions: sometimes the questions must use vocabulary from the chapter; sometimes the questions involve grammar ("what is the je/yo/ich form of *to go*?"); or culture ("Where are the tallest mountains?" "What painter is best known for...?").

Toward the end of the semester, we always play Hot Seat, but I supply the questions on cards, which we also use for the oral portion of our final exam. With one student being interviewed, team members take turns drawing cards and asking the questions on the cards, which are drawn from our text and/or sponge activities we have done that semester. Students take turns reading and being questioned. The two not currently involved as questioner or questionee serve as Checker and Researcher (looking up the answer as needed). All of the students know that they will, for the final, draw 10 of those cards and answer the question on them, so they are all highly motivated to learn the stack of questions.

One last variation of Team Interview is *To Tell the Truth*, just like the old game show. For this, students must write down unusual things that they have done or experienced. Pick one, and have that student and two others step outside. Bring them back in and say: "One of these people did ___." Each student would then step forward and claim: "I, (name), did ___." The class should then question them, trying to determine who did it and who is lying. At the end of a suitable amount of questioning, ask the students to vote by raising hands for the one they believe is telling the truth. If the students guess correctly, they get a point, and if they were all stumped, the players get a point or reward.

TEAMS GAMES TOURNAMENTS (TGT)

This cooperative teams activity (Johnson, Johnson & Holubec, 1993) was developed by Slavin in 1986, and many books suggest this as a wonderful activity for classes on the block schedule. I have not used this, but will briefly summarize it.

To students grouped in teams of four to five students selected by their classroom performance/ability level (one low, two middle, and one high to encourage peer support), the teacher teaches a lesson, using (usually) the traditional lecture method, chalkboard demonstration, and possibly audio- or videotapes. The teacher first makes it very clear to the class that paying careful attention will be instrumental to student success. Teachers should also teach only the material that will appear on the quiz. The group then does a series of worksheets and group activities, after which they play games to display/check for mastery of this material. The games actually physically split the teams since students are seated by ability level, and compete against students of their own ability level, but students are earning points for their team. At the end of a round, the highest scorer in the middle or low ability groups is bumped to the higher level ability group, and the lowest scorer at all three levels is dropped to the lower ability grouping. Teams with the most points are rewarded. The games sound similar to Jeopardy, Trivial Pursuit, or other game shows with questions based on knowledge. After the games, students are tested individually over the unit; grades are based only on individual performance. Teams usually remain together for a grading period.

Like Kagan (1995), I have a few reservations about this method as I don't like the idea of separating students into ability levels; they are probably quite aware they are the lower-performing ones, but labeling them as such cannot be good for self-esteem. However, it is true that some students do respond quite well to competitive games and would strive hard to be able to move up to the next level; I remember competing for "chairs" in high school band, which is a similar concept, and in France, students receive their class rank (e.g., 2 of 24) for each of their subjects individually on every report card, so this sort of competition is a common practice.

STUDENT TEAMS ACHIEVEMENT DIVISIONS (STAD)

This activity, also developed by Slavin, is basically the same as TGT, except the competitive games at the end are eliminated and there is a pretest before the unit is begun. After students have taken the quizzes on an individual basis at the end of the practice activities, the team is rewarded according to whether its members' scores improved from pretest to posttest, and on how much improvement there was. (See Chapter 5 on Assessment for suggestions on how to do this.)

"Teaching is the process of building communities of learners who use their skills to educate themselves" (Joyce, 1996). The next three teaching strategies have this goal in mind: teaching the students how to process data and extract meaning from them, themselves.

CONCEPT ATTAINMENT

This activity, which begins on the individual level, proceeds to pairs work, and ends as a group activity, is used to introduce new material, replacing the traditional lecture method. Prior to beginning the activity, the teacher selects the concept to introduce, and also chooses and organizes the examples that contain characteristics of this concept. At least 20 pairs are needed, especially for more complex concepts. Few, if any, texts provide such lists, so it involves a bit of work and thought. Concept Attainment works well for introducing concepts like masculine/feminine/neuter endings, teaching students to identify a particular style of art or that of a particular artist, or learning how to form a new verb tense. (Examples will follow in the explanation of how Concept Attainment is structured. Figure 4.6 contains a list of positive and negative examples for a lesson on the *conditionnel* in French.)

In Phase One of the activity, in class the teacher lists several examples, either on the board, on an overhead, or on a handout. The examples are labeled as positive (good/"yes") examples of the concept or attribute, or as negative (bad/"no") examples. The teacher asks the students to contrast the positive examples with the negative (to themselves, not out loud), and to take notes on those differences. (*Note:* This is a good sponge activity.) If he/she wants, the teacher could underline portions of the example in order to call attention to the important portion to examine. Then the teacher adds a few more examples, asking students to make a hypothesis about what the difference is between the positive and negative ones. Then, a few more examples are given, to test the hypothesis and refine it. Then, a new step: unlabeled examples are presented and students (still working on their own, and not out loud) are asked to guess, using their hypothesis, if they are positive or negative. (Students love this approach: it is challenging, yet game-like.)

FIGURE 4.6. HANDOUT FOR CONCEPT ATTAINMENT EXERCISE ON THE *CONDITIONNEL*

1. Il *entrait* dans la salle de classe.
2. Elle *arriverait* en retard.
3. Nous *aimerions* un sandwich.
4. Nous *parlions* français.
5. Ils *chanteront* bien.
6. Elles *finiraient* vite.
7. Je *mangerais* à midi.
8. Je *prendrai* mon livre.
9. Tu *visiteras* Paris.
10. Tu *vendrais* ton vélo.
11. Vous *choisiriez* Marc.
12. Vous *couriez* très vite.
13. Elle *conduirait* rapidement.
14. Elles *grossiront*.
15. Ils *se laveraient*.
16. Je *me marierais*.
17. Nous *nous parlions*.
18. Tu *regardais* la télé.
19. Vous *alliez* au café.
20. Elles *feraient* du café.

(These were presented: first four to compare/contrast *imparfait* with *conditionnel*. Second four to compare/contrast with *futur*. Then, mixed examples (#9–12) presented as pairs: one is and one is not. The rest were used to test the theory they had developed, #13–16 with a partner, #17–20 in a team of four. Students were then asked to generate some of their own examples, and, finally, to consult the text.)

Phase Two begins when it looks like most of the students have a workable hypothesis. (Use body language to identify this: nodding heads, smiling, etc; or use signaling—cards, tap on desk, etc.—for feedback on who has a good idea/hypothesis.) Pair the students and have them share hypotheses with their partner. Test these new, combined/synthesized hypotheses with a few more unlabeled examples, and then ask groups to share their methods with the class. At this time, the teacher confirms the correct hypotheses, refining how they are stated if necessary, and supplies the name of the concept (e.g., "This is called the future tense, and you have correctly identified how it is different."). Now, have the student pairs (or combine two pairs into a team, perhaps using Roundrobin) generate their own examples of this concept, or assign this as homework.

Phase Three is to check these new examples for accuracy, and to have students describe what thoughts went through their minds as they attempted to identify the concept. What did they concentrate on first, and reject? How did they modify their hypothesis based on additional examples? This is very important to voice, either to the entire class, or within their groups, because it more firmly fixes the concept by reviewing the steps they went through to find it.

Concept Attainment is also an excellent review tool or evaluation tool if you want to check to see if some material you covered previously has been mastered. By giving good and bad examples of the concept, you will determine the students' depth of knowledge by how quickly they catch on, and will also reinforce their understanding of this concept.

CONCEPT DEVELOPMENT

There are three basic steps in this method, which was first used in scientific investigation: First, a set of data on the topic are created, either by the students or by the teacher; second, these are grouped into categories based on similarities observed; and third, these categories are labeled or named. When students identify the similarities, they are using many higher-level thinking skills (interpreting, inferring, generalizing), which lead to a greater ability to manipulate the category and apply it to new situations, so this strategy is very often used to teach basic grammar concepts.

English teachers have developed many lessons to help the students grasp how an adjective, adverb, phrase, or clause functions and how it is different from other parts of speech. In a foreign language, these same activities could serve a similar purpose, *without* having to teach the concept in English or use grammatical terms. Students provided with sentences with all the adverbs underlined, for example, would group them into categories such as location, time, or description, and then, still using the sample sentences, would discuss how any words that would fit these categories are placed in a typical sentence (i.e., immediately after the verb) without having to use the word "adverb."

A couple of warnings are needed here: the more examples you give the better, and, even more important, the simpler the better. Beware of "false decoys" such as sentences with some noun subjects and some pronoun subjects, or with adverb clauses alternating with simple adverbs. Make sure the only element that varies is the adverb, or whatever concept you are presenting. Use the words in a sentence, so the students learn to handle them in context.

I like to use the Concept Development method in French for the simple IR verbs (*dormir, partir, servir, sortir,* etc.), which are rather confusing for my students when simply presented separately in the book. A similarly useful activity is to present students with sets of irregular verbs whose nous/vous forms closely resemble the infinitive (*vouloir* and *pouvoir*, followed by *aller*, *boire*, and *devoir*) and have the students discover this pattern for themselves (using concept development) and then apply it to new verbs.

But my favorite lesson, either to introduce or review, is one in which I provide a brief story with its sentences scrambled (Step One: List) as shown in Figure 4.7, and ask students to categorize the sentences by sentence TOPIC (Step Two: Group). After this is done (and yes, I often have teams that have categories called "miscellaneous"), we look at each sentence in a particular category, for example, "Moving around," and discover that within that category, the sentences are all in the same verb tense. Then I ask the students to group the categories by verb tense (Step Two: Regroup, if necessary), and rename the resulting categories (Step Three: Label). This is a wonderful way for the students to discover that, in French, the *passé composé* tense is used for action, and the *imparfait* for descriptive passages (Step Four: Generalize). After we voice this generalization (I say, "Look at these two groups and make a general statement about each."), we evaluate our statement by trying it on a new story, *Le Petit Chaperon Rouge* (*Little Red Riding Hood*), predicting what tense each verb would be in if it were told in the past tense, and checking our answers afterward. Using Concept Development and letting them find out for themselves how these tenses work has cut the time I need to teach this unit practically in half, with many fewer practice activities needed. Because they found it out for themselves instead of my just telling them, even though a lot of time was spent in the discovering, their ownership of the concept was much more permanent and much better understood.

**FIGURE 4.7. CONCEPT DEVELOPMENT HANDOUT FOR FRENCH 2
INTRODUCTORY OR FRENCH 3 REVIEW**

---

1. Une fille est sortie de la maison.
2. Elle était jolie.
3. Ils ont vu un film.
4. La voiture est partie très vite.
5. Il était midi.
6. Le garçon l'a invitée au cinéma.
7. Après, ils ont mangé une pizza.
8. Il faisait chaud.
9. Une voiture est arrivée.
10. Elle a parlé avec le garçon.
11. Il portait un jean et un pull.
12. Elle est entrée dans la voiture.
13. Elle portait un short et un tee-shirt.
14. Le chauffeur était un garçon.
15. La voiture était rouge.

Most research shows this method to be the most effective when done in a whole-class setting, because the more input there is, the better. I find, however, that Steps One and Two are good pair or team activities, with a Roam Around the Room and then time for revising categories, before the class unites to list these categories and make our final Step Three and Step Four discoveries about the concept.

One small variation is to have the students create their own data file (Step One), perhaps by looking at a page in a text, and making a list of what they see/read. For example, in French, by making a list of fruits, they might discover that all fruits listed are feminine in gender, and end in -e, a useful generalization.

MEMORY MODEL

Like the two teaching strategies mentioned previously, this method is good for learning new material as a group, but Memory Model is better for memorizing data such as names (both from novels and geography) and vocabulary lists. Memory Model is a form of mnemonics, also called Link-Word, which attempts to make it easier for students to recall words by drawing from their own personal experience to form word associations.

In Step One, the students select the terms they must know by reading and then underlining or listing unfamiliar words, by choosing the key points in a story or speech they wish to memorize, or by looking at a list the teacher has given them. Step Two is to link the unfamiliar material to something they know. To make the image memorable, the new idea must be sensual (using senses such as taste and smell), motion-oriented, very colorful, or very exaggerated in size—in short, the student should be as creative as possible and as humorous, outrageous, absurd, or downright silly as possible.

In Step Two, therefore, the students, working in teams, will look at the vocabulary list and try to make as many crazy connections as possible. For *haricots verts* (green beans), my students have come up with things like "green haircuts," a translation of one word and a lookalike for the other, which they then made into a poster of a punk with a green Mohawk haircut, ring in his nose, and so forth. That is Step Three: make it concrete. Draw a picture of this idea, making it visual, auditory, and as exaggerated as possible. A Spanish student, in order to remember *carta* (letter), uses a connection to the English word *cart*, and draws a huge letter that barely fits into a shopping cart. Step Four is to practice the words with their associations until they become familiar.

This method can also be used to memorize the countries in Central America and information about them: for example, Guatemala has the largest population, so students remember Gotta Lotta, and draw a picture of a group of people all squished into a small space. To learn the position of the countries the students might make up a story, where in Nicaragua they pay a nickel for water when thirsty (Nicaragua = Nickel Water) and they have a Honda Race across Honduras. Then they rehearse the story, using the pictures, until they remember it well.

In this way, an elementary school teacher helps her students remember some basic Spanish: *buenos días,* which means *good morning,* they remember as "bonnie day"(bonnie is Scottish for pretty or good); *buenas tardes* (*good afternoon*) as "bonnie LATE day" (late = tardy); *hasta mañana* (*until tomorrow*) as "no haste, man." No matter how silly, the students will only remember these associations well if they are the ones who thought of them, although occasionally a really good one will help anyone. Even if they are a bit off-color, let the students use whatever works. For example, one group linked the French word *piscine,* pronounced *pee-seen,* with a "No 'pee-seen' in the pool" sign. It worked like a dream. Others linked it with Pisces, the fish symbol from the zodiac. Guess which group got 100 percent on the quiz! (Yes, the first one.)

Given the following list of vocabulary, *une fois, plusieurs fois, parfois* and *quelquefois,* one group developed a story about a Mr. Fois, who plays golf, but he's really not very good. *Une fois* (*once*) he got a hole in *one. Parfois* (*sometimes*) he shoots *par,* but *plusieurs fois* (*several times*) he got more than par (plus +), and *quelquefois* (*sometimes*) he quits before he even finishes (in this last portion, the students had noticed that both the vocabulary word and the word "quits" begins with "qu-."). That story, after drawing pictures, and having rehearsals, earned them all perfect scores on the quiz, over very difficult and very similar looking and sounding words. That is how Memory Model works, and with it you can present more vocabulary more often, and with greater retention.

SIMULATION

Simulations are probably what foreign languages have always done best: how you make students see that the vocabulary and behaviors you are teaching them are really useful. Most kids know that movies are not real life, so videos have some, but not significant, impact on their perceiving grammar or vocabulary as relevant. But put them in a situation where they must actually perform, using the language in a life-like "reality" situation, and they suddenly see the relevance of what they have been learning, as well as get feedback on how well they have mastered these communications skills.

In short, simulations are the "meat" of foreign language teaching. A simulation must be carefully planned to be useful, and the block schedule gives more time for both the planning and the performing of a simulation exercise than the traditional class period. Here is where you will really see the block schedule pay off, in increased time for participation, and in being able to do simulations you never had time to complete in just one class period.

A good simulation has several different parts. When choosing a simulation, a teacher makes several decisions based on time available: what classroom resources are needed (and finances); how to assign teams (small groups of no more than five are best, says the research. I prefer even smaller ones); and, especially, how to distribute the high-status roles in a manner the students will perceive as fair. The teacher must also decide if this activity will be graded, and, if so, how the grading will be done. Of course, a simulation usually follows extensive preparation by the students (learning vocabulary and practicing skits and conversational skills), and preparation of the students by the teacher, who explains the goal or goals and the rules of the simulation, as well as assigns the students to teams, models the correct behavior, and gives the students a small practice session before beginning the actual simulation.

EXAMPLES

Start with a short simulation first, one that can be completed in one class period or less. A very short example is one that can serve as a good introductory set for a unit on the feudal system. Give every student a small sack with 10 to 12 M and M's (or similar candies) in it, and a spoon (for finicky students who don't want their candy handled by classmates). In each bag is a strip of paper with the name of a social role: one "king" strip, three "dukes," six "counts," and the rest are" peasants." Now, have students line up, with the king at the back of the room, the dukes nearby, two counts near each duke, and the peasants evenly divided under each count. Have the peasants hand all but two candies to their count, the counts pass on six of those eight to the duke, and the duke passes on three of the six to the king. Ask the peasants how they feel, then the counts, the dukes, and the king. Of course, the peasants don't like the situation, and the king is very happy. Now, ask the king to levy a tax on the dukes and see what happens. This is a good, short simulation of how the feudal system works, which can then go to the text or whatever support materials the teacher wants to use next (as well as sharing and eating the candies, of course!). It is very typical in that it involves a lot of planning by the teacher and illustrates history in a lively, but open-ended way—the results are never quite the same. Sometimes the dukes or counts cheat, sometimes the peasants rebel, or appeal to the king. Because it is based on personalities, the activity can take on many different characteristics, any of which are good and can be related to real history.

A good, longer simulation has two characteristics: it is like real life and it involves an ongoing process or series of necessary behaviors. In a game called El Mercado/Le Marché/Das Kaufhaus, students go shopping. First they study vocabulary on clothing, which is sold at the market, as well as the tradition of bargaining ("too expensive," "3 for 10 pesos/pesetas/francs/marks"), which is in the text and videos. Then the students are divided into teams. Some are the store owners, and their aim is to sell as many items for as much money as possible. Other teams are shoppers who want to buy clothing "outfits" (what good is a shirt if it doesn't go with anything else?) for as little as possible. Stores are given identical sets of cards with clothing items pictured, and money for making change. Shoppers are given money to spend. After a brief planning period when stores set prices and shoppers plan strategy, the teacher must explain a few more rules. Since I have done this simulation over the years, the rules get longer: I now add "No armed robbery" and "No shoplifting" to my usual "No English" rule. I also explain the scoring system.

After handling any questions, the stores open and shopping begins. During this time, the teacher has two roles: Referee, to see that rules are followed, and Coach, to give advice in a supportive way, while still allowing the students to make mistakes. Because most stores close for a noon break, or a siesta, a closing bell is rung after about 20 minutes; shoppers finish their current buying and everyone regroups. The teacher can use this time to highlight common errors observed, the stores to mark down prices, and the shoppers to lay out their outfits and see what is still needed. Then, shopping begins again. When time is called, the exercise is over, scoring is done, and the winning stores and shoppers are rewarded.

Then comes the most important portion of a simulation: debriefing. How closely did this exercise resemble the real world? What difficulties did shoppers encounter, and what solutions did they find? What cultural differences did they observe? What would they do differently next time? Students need time to analyze what happened, compare it to their previous experiences, and appraise their performance, planning how to redesign it for future simulations, or, hopefully, for a real trip to that country.

EVALUATION

Grading a simulation is up to the teacher. It could be a simple participation grade based on the teacher's observations while circulating: 4 points for participating fully in the target language/3 if English was used/ 2 if student had to be encouraged to participate/1 if student broke rules. The activity could culminate in a written exercise that could be collected. Another option is observation: I often have a simple check sheet I use when I stage a simulation that I control.

A good example is when, after practicing vocabulary and culture, I have my students check into my "hotel." As they enter my classroom, singly or in small groups, they ask for a room, specify the type of bed and bathroom facilities they want, ask the price, whether or not breakfast is included, and any other information they need. I hand them a room key, and they fill out a form like those used in most hotels, with passport number and other relevant information, which they return to the desk. There, they pick up a sheet with vocabulary about a standard hotel room which, at the bottom, tells them that there is a problem with their room, and that they must complain to the desk clerk. My check sheet for this activity looks like this:

CHECK-IN	Began conversation	Yes	No
	Answered questions	Y	N
	Asked price	Y	N
	Asked/breakfast	Y	N
	Said thank you	Y	N
FORM	Turned in to clerk	Y	N
	Filled out correctly	Y	N
COMPLAINT	Registered	Y	N
	Understandable	Y	N
	Polite	Y	N

Each *Yes* is worth one point.

I have similar forms for when I have them enter my country through customs (I am the customs officer), order from the waiter at my "café," buy movie or metro tickets, and for other activities.

There are many, many different ways to use simulation. Wish you could find a guest speaker, but don't have one? Simulate one: have students write questions they would like to ask a guest speaker, and then research the answers. For example, have students prepare questions for a German/French/Spanish exchange student, and then, using encyclopedias, letters to embassies, or the Internet, try to find answers. I have a video called "Speak French and Double Your World," purchased from a school in Buffalo, New York, that interviews people who use French in their jobs here in the United States. Before the video, I have students write questions for a business person about how French is used, then I show the video, and, as the people are interviewed, the students find answers to their questions. Afterward, we research any unanswered questions on the Internet, by posting e-mail questions to various lists, and waiting for answers. Other simulated interviews could be a famous politician, athlete, or writer. Another option is to have students each take turns being the guest, researching in order to role-play the guest speaker—what might he/she say? You could have some very famous "people" visit your classroom through simulations.

ELABORATING

Simulations do *not* have to have a lot of props, and a good simulation need not even involve a lot of preparation, because in real-life situations the outcome of a conversation or situation will depend on the other person's reactions and responses. It is this unknown factor that is both a little scary and a little exciting for the students. Simulations can be simply setting up conversational situations. I have several of these I like to do primarily with upper-level classes. One is called Elaborating. In it, students are not allowed to simply answer *"yes"* or *"no"* to *yes/no* questions. For example, asked if they live in town, they may reply *"yes,"* but then they must volunteer more: how long they have lived there, what color their house is, or what street they live on. Then they must turn the question around on the interviewer: Do you live in town? Do you like living in town? I usually provide question cards for this type of activity, based on whatever topic we are studying: where to shop, driving cars, studies, or whatever.

MULTIPLE RESPONSES

Another variation on Elaborating is Multiple Responses, where students are asked to provide a variety of responses. In *la aduana* (customs), to the inspector's statement *"Su pasaporte, por favor,"* give as many appropriate responses as possible: (it is fun to play this in teams) *"Cómo no," "Claro," "Aquí tiene Ud. mi pasaporte," "Un minuto, por favor. Está en mi maleta."* Translations: *Why not?, Of course, Here's my passport, Just a minute please. it's in my suitcase.* See how creative your students can get!

REACTIONS

Another variation is called Reactions. After reading or hearing a description of a situation, students are asked to play the roles of different people, and react to the event, for example:

> *Ein junger Arzt, der eben aus dem Krankhaus gekommen ist, lauft uber die enge Strasse, die mit den vielen Wagen des Hauptverkehrszeit verstopft ist, ein unvorsichtiges Benehmen.* (A young doctor has just left the hospital, running across a narrow street that is full of rush-hour traffic, very careless behavior.)

Roles to assign for this would be accompanied by a suggestion as to what type of reaction is desired: *ein Politzist/Frage* (a policeman/ask a question such as, "What do you think you are doing, young man?"). The policeman could also exclaim, or could question another person. Other roles would include such people as *ein Kind zu seiner Mutter/Frage, Bemerkung* (child to his/her mother/question or observation), the child's mother/reply, a bus driver/exclamation (*Ausruf*), the doctor's wife, a pedestrian, an elderly woman to the child/negative question, a merchant at the door to his shop, and so on.

EAVESDROPPING

Perhaps you wish to create a simulation involving native speakers and the only ones you have are on the tapes provided by your text. Try Eavesdropping. Pretend that the students overhear the conversation on the tape. Then they should tell someone else what they heard: who was talking, about how old they were, where they were, what the topic was, and what they said about it. Reporting information that was overheard is good practice, especially for changing verb forms from "I" to "he/she/they."

A simulation should not be confused with a skit. A skit is a conversation or situation that is completely planned beforehand, with time to prepare what is said and for memorization; the previous activities are *not* simulations if you give students time to look up words and write down what they want to say. It is a skit, for example, if students bring pictures of animals and stage a "pet show" with them, speaking prepared pieces about their "pet." It is a simulation if, in teams of four and with no planning time, the two "children" are told to try to convince "mom" and "dad" that they can have a pet, suggesting a variety of animals and promising to care for them. Broken speaking quickly becomes more fluent with practice in which the unknown (other's reactions, statements, etc.) play a part. Some teachers think dictionaries are okay occasionally, but not for entire sentences.

Elizabeth D. Morie, in her chapter in *Teaching in the Block* (Canady & Rettig, 1996), lists these advantages to using simulations:

- ◆ Student interest and enthusiasm "for the content, the teacher, greater motivation for learning in general."

- ◆ Better attitudinal changes. Students more empathetic and tolerant. Increased peer and student-teacher interaction. A more relaxed, open classroom.

- ◆ Skills enhancement. Improved coping and decision-making, bargaining, and persuasion skills.

- ◆ Factual learning. Knowledge more relevant and understandable, leading to more transfer and long-term retention of material.

- ◆ Variety and change of pace, because the activity's outcome is unpredictable and because simulations are not done as often. An opportunity for movement, also.

- ◆ Responsive environment. Immediate feedback.

- ◆ Safety. A perception that it is okay to make errors and keep going.

Simulations are the foreign language equivalents of a science lab experiment, a form of hands-on (tongues-on?) learning, and students love doing them.

SYNECTICS

Synectics is a method to stimulate creative thinking and is best done in groups until students have mastered the steps. It teaches students to think metaphorically, comparing things that have no logical connection to each other. It is useful in the sciences and math for reexamining data, but in arts and languages, it is used primarily for its creative aspect, making creative writing, in particular, much more interesting to read, and to correct (We all can empathize with grading 30 very similar reactions to a play, or 30 hardly distinguishable poems about love.). Synectics can also be used to explore social issues (culture, prejudice, etc.) and to make prize-winning artistic projects such as posters and advertisements.

First, describe the object/person/idea, with the class brainstorming ideas and with you or a helper listing them: use the words, "You are a... (king/ peasant/ cloud/ German boy). How do you look and feel?." At this point, answers will be highly stereotypical. So, Step Two is to make analogies. "If (Fritz, Paco, Pierre) were a (plant/ animal/machine/hat or whatever), what kind would he be?" Write down the suggestions. Fritz, for example, could be a Porsche, a cuckoo clock (both still stereotypical), a telescope, a robot, a tank, a bulldozer, a typewriter. The class will vote on the strangest/most creative one.

Now, reuse Step One: "You are a... (whatever the class voted for in Step Two; for example, a telescope). How do you look/feel?." The groups or teacher would record the answers, such as (for telescope): all-seeing, helpful, steady, precise, technical, adaptable, long, polished, bored, strong, distant, impersonal.

Next, seek Compressed Conflict: see if two items on the list can form an oxymoron (almost opposites)—in this case, *distant precise, helpful impersonal*, or *steady adaptable* might work—or take a really good word off the list, and put its opposite with it. Then have the class choose its favorite.

Now, reuse Step Two: What type of plant (animal/food) is "helpful impersonal?" Answers might be a tree (its shade is helpful), an aloe (its sap is helpful), a corn plant (there are so many in each field).

Finally, give the students the assignment: Using this last analogy, or another they found during the synectics exercise, they are to write a creative composition on what a (topic from Step One: king/cloud/German) is. You will get a wide variety of papers, sometimes with startling insights into whatever you asked them to investigate (in this case, the German national character).

DIAMANTE

In groups, or singly once they have mastered this technique, I have my students write a poem called a "diamante:"

In the first line, they use a noun;

In the second, 2 adjectives to describe this concept;

In the third, 3 processes connected to it (participles);

In the fourth, 2 nouns related to it, followed by 2 for line 7;

In the fifth, 3 processes related to Line 7;

In the sixth, 2 adjectives describing Line 7;

In the seventh, a word meaning the opposite of Line 1:

Noise

Loud   Uncivilized

Smashing   Shrieking   Booming

Bang   Crash   Chord   Note

Moving   Flowing   Singing

Fluid   Beautiful

Music

The poem has the shape of a diamond (diamante), and it is easy to see that the words from the poem are easily drawn from the brainstorming using synectics: If you are noise, how do you feel? The students are often surprised at how easy it is to be creative. Diamante can be written as a class, in teams as a group, or, in an advanced class familiar with synectics, as an individual, with a team/share afterward for feedback.

This is easier to do in English, and then make it a vocabulary-learning activity as the students look up the words which best translate their lists of words.

QUINTAIN

A quintain is another poem that lends itself well to synectics in a foreign language. As its name suggests, it has five lines. Line 1 is the poet's name (or another person's). Line 2 has two adjectives to describe that person. Line 3 has a comparison "like a _____." Line 4 has two adjectives that describe Line 3, and Line 5 finishes with a word or group of words that describes both Lines 1 and 3, and summarizes. An example in English might be:

Marie

Small, moving

Like a feather

Thin, flexible

Dancer.

An example of an artistic product might be a poster to advertise a product. When we do a chapter on bathroom items we develop an ad campaign for an item of choice, with a product name, description, and slogan. Because creativity counts in advertising, as the most interesting gets a prize, we use synectics. Classes entering the state "Learn a Foreign Language" contest might also try using synectics to have more interesting posters. Using synectics definitely has creative results.

Socratic Seminar

Socratic seminars, like synectics, are also useful in your classroom on a limited basis. The purpose of a Socratic seminar is not to teach facts or to coach skills, but to explore ideas found in a text, through thoughtful dialogue about a shared reading. Here is how it works: after a reading assignment, students sit in a circle and, prompted by open-ended questions, engage in meaningful dialogue with each other about what was read. The circle formation is critical, as it emphasizes eye contact, a feeling of openness, and equality. The teacher usually joins the circle as the students' equal, and does not participate in the discussion.

Usually, a Socratic seminar is based on a common reading: a story or a book that everyone in the class has read. However, if the intent is to know an author's style and belief system rather than a specific work, students could be grouped, with each group given a different work to read: for example, several of La Fontaine's fables, several short stories by Thomas Mann, or several poems by Miguel de Unamuno. Then discussion would probably center around the author's views on certain topics.

Before beginning a Socratic seminar, the teacher should make clear to the students the purpose of the seminar, its rules, and the grading system. The rules for the students are simple: disagree with someone's idea but not with them (no personal attacks or statements), take turns, and be courteous. They are accountable for their performance, not based on how many times they talk, but on the quality of their input.

The key points of a Socratic seminar are the questions, which the teacher carefully chooses for their ability to stimulate discussion. In a textbook Socratic seminar, the teacher provides the questions one at a time, beginning with one broad question which has many possible answers, and which should lead students to the text to support their position/opinion. Two to five more "core" questions follow. A core question may be defined as one that would not be answerable without having read the text; it may ask students to interpret a quote, or to tell how or why something happened. The closing question should try to connect what was read to the students' own lives, the "real world"— it will establish the relevance of the text, and it can be answered based on the students' own experiences.

I have my own variation on this questioning process, suggested by Marcia Powers, an English teacher at my high school, and I like the way it involves students more fully. Instead of my asking questions, I let the students lead the discussion completely, in the following manner: I put them in pairs, and provide each pair with a question and about seven minutes to discuss this question and what their answer is. Then, one pair at a time, they ask their question of the group, but do *not* give "their" answer. Instead, if a member of the group supplies an opinion that is different from theirs, they may thoughtfully compliment the student if they like it as well as or better than theirs; or, if they don't, they may say one of these prompts: "Where in the text do you find support for that?," "What do you mean by…?," "Are you saying that…?," "But what about where it says…in the text?," or a similar question to try to lead the person to see their viewpoint. After the question has been exhaustively discussed, or when the pair leaders are satisfied with the answers given, or when discussion has reached an impasse, the next pair will volunteer their question for consideration. I usually indicate which one I wish to use to begin and end the discussion, but the others may supply their questions whenever they wish. Using this method, my fifth-year class had a wonderful discussion on Camus' *The Stranger*. It guaranteed that they all would find an opportunity to talk, because they could present the question or prompt other speakers if they did not wish to give their opinion. Since I was more interested in the quality of discussion and the depth of their understanding of the philosophy (because they had read the book in French), our Socratic seminar was in English.

TROUBLESHOOTING

There are a few difficult things. One is that the teacher *must* remain completely neutral. It is *very* hard not to smile if someone makes a good point, or nod one's head when agreeing, but the students look at the teacher for positive feedback at the beginning, not at each other, and to react is to tacitly establish the teacher as the authority figure. The students should be concerned only with each other, and want each other's respect and opinions. It is also not a good idea to take any notes whatsoever, because the really grade-oriented students will worry themselves silly if you take fewer notes when they speak than when someone else does. Audio- or videotape the discussion if you intend to grade the seminar based on a checksheet or something similar.

Other problems could include one highly opinionated student who attempts to monopolize the discussion. One way to avoid this is to have a circle with two or more empty chairs in the middle; persons wishing to speak must sit in a chair first, and leave it as soon as they finish speaking. If someone remains in the discussion too long, the teacher also could gently ask that person to be the Monitor or Checker who makes sure everyone has a chance to speak, and that everyone understands what was said. (Such a position of authority is often what that student was seeking.) Another method that seems to work is to have some object that the speaker must hold in order to speak, which is passed clockwise or counterclockwise around the circle; students have the option of speaking or just passing it, but the talkative ones must wait until the object makes it around the circle and back to them before it is their turn. Objects could be a model Eiffel Tower, a stuffed school mascot, a beanbag or ball, or whatever is unbreakable and available to be passed.

There are many positive aspects to the Socratic method, but my favorite is found in Canady and Rettig (1996), where a teacher commented that this method particularly appeals to lower-level students: "At-risk students particularly enjoy this process so much that they behave for the seminar....They likewise will prepare their assignment for seminar." That motivating aspect of a Socratic seminar is what makes it worth using at least once or twice.

LEARNING CENTERS

Learning centers involve different activities for students to do that are set up at various locations in the classroom. They are least effective when used to introduce a new skill, and so are better used to practice a skill, extend knowledge about a topic, rehearse a skill before assessment, or to continue practicing skills the students have not successfully mastered in an earlier unit (remediation). In a learning center activity, students are independent, actively engaged at all times, and self-directed. A good learning center activity should appeal to a variety of skill levels, interests, and attitudes. In fact, the primary purpose is to help students learn how to be independent language learners. This requires a different perspective and affects the preparation of materials. To help the students, part of any learning center activity has to be practice with self-help resources such as dictionaries, grammar books, and encyclopedias.

Exercises must be adapted to include more complete instructional guides, and students need to have access to correction sheets once they have completed their work.

First, decide what it is you wish to accomplish—practice, review, extensions—and on what topic. After setting up the centers, introduce the students to your learning goal, group them, and inform them of your expectations as to correct usage. Then turn them loose to learn at the various centers. During their participation time, it is always a good idea to stop everyone periodically to point out positive examples of your expectations (both usage and goal). Students will use some sort of recording sheet, which can be used by the teacher as a form of assessment and that also serves as a good classroom management device, particularly if you wish the centers to be visited in a certain order.

Here is an example of a learning center I use at the first-year level when we learn how to make questions. There are seven stations in my learning center. My students are told that they may visit them in any order as long as they visit all of them. They are provided with a recording sheet and count off from one to seven (in the target language) to receive their assignment for the first station they will do. When they are done, the completed recording sheet goes on my desk and I usually have a sponge activity for them, although I can also assign early finishers to help the slower ones.

- ◆ Station One has paper dice. Each side of each die has an interrogative expression on it. The student's sheet and an instruction card at that station instructs the student to take one die, throw it, and construct a question using that expression, writing it on the sheet.

- ◆ Station Two is a Graffiti Wall. A large piece of paper with a big Q and an A at the top is taped there. I start the wall by writing a question. The first student to arrive must answer that question and initial the answer. The next student must supply another question, and the third student an answer, and so on. They seem to enjoy reading each other's responses, so it is good practice.

- ◆ Station Three has several sets of index cards. Students get a partner, shuffle the cards, lay them face down, and, as their partner begins to time them, turn them face up. Half the cards have questions written on them, such as "What time is it?," and half have answers. Student A pairs as many questions and answers as possible in three minutes after which Student B verifies the total number of pairs, writes it on Student A's recording sheet, and initials it. They then switch roles. I usually stay close to this area to help verify the pairs.

- ◆ Station Four is a Scavenger Hunt. With previous permission from the office, my students, in pairs, take a hall pass and a question sheet, and go into the halls to find the answers to such questions as, "What color shirt is Mr. X wearing today?" and "How many trophies are in the window opposite Room 400?" Questions use a variety of interrogative expressions, and answers are written in French. I also have more than one Scavenger Hunt sheet, so student groups are not constantly answering the same questions. To avoid major dawdling, students have only 10 minutes to do their scavenger hunt, writing their time in and out on the sheet. (I try to monitor, also.)

- ◆ Station Five has a pile of magazines, scissors, and glue. Students are instructed to cut out a picture, glue it to their recording sheet, and write four questions, using a variety of interrogatives, about the picture.

◆ Station Six is my computer. The software provided by my text has an interactive portion where students may move and pose figures on the screen, filling in bubbles over their heads with a conversation. I have students construct a conversation, in groups of four, at this station, saving it for later viewing by other groups and me. So that I know who worked on the conversation, they use each other's names in the conversation.

◆ Station Seven is a tape recorder. The first student there records a question, the second listens to it and answers it, the third asks a question, and so on. It is an auditory version of the Graffiti Wall.

After students are done with these centers, I look over their papers, listen to the tape, review the computer work, and read the wall; the next day I have several possible follow-up activities. I can put the computer skits on the screen for us all to see (and for me to point out common errors). I can do the same with the audiotape. I can pass back the recording sheets so each student gets someone else's and have them all answer the four questions about the picture glued to the Station Five portion, and either re-collect them for grading the answers or have these students return the paper to its original owner and give them some feedback on their questions. I can use my favorite pictures that were provided for show-and-tell, question-and-answer practice. I can also give students who did poorly, for example, on Station Three's card sets, additional practice time with those while the rest of us do something else.

Other learning center activities might ask students to read something and either answer questions about it, or summarize the main point. There are other tape recorder-oriented activities that may ask students to listen to a speech and fill-in-the-blanks in a script with the missing words they hear, or to convert the sentences they hear from the present to the past/future/whatever tense (perhaps with an answer sheet for checking their answers for immediate feedback). Other stations may have students look at a slide, or a series of slides, and describe it, or watch a video and summarize it. I have developed learning center activities for Christmas and Mardi Gras (Carnival/Fasching), and for adjective usage, and like to try to develop a new one every year. The possibilities are infinite.

Another variation on Learning Centers is to have a permanent learning center in your classroom. My foreign languages colleague has a desk set up behind a screen with a tape player and headset/microphone attached. She uses it to catch up students who have been absent, and for remediation and extension purposes.

Bulletin board centers also work well; I like to have a bulletin board center for students who want extra credit. There are three pocket folders on the board. One holds newspaper and magazine articles that I have cut out. Students select one to read. The second folder has a form they fill out, stapling the article to it; the form asks basic comprehension questions about the article, and the student's own view on that topic. The third folder is where completed work is put by the students. (Note: my extra credit is only given to students who have completed all regular work first.)

My computer is also a good learning center source, particularly for mixed classes. I have often, due to enrollment, taught a 3/4 or a 4/5 class. While one group is working with me, I often assign the others, on a rotating basis, to do a grammar review activity on the computer, or a vocabulary-building exercise, a research project, or a report.

USING MODERN TECHNOLOGY

COMPUTERS

Computers are the cutting edge of modern foreign language technology. For 10 years or so, new programs have been available that drill students on language, enable them to play matching-type games, and enable them to put out a student newsletter using a desktop publishing program. Programs today enable students (or teachers) to create video-quality skits with moving figures, using their own voices to tape the dialogue (the DC Heath *Dime* and *Discovering French* series has this capability).Others allow them to create multimedia reports that combine videos, music, animation, and graphics, which can be shown from the computer onto a screen (Powerpoint is an example), as well as generate their own handouts and even a quiz on the material.

When using computers or any other technology in the classroom, several basic rules are good to keep in mind. Place students in small groups for more interaction (of course, the ideal is one student per computer). Set a realistic time frame for accomplishing the goal by breaking the goal into smaller portions with a deadline for each. Establish a set of grading criteria (a rubric) that the students see immediately when the assignment is made. Always be available to monitor what students are doing, and to provide technical assistance.

The most common use of computers is for students to do self-paced tutorials, practicing vocabulary, verb tenses, and other grammar concepts. These tutorials can serve to introduce a new topic or practice new material, or for remediation purposes through frequent repetition. A good tutorial program has a student repeat his/her most-often-missed questions, and provides a variety of options for practice: true/false, multiple choice, pair matching, and essay. I like a shareware program called Total Recall, available from Zoft Systems (see address after References at the end of this book). It has characters and accents for French, German, and Spanish, but you supply the data, creating your own review program. Students can save their scores for you to see. There are many such programs. These actually decrease the instructional time needed, because individuals can progress at their own rate with immediate feedback and rapid generation of examples for practice. The benefits are obvious. Also, the class need not slow for one or two students to catch on; they can be assigned extra practice on the computer for remediation.

Students also often use computers when writing research papers, both for the research and for typing the paper (although few word processors have a spellchecker for foreign languages). My students have found information as well as pictures for reports on famous people, countries that speak French, art movements, and historical events. My favorite so far has been an imaginary trip around the country: the Internet provided actual photos and descriptions of hotels, cafes, and museums to visit!

Here are a few more creative uses. First, a short one: Assign groups of students a survey topic such as how their classmates get to school, music preferences, or favorite sports. When they are done, have them go to the computer and, using Excel or a similar program, quickly graph their results for the class to see.

Use the computer lab for an electronic debate. On a chat network mode, the teacher posts an open, debatable question. As students respond (in the target language), everyone sees and can respond to their response. The teacher circulates as they work and points out errors. There are several advantages to doing this rather than assigning a written essay on the topic: immediate feedback on their ideas is better than a delayed reaction to a written essay; however, there is still a permanent record that the teacher can print out, choosing common errors to comment on later. An intermediate level class of 20 will generate an average of over 100 responses in about 45 minutes (our lab has half-block usage due to demand). In addition, absent students can access the conversation and still participate days later; some students even go back after class and finish conversations they liked!

THE INTERNET

The Internet has become a wonderful source of materials for any foreign language classroom. It is still difficult to establish any sort of penpal set-up because of the lack of computer access in other parts of the world, but there are addresses to contact that will, at the very least, put your students in contact with "keypals" who will write in the target language (often fellow students of the language, but sometimes from England or another country). A list of these addresses is at the end of this chapter, in the Resources section.

There are also databases all over the world that can be accessed for information on music, movies, art, subways, travel, and thousands of other topics. At the end of this chapter is a list of video sites I have found for foreign languages in general, as well as some for specific languages, which are good teacher resources. But why not let your students roam the Internet and find sites that they think are fun to visit? I like to have lower-level classes look on the Internet for sites about French or French-speaking countries, and write a short paper that supplies the following:

- Internet address of the site;

- Brief summary of what materials the site contains;

- Students' favorite item on the site;

- The students' assessment of the educational or entertainment value of this site; and, finally;

- Their favorite sites and why.

I then add these to my list of good sites.

My intermediate classes travel on the Paris metro (subway) via the Internet, plotting the shortest route to visit monuments and museums they wish to see, and have learned to book plane and train tickets to various locations. My advanced classes generally pick a topic, such as a French city other than Paris, and do a multimedia presentation on that place, based on Internet information and photographs. I researched a video I received, supplying students with information on the actors and the setting of the video, to make a whole unit based on it. The possibilities are enormous; use your imagination.

Also remember that the more specific a site, the more interesting it will be to your students. There is an entire site just on the Alpenhorn in der Schweiz, an interesting musical instrument that German classes would like to see. It is easy to ask your class to visit a specific café/Kaffehaus or restaurant, and list what they would like to order from its menu, which subway stop is closest to it, and other information. These are the sorts of small details that the Internet can bring to life in your classroom.

Another teacher provided me with this unit: She divides the class into groups in which at least one student has Internet access at home. Each group chooses a country and a newspaper from that country. Each student in the group is responsible for one section of the paper: sports, editorials, arts, or local news, and has to download that section for four days to a week. As homework, they summarize the articles in writing and in Spanish. During the second week they work in groups for two days, discussing their articles with each other. As a final presentation, each student gives an oral summary of the most interesting articles he/she has found and chosen, along with what the student has learned about the country from the article, pointing out similarities and differences between that country and ours. "The project was the favorite work of the year for many students."

There are ways to use the Internet even if your classroom is not connected to it. Without getting extremely technical, it is possible to access a Website, download it and save it on a disk, and then either print it out in hard copy (but be careful; some sites are bigger than they seem!) or show it to students on your classroom computer screen from the disk.

VCRs

Videos have been used for years to provide students with good visual examples of the target language, its usage, and the countries that speak it. What is new is to combine video with one of the new techniques such as Jigsaw: first, the teacher previews the tape, and identifies (perhaps by outlining) the main topics. For example, if the video is on Spain/Tahiti/Liechtenstein, these areas would be included: culture, geography, climate, history, government, and the educational system.

For Jigsaw, the teacher would organize students into expert groups, and as they watch the video, assign each group to take notes only on their area. After viewing the video in groups, they would decide on the key concept/idea for their topic, based on the information in the video, and on how they are going to present it when they teach it.

Student experts then return to their cooperative groups, share their information on their topic, and take notes as others share their expert fields. As an assessment, the team could do a poster, a newsletter, a written report, or take a group (or individual) test on this topic. This method increases the usefulness of the video because its information is more fully assimilated when it is discussed repeatedly, than when it is viewed only once.

We all receive catalogs from the commercial companies that publish videos, but I suggest that most embassies have quite good collections of tourist-oriented videos as well. Most teachers' texts list the addresses of embassies in countries that speak that language; it is well worth your time to contact them. Museums usually have such resources, but for sale only. Art museums, however, often lend small numbers of slides on a short-term basis. Send a letter on your school letterhead, if possible, to request a list of what is available.

CAMCORDERS

Videos are of especially high interest to students when the video was made by classmates. When doing a unit on clothing, students may produce a video fashion show, with students taking turns showing and describing clothing. When studying left/right and body parts, why not do an exercise video? For the chapter on toothpaste and shampoo, produce a video advertisement for a product. Take any fairy tale, write a script for it, and film it (Incidentally, student-produced videos are excellent sponge activities. I particularly like to put on an exercise video and have the students do it, especially when they need some out-of-seat time built into my lesson plan.)

The teacher's role is to establish teams, set a realistic time frame for the project, state the goals (how many minutes long, etc.), establish the grading criteria, and provide technical assistance to the students. To make this a good experience for everyone, I strongly suggest using a team proposal form for the video. I use one that looks like this:

> What is the TOPIC of the video?
>
> Who is making the video?
>
> Who is being videotaped?
>
> When will video be made?
>
> Where will video be made?
>
> What equipment is needed?
>
> What are the DETAILS: (how long will it take, etc.)

After students complete the proposal form and it is okayed by the teacher, they have a strict time limit for submitting a storyboard (visual or written outline of what will happen first, second, third) and a written script. This ensures that they are ready to film when they get the equipment. Of course, everyone has a due date for their final product, also.

I was fortunate to be able to arrange a video-penpal relationship with two high schools in France. We have been corresponding for six years, with each school sending a video per year, which is both a response to the previous video and suggests new topics to cover. We have also exchanged school papers, calendars, TV guides, and other realia. Our video contribution is always student-planned and executed, with my advanced classes doing their portion for a grade. Past topics of conversation have included typically American subjects such as school sports, cheerleading, proms, graduation, hayrides, sleepovers, and drive-in places of various sorts, as well as holidays, vacations, jobs, cars, music and movie preferences, leisure time activities, a typical house, a tour of the school, a typical day in a student's life, elections, churches, future aspirations, student pregnancy, and school violence. I now have a shelf full of tapes from France about the same topics, or their own variation or reaction to them. I arranged this video exchange through the AATF penpal service. Other groups (AATG, AATSP) probably have similar opportunities. The videos we send are in both English and French, as are those we receive (our videopals are English classes in a Paris suburb and in St. Etienne in south central France).

INTERDISCIPLINARY LEARNING

On a block schedule with only four blocks per day, at any given time, one-fourth of the school's teachers should be available at the same time you have your planning period. This is ideal for planning shared units or activities. Look at your schedule and see if there is a colleague with whom you could plan an interdisciplinary unit. Foreign languages can combine with almost anything. Of course, art, history, and literature classes are the easiest, but why not health (body parts, illnesses, AIDS issues, or whatever), math (story problems in the target language), or science (famous scientists/discoveries—France has the Ariane space program)? Make a guillotine with the shop class, construct a bridge with the physics class, or bake and assemble a gingerbread replica of a castle with the home economics class (ours has won the local contest twice). Use your imagination!

Projects may be short-term, taking only one block, such as writing a poem using synectics with an English class. It may be a week-long series such as Reading Week, where a theme is chosen and students in all subjects are asked to do readings on that theme; or assemblies for storytelling or reader's theater groups could be scheduled, as well as a dress-up day. Long-term projects might include AP English classes reading the play *No Exit* as the French classes do and then meeting to compare journals and produce a paper, a video, or to participate in a Socratic seminar. (Of course, English classes could just as easily read *Don Quixote* or *The Tin Drum* when the Spanish or German classes do.) Some themes are year-long. One local middle school chose Ancient Rome, with students making togas, studying history, geography, science, sports, and so forth, and culminating in a Coliseum Day where everyone dressed, ate, and acted as much like ancient Romans as possible. Why not do the same with a modern country, especially if the school has an exchange student from there?

INTERDISCIPLINARY STRUCTURES

There are several different methods for interdisciplinary teaching. One is obvious: the joint method, where two classes actually meet and learn in the same room with both teachers present. This is fine if classes are small in size. Easier, but similar, is the "shared" method, where students are taught about the same topic in two different classrooms. Examples of shared teaching are history classes covering a time period while foreign language classes read a novel set in that time period. Teachers from each class could switch classrooms as guest speakers to each other's class, or class projects could be shared by selected groups or members. Jigsaw would provide expert groups who could recombine into groups from each classroom for presentations. A Socratic discussion held jointly could deal with issues from that period.

An "integrated" unit is a collaborative one, similar to the "shared" except that more than two types of classes are involved, and the topics overlap. While foreign language classes study the World War I time period, so would the history classes, art classes, music classes, and whoever else could contribute a new and different perspective. Teachers would provide each other with an outline of what they covered, so that the history teacher could point out that art/foreign language/music students had studied X, and ask members of the history class who take those subjects to share what they had learned; in art, the teacher could ask history, foreign language, and music students to share any insights or knowledge on that topic. Students enjoy being "expert" representatives from one class to another on a chosen topic. Overlap in material covered from one course to another reinforces what was being learned, and is expected and encouraged.

A "webbed" interdisciplinary unit is one with a central theme. Each teacher constructs a lesson using that theme so that students, all day or all week long, in each of their classes study a different aspect of that theme. A theme such as Earth Day, Martin Luther King Day, or a space shuttle launch, with every class doing a relevant lesson, are obvious examples. Foreign language teachers merely need to find some materials on that topic in their language, make posters, or teach some new vocabulary to conform with such a unit. An example of a week-long unit would be a Careers week, with students learning about various careers from guest speakers, and reading and writing about their hopes for their own futures. Durham, Carmines, and Lewis (1990) published an account of an integrated unit they had done with their advanced-level foreign languages classes, part of a process they call Teaching for Synthesis. French students read Molière's *Dom Juan*, Spanish students read Zorilla's *Don Juan Tenorio*, and German students read Frisch's *Don Juan*. All three are significant literary works with audio and/or video performances available on tape, and are also related to Mozart's opera *Don Giovanni*, Byron's poem "Don Juan," and Shaw's *Man and Superman*, involving the English and music departments as well. Using the play as a device enhanced the understanding of the culture they were reading, as well as a cultural commonality that crosses national boundaries. Student evaluations said, among other things, "Language seemed to have a purpose for the first time....The key factor was the utilization of the interdisciplinary method."

INTERNET RESOURCES

BE VERY CAREFUL not to insert any spaces or change any punctuation or these addresses will not work! These sites all existed and worked well in October 1997.

PENPAL ("KEYPAL") LISTS

www.vcu.edu/cspweb/,icp/009.html

   Interclass Web sites

www.stolaf.edu/network/iecc/

   Intercultural e-mail classroom connection

www.advertising-america.com/club.htm

   International Penfriend Club

www.ling.lancs.ac.uk/staff/visitors/kenji/keypal.htm

   British group that connects students individually

tandem.uni-trier.de/Tandem/email/infen.html

   German site but has Spanish and French, too

www.pntic.see.mec.es/recaula/expe tel/index.htm

   Experiencias Telematicas: Spanish site

www.slf.ruhr-uni-bochum.de

   Tandem Keypals; matched by language studying

www.vcu.edu/cspweb/,icp/ipi.html

   Tells how to structure keypal usage; lesson plans

GOOD SITES FOR TEACHERS OF ANY LANGUAGE

www.cortland.edu/www root/flteach/flteach.html

   FLTEACH web page. Foreign language teachers share ideas, concerns. Good archives. Links to many other sites. My favorite place to start a search.

polyglot.lss.wisc.edu/lss/lang/teach.html

   Teaching with the Web. The absolute best site I've found so far to list sites, lesson plans, and suggestions on how to structure an Internet-based lesson. WONDERFUL!

wsrv.clas.virginia.edu/~iad4c/www.html

   Teaching with the WWW. Suggestions and lesson plans in many languages.

www.city.net/countries

Maps, travel, and hotel information, for hundreds of countries (for example, in Germany, it will give maps and info on over 20 cities).

www.vtourist.com/vt/europe.html

The Virtual Tourist

www.travlang.com/languages/

Languages for Travelers: At this site, you can select from 17 different languages, including Hawaiian and Esperanto, and you will learn phrases and words often needed for travel. There is also a dictionary function, a chat room, and a message board.

www. mapquest.com

Worldwide Atlas. Maps galore.

GERMAN SITES

www.uncg.edu/~lixlpurc/german_WWW

Children's story pages, a chat room, *and* 10 teaching units for the Web, with exercises ready to print out for use. AUSGEZEICHNET!

wsrv.clas.virginia.edu/~iad4c/webex.html

Web exercises for first through fourth year German students, with worksheets and teaching suggestions.

www.kultur-online.com

Kultur Online: museums, shows, movies, etc.

www.schulweb.de

Schulweb: info on German schools, chat lines for students, etc.

www.entry.de

German Server map, by regions, of *all* Websites in the country; great if you need info on regions and towns.

www.spiegel.de/index.html

Der Spiegel, the magazine: even the cover page. IN GERMAN!

www.dwelle.de

Current news and information in German or English.

128.172.170.24/menu.html

19th century German stories (in German or English), with accompanying music and illustrations. LOVELY!

FRENCH SITES

www.utm.edu/departments/french/french.html

Tennessee Bob's Famous French Links, a 5000-Link Supersite. Almost anything. A neat unit on Chateaux is the latest addition I've seen.

www.challenge.state.la.us/lessons/foreign/index.html

Lessons using the Web.

www.info-france-usa.org

The French Embassy's Web site: a news digest, demographics, a "Just for Kids," and many more useful tidbits.

www.AdeTocqueville.com

A weekly newsletter, in English, on issues of common concern to France and the U.S. Up-to-date French news and analysis, good current events, with extensive archives that include recipes, too.

www.paris.org/parisF.html

"La Boutique des Pages de Paris." English or French, Monuments, museums, shops, shows, cafés, the métro: EVERYTHING!

www.mmania.com

The Virtual Baguette: weird trivia on everything from bidets to gastronomie. In French; English is available but is not good.

www.wfi.fr/volterre/home.html

Volterre. Wonderful site for everything French.

www.bpi.fr/autres/index.html

Pompidou Center library links to other French sites. Very new.

www.culture.fr/culture/services.htm

Find out what's happening in France; concerts, museums, etc.

www.france.co.nz/~ftfw/tips.html

Planning a Trip to France, renting a home there, many tips for the traveler. English only.

www.cyberie.qc.ca/chronik

News on anything French-Canadian.

www.sirius.com/~alee/fmusicl.html

Anything on French music.

www.mygale.org/11/scarabee

Anything on French celebrities.

www.bertrand.com

Sells food from France.

SPANISH SITES

www.bbk.ac.uk/Departments/Spanish/TeclaHome.html

A text magazine for learners and teachers of Spanish. Has vocabulary lists for reading articles and all sorts of useful and interesting things. Educational site.

edb518ea.edb.utexas.edu/html/LatinAmerica.html

Latin America/Spanish Speaking Countries Pages. Links to over 15 countries, including Mexico.

donde.uji.es

Online directory to Spain, by regions.

www.udg.mx/cultfolk/mexico.html

Arte y Cultura Mexicana: music, art, and culture, including cooking

LanguageCenter.cla.umn.edu/lc/surfing/spanish.html

Elsie's Bookmarks Language Center. Links for many Spanish sites. MUY BIEN.

members.aol.com/maestro12/web/writing/html

Three Web activities for beginning students in Spanish. Written by teachers in California.

www.uco.es

Spanish site; Guide to the City of Cordoba (multimedia!).

mld.ursinus.edu/~jarana/Ejercicios

Spanish language exercises.

5

ASSESSMENT, GRADING, AND REPORTING

"Look and you will find it...what is unsought will go undetected."

Sophocles

Grades serve many purposes, but first and foremost they serve to give students a chance to prove to everyone that they are doing a good job. Grades also give teachers a measure of the job they are doing. Good grades are most people's definition of success. For some, they come easily; others strive mightily to achieve them, and others are less motivated; but for all, the task is easier if the objectives are clearly defined.

Every teacher determines grades in his or her own fashion, according to his or her own judgment of what is most important. Should one stress written or oral proficiency? Grammar skills or communication? What percent will tests, skits, daily work, quizzes, and projects represent in the student's total grade? Should the grade be based on points or percentages, use straight percentages, a bell curve, or the newer "J" curve (all grades either A, B, or incomplete)? Should classroom behavior (attendance, participation, doing work on time, etc.) be a part of the grade also? If so, how does one quantify behavior? What sorts of products should be graded? What will the teacher have to show a parent requesting a conference?

So many decisions! Some standards have recently been set for us via national and state proficiency guidelines (these are discussed in Chapter 1), which stress the communicative aspect as the most important. Some are made for us by our administration: attendance policies, grading scales, and percentages for semester exams are often included in the student guide on a schoolwide basis. Other aspects are based on what other teachers in the foreign language department are doing (often a wise strategy because it is perceived as more "fair" due to consistency from level to level, and language to language). Yet many others are still left up to the individual teacher. In this chapter, I present several different teachers' opinions on grading methods they like and use. Consider them suggestions and adopt those that are likely to work for you.

It seems clear, however, that all too often a distinct line has been drawn between the instructional process and the evaluation process; that is to say, that tests are used to label students, and not as a learning tool. If all we record about students is how well they perform on a test, we are not evaluating everything that takes place in our classroom. The block schedule affords more opportunities to arrange, observe, and evaluate behaviors such as conversations (the Communication component so highly valued in the national standards), simulations, and research projects (Culture component), in addition to the usual listening, reading, and writing found on standard tests. There is also more time for testing and assessment in the block, with more types of assessment (variety) possible. Once again, the block schedule's main strength, more time for greater variety, is an asset.

If you are setting priorities when going to a block schedule for the first time, however, postpone assessment changes until you have a good feel for the type of activities you enjoy doing in the new schedule. It might even be best to evaluate your assessment process the summer after your first year on the block. After seeing how much you can accomplish, and evaluating what was successful, as well as planning what changes to make for the next year, you can reassess your grading policies and procedures, and work on feedback forms, assessment scales, and some of the other instruments found in this chapter. Nevertheless, there is one step that is essential—because it is a part of establishing your classroom rituals and daily procedures—your course description handout for Day One.

CLEARLY ESTABLISH YOUR EXPECTATIONS

The first step is to clearly establish the course objectives, rules, and requirements. The listing of class offerings for the school should state, as clearly as possible, a *very specific* description of each course. For example, "Students in Level 1 will be able to communicate clearly about the following topics:...; Students will: write a report on...; perform two skits per week...; read X short stories and poems...." In this way, students will know the course content. The listing should also state specifically the requirements for entry into that class, for example, "A grade of C– or better in Level 1 is required for entry into Level 2, or written permission from the teacher," or whatever your administration will allow. I *strongly* advise that you state in your course requirements that Level 1 and Level 2 should be taken consecutively or severe learning difficulties will be encountered. (This was discussed in Chapter 1 and is based on many different teams' observations of retention.)

The teacher needs to write a class description sheet to be given to students on the very first day. At the top, list your classroom rules. Assertive Discipline trainers give very strict guidelines on these rules, which I find quite reasonable: they should be simple, few in number (five or less), and easily enforceable (i.e., black and white: student does or does not have a pencil, for example), except for the last one, which can be phrased however you wish, but should read something like, "Students will do as the teacher tells them." This last rule is a catch-all for unforeseen circumstances.

My class rules are:

---

1. Come to class prepared to work.
2. Do French first.
3. Show no disrespect.
4. Do what the teacher asks.

♦ Come to class prepared to work.

As I explain the first rule to them, I show them my attendance policy: at our school, on the block, students must not miss more than five days or they may not receive credit for the class unless they can prove mitigating circumstances. That is also my rule; however, I also require that time missed be made up in my classroom, either with me, or on the computer, or with a student tutor, or by viewing a video. I tell them that a foreign language is the oral, visual, artistic, and communicative activities that we do daily and which will be quite difficult to make up; we cannot restage a simulation, or a guest speaker, or group reports just for them. However, the time spent practicing the language is vital and should be considered a minimum requirement for passing the class. NOTE: my administrators approved this policy, which is vital for its success, and I do not give a student any grade whatsoever until the time has been made up to my satisfaction. Instead, I assign an NG (no grade), which becomes a failure one semester later. This NG concept, as well as the attendance requirements, are typical at our school. I find they are a necessary "weapon" to force students to make up time missed, and result in increased proficiency for absentee students.

The second portion of my first rule is "prepared to work." I train my students to expect a sponge activity every day (these are discussed in Chapter 4), and when they enter the room, they are expected to have begun it by the time the bell rings. This rule also applies to having all necessary equipment (paper, writing instrument, text, workbook) with them at all times. Even if class is shortened to 15 minutes for an assembly, we will find several things to do, and I want them to know that. I never allow students to go to their locker for forgotten items.

- Do French first.

The next rule is that they are expected not to attempt to complete classwork for other classes before they have completed their assignment for me. They need to know that I will not honor a pass from another teacher until their assignment is turned in to me, and that restroom requests, and so forth, must be made after they have completed whatever we are currently working on (except in dire emergencies, of course).

- Show no disrespect.

The third rule is basic. Speaking a foreign language sometimes requires us to make funny noises, perform somewhat silly actions, or make personal statements, and an atmosphere where students feel free to be different and to make mistakes is essential. Students are told that they may criticize an idea but never a person, and that personal attacks are strictly forbidden and will be punished (I leave the punishment vague as I usually make it fit the circumstances). I model for them statements that I never wish to hear in my classroom, so they have a good idea of what I do not want.

- Do what the teacher asks.

The fourth rule is the catch-all rule, and it tells the students that I expect cooperation at all times. Setting rules on Day One is very important. The teacher also needs to decide how to have proof that students have seen these rules and been informed of them. I have the students sign them, and then I collect and photocopy them, returning them to the students. I usually give an extra point to any student who can staple his/her copy of the rules to the semester exam, which I find to be a good motivator.

In addition to my four rules, I also include my grading scale, as well as percentages (which vary according to the level), such as tests 50 percent, daily work 25 percent, projects 25 percent, and my extra credit policy, which states what sorts of extra credit I accept. I also tell them a little about French club, the pétanque team, and some other fun activities they may expect, especially if I have dates for restaurant visits, tournaments, language fairs, and fund-raisers already set.

To summarize, assessment/evaluation is not valid if students have not been properly informed about what your expectations are, and what skills are valuable and will be taught and tested. Most teacher-training classes stress informing students of your instructional objectives as the most important part of teaching. Otherwise, students must feel their way slowly, wasting valuable time trying to figure out what is required of them. Once they know what to do, they are ready to go.

Another foreign language teacher put his RARE on the Internet for others to use. This acronym stands for Respect, Accountability, Responsibility, and Effort. He tells his students, "First, respect yourself, your classmates and the administration. Without respect, our class would not be successful." He goes on to say the student is accountable for homework, behavior, and other class requirements. Responsibility means not blaming someone else for failures, and the Effort to always do one's best is expected. In return, he promises to be a RARE teacher.

FEEDBACK

There are many different ways to provide feedback to students on whether they are fulfilling your expectations. One is a daily grade for work done. In Chapter 3, I discussed methods for letting students know what they have missed when absent. These included a classroom checklist, a folder with assignments listed, a list on the board or the wall somewhere in the classroom, a "study buddy," or a designated note-taker.

CHECKLIST AND HOMEWORK CALENDAR

The checklist on the wall works well for me because it records assignments for the entire grading period rather than for a week at a time. But recently, I came across several teachers (via FLTEACH, an Internet site for teachers) who have a similar approach that would inform those absent and would also clearly show all students if they have done the required work: a calendar in the target language with big spaces for each day is distributed to each student. They may use it to write due dates, birthdays, and so forth, but the teacher uses it as an assignment record. As students are quietly working on something else, the teacher will scan the student's assignment for accuracy and stamp that spot on the calendar. If the assignment is incomplete or missing, no stamp and no points are given (some teachers give points for late work, and others do not). Calendars are usually kept in the room, in a folder which the students pick up as they enter each day. Students who were absent clip their calendar to the make-up work for full credit. Teachers collect these calendars at the end of the month.

Mary Jo Eide takes the additional step of also stamping the homework paper since few students would lose both the paper and the calendar. This way the calendar can be resurrected if lost. It also makes it harder for students to pass a completed assignment to a classmate or someone in another class. And, of course, creative writing and nonroutine assignments are not put on the calendar in this way. Another teacher adds, "This has been one of the best time-management tools I've discovered over the years," because it eliminates her paper load of rote work; changing daily grades to just a quick check to see that it was done, with each assignment having an equal number of points.

Of course, the logical activity after a calendar-stamping check of homework would be some sort of pairs-check, Roundrobin sharing, teamed boardwork, or other form of looking at the actual answers to talk about how the work was done and why, fixing it more firmly in the students' minds. Chapter 4 provides many different strategies for checking homework.

BEHAVIORAL EVALUATIONS

But what about assignments that are not pencil-and-paper ones—skits and other performance activities such as working in groups, learning stations, and simulations. A second way to provide feedback for your students is to use feedback forms, or behavioral evaluations. In the section about active versus passive learning, Chapter 4 discussed one type of feedback form in the case of an oral report, in which the teacher and the other students all provided feedback by checking an easy form similar to this:

Talked loud enough	Yes ___	No ___
Could see the project	Yes ___	No ___
Looked at me	Yes ___	No ___
Liked the report	Yes ___	No ___
Comments:		

For a performance such as any teamwork, some teachers use an anecdotal record. This is when a teacher circulates among the students as they work, recording observations on a clipboard as specifically as possible. That is to say, writing "John: good" is not enough. Comments should be more like, "D.B. has made real progress, 100% on the quiz, and today used the lab to work, not to talk to J.V.," or "T.M. seems confused at times and does not ask for help." These comments should probably be stored via some sort of software program (my grade managing program has a comments section) for retrieval if the teacher needs to discuss areas that need attention with that student or his or her parent(s).

Another alternative to such comments is a checklist; decide on a behavior to look for (praising, for example) and make a check mark each time you hear a student praise someone else. Stand between several groups and eavesdrop for a time. At the end of the activity, share your checklists with each group.

Sometimes you may wish to grade students on their behavior. Figure 5.1 is a rubric I adapted from several I have seen, and which I use for activities such as simulations and learning stations. Make sure you share your rubric with students before the activity so they know your expectations. Sharing will eliminate problems when the grade is assigned and will result in a more cooperative classroom exercise.

FIGURE 5.1. GRADING SCALE FOR CLASSROOM BEHAVIOR

4 points "A"   Works until finished; always on task.
Completes all required work to specified standards.
Shows initiative by helping others.
Asks for assistance in an appropriate way.

3 points "B"   Works until finished but needs support to remain on task.
Needs a little prompting to complete work.
Works and helps others with some guidance.
Usually asks for help in an appropriate way.

2 points "C"   Needs regular prompting to finish work.
Does not consistently complete work as directed.
Works with others with little prompting; does not help others.
Needs reminding to ask for assistance in an appropriate way.

1 point "Unacceptable"
Often off task.
Often gains attention through inappropriate means.
Seldom completes work, or does not complete it according to directions.

COMMENTS/OBSERVATIONS:

Behavioral rubrics come in many forms. In the "real world," they are often used in employment evaluations. I know of many people who are rated and receive raises based on their punctuality, their cooperation with fellow workers and helpfulness to clients, their ability to complete work accurately and on time, and so forth. Ratings forms are quite defensible for use in assigning grades in the classroom, just as they are used to rate students on skills needed for success in college, on the job, and as a citizen.

A third way to give students feedback is by using role-playing or simulations. If they have the skills to do what they must/get what they want, they have immediate feedback on how they are doing! No grade is needed; however, students may be asked to evaluate themselves on a short form such as this:

SITUATION: _____

I did: Quite well   Somewhat okay   Not too well

I was proud that I could: _____

I wish I had known the word for: _____

What I would do differently next time: _____

These could be turned in for "calendar credit" so that the teacher could see areas of weakness, or saved in a folder or portfolio to show parents the progress and types of activities used in communicating. It also is good for students to look over the forms before a semester exam to review the types of situations practiced during that grading period, or at the end of a course so they can see how far they have come.

Students can also evaluate each other, and surprisingly accurately. I tell students that they each have FF 100 (French francs) as a "bonus" for the team, including themselves. They determine how much they each deserve based on their contribution to the project; if all members on a team of four contributed equally, each would get FF 25, for example. Students will usually be quite fair in apportioning this bonus and, amazingly, within the group will agree who worked and who did not when their answers are compared. An advantage to this method is that students receive peer recognition (or censure) for a job well (or not) done.

Another easy way to provide feedback from the teacher is a regular update via computer. I use a grade manager program to calculate my grades, and provide a printout for each student every time a test is taken, which is at least once a week. One year, I did this every Friday. It uses a fair amount of paper, but the student has something to take home and show off, and parents have commented very favorably.

Although feedback is not usually part of a student's grade in the gradebook, it is a good assessment of behavior and progress, which the student recognizes as such, and which serves as a good motivator and reinforcer.

PARENT CONTACTS

Your school will also probably adopt some form of progress report or deficiency report, which is sent home on a regular basis. You could attach a computer printout easily to one of the school forms, or send a printout home for a parent signature if a student is having difficulty. However, parents also like to be contacted when a student does something really well. Weekly computer printouts could provide this positive communication, as well as telephone calls, stickers, or prizes a student could show off, or perhaps you might consider making an award certificate on your computer (or purchasing some from one of the foreign language catalogs, or having a student contest to design one) for work above and beyond the call of duty.

PORTFOLIOS

Having students keep a folder portfolio is also an excellent idea borrowed from the grade school. A portfolio is a sampling of a student's work, projects, comments, and tests. Students are periodically asked to place favorite assignments, or work they feel is important, in a storage area: folders, notebooks, or some sort of container. Teachers may also decide to place certain things in the student's portfolio. Class time is used occasionally to look over, improve, and/ or comment on the items in the portfolio.

A typical portfolio might contain a passport, a self-description, a coat of arms, an advertisement, two quizzes, an oral performance evaluation sheet, four examples of daily work, a cassette recording of a skit, one letter written to a pen pal and the answer to it, an extra credit assignment, and a self-evaluation sheet (Bartz, 1997).

Here are two of examples of portfolio use from two rural New York schools: For their portfolio, Cindy and Lauren did a study on "arroz con pollo," a typical Mexican dish, and gave an oral presentation on the ingredients and how the dish was prepared, bringing a sample for classmates to taste. Before placing this report in their files, they decided it could be improved, and added sources for the ingredients, the region in which this dish originated, and the routine associated with the meal itself.

Chaz, a seventh-grade student who was originally from Quebec, did a study on "Greetings and Leave-Takings" in French. He and his teacher found eight French speakers in the community, and Chaz interviewed them using a video camera. He asked them how they and people from their French community greeted or said good-bye to each other, what gestures they used, and whether these varied depending on the age or sex of the speaker and the person being addressed. As he did this report, he developed more positive feelings about himself as a Quebecois, and learned more about French cultural patterns. It also gave him practice in speaking, and, because he used a camcorder, it developed his ability to use the equipment as well as the opportunity to combine artistic taste and content in his final product. Chaz added a brief comment sheet to the video that detailed these benefits he had derived from the experience (Moore, 1994).

Types of comments students could add to portfolio items are these: "This is my favorite piece because…"; "I'll remember this piece 20 years from now because…"; "This piece was my greatest challenge because…"; "My parents liked this piece because…"; "If I could do this over again, I would….."

Kathy Shipley, a French teacher in Evansville, Indiana, supplied her "Questions for Student Reflection and Self-Assessment," which I adapted as follows:

♦ Write a table of contents for your collection, starring the ones you think are the best.

♦ Make a list of the cultural information you have learned through making your portfolio.

♦ Comment on what you have learned this year about this foreign language.

♦ Give yourself a grade on this subject. Take into consideration your preparation, attitude, motivation, performance, and the progress made. Give reasons why you deserve this grade. (Bartz, 1997)

Portfolios have these benefits: they show the processes as well as the products; they provide students with time to reflect about their own learning and promote self-sufficiency and active involvement; they represent what students can do in real-life situations; and they are a tangible basis for discussions among students, teachers, and parents (Evansville-Vanderburgh, 1993).

Portfolios may be kept for years, and updated and used for college applications or employment purposes. They also may be graded (discussed in the Assessment section of this chapter).

Figure 5.2 is a form I use for culture projects that includes both the project proposal and a final self-evaluation. I find it useful to have the proposed project description to compare with the actual product, and the student's evaluation helps me assess the project more completely; students are often harder on themselves than I would be.

KEEPING A JOURNAL

A journal is a special tool often kept by writers. In it, they record daily events and various impressions of the world around them. A journal is also a very useful learning tool in foreign language, and is usable by the teacher both as an

---

FIGURE 5.2. CULTURE PROJECT EVALUATION FORM

Culture Project:

Name: Class:

Due 9/5   1. TOPIC:

   9/10   2. CONTENT:

        a. What is/are my objective(s)?

        b. What do I hope to learn?

   9/12   3. FORMAT:

        What is the end product of the study? (interviews, a clay model, a video, a written paper?)

   9/15   4. STRUCTURE:

        a. How am I going to do the study?

        b. What steps are involved?

        c. What materials and resources will I need?

PROJECT DUE 10/2, including this sheet, completed above and below

        5. EVALUATION:

        a. How did the study come out?

        b. What improvements can I make?

        c. What would be a good follow-up activity for this study?

Rank your performance by circling a number from 1 to 5, with 5 the highest or best.

| CONTENT | Self | 1 2 3 4 5 | Description: At least 2 sources, with bibliog. |
| | Group | 1 2 3 4 5 | Had accurate information, communicated clearly |

PREPARATION:			Completed outline promptly.
	Self	1 2 3 4 5	Had regular conferences with teacher
	Group	1 2 3 4 5	Was always on task

| CREATIVITY: | Self | 1 2 3 4 5 | Used information in a unique way. |
| | Group | 1 2 3 4 5 | |

ORGANIZATION:			
	Self	1 2 3 4 5	Presented ideas clearly
	Group	1 2 3 4 5	

assessment grade and for feedback purposes; and by the student for self-assessment and for recording his or her progress in the language. At the lower levels, students may keep the journal in English, recording things they learned and enjoyed, mistakes they made, and so forth. Recording things such as words they had to look up (or ask the teacher about) in order to understand an assignment will also fix that word or phrase more firmly in the students' minds, in addition to being there in black and white if the students have difficulty with it again.

The teacher may collect these journals periodically and write notes to the students in them about something they had written, or about how they are doing in the class, and make the journal part of the students' grade. Students may create their journal's cover as an art project: one teacher had the students draw a simple design on sandpaper with crayons, and then ironed the paper onto construction paper—an instant pointillist "masterpiece" for the cover.

In the upper-level classes, a journal is often used as a weekly writing assignment, to which, after reading the student's entry in the target language, the teacher replies, asking questions for the student to answer; a dialogue is established for both reading and writing practice. In multilevel classes, this is a good way of increasing teacher-student contact in a positive and fairly enjoyable manner. (Note: the teacher should be very careful about making corrections. The journal's purpose is communication. Only major errors in the student's entry should be commented upon. The teacher should, instead, consider modeling the correct way of writing in his/her response to the student.) A journal serves as an evaluation instrument, a record of progress made in improving writing skills and, after correction, as a good manual of correct usage for everyday words and phrases, for use in "real life" conversational situations.

ASSESSMENT

The important thing to keep in mind in assessment is that every student is responsible for his or her own grade on an individual basis, not as part of a group. Any assessment must be designed to determine if the individual student has learned the minimum competency requirements; however, it is still possible to involve a team or a group in the assessment process. This section discusses several options for both situations. However, let's talk about adapting testing to the block.

ADJUSTMENTS FOR THE BLOCK

First, there are more possibilities for assessment on the block schedule, and you may wish to make some adjustments. If, on a regular schedule, you were in the habit of giving vocabulary quizzes every other day, or once a week, and a chapter test every other week, and if you simply compress the lessons, you would find yourself doing some form of testing almost every day. It will seem to you (and to your students) that testing is all you do. So, there are several ways to get around this perception. One is to continue to give vocabulary quizzes, but over twice the vocabulary; it will be a longer quiz, but this could encourage students to remember these words longer. Giving more opportunity to practice these words, over a longer, more intense form of instruction should serve to imbed the vocabulary more firmly in the student's mind.

ADJUSTING TESTS

Another option is to change the format of the quiz. Instead of a dictation-style quiz, make it a crossword or a wordsearch, with the definitions in English (or the target language), or consider a Roundrobin or group quiz (more on that later). Remember, those words will still be tested on an individual basis on the next unit test! To test verb endings, Don Houghton has his students translate "creative conjugations." After providing a list of verbs, he has the students translate series such as: "I smoke, you smoke, he coughs, we continue, you cough, they cough" or, " I sleep, you snore, he yells, we wake up, you laugh, they laugh," or "I ran, you fell, he won, she was second, we lost, you yelled Bravo, they celebrated" (Houghton, 1997). Use your imagination and make the quiz more like a game; tell them it is for a grade, but don't call it a "quiz." This will be more work for you, but only during that first year on the block, almost like the first year after you adopt a new textbook.

To avoid so much work, try having the students make up the quiz. Have them write sentences using the vocabulary; choose your favorites, and retype them, leaving out the vocabulary word, and have the students figure out which word goes in the blank. That would test both spelling and reading comprehension. Or, have them write stories, in groups, if possible, using every single vocabulary word. Then, making sure they get another group's story, have them, either individually or in groups, translate a story from another group without a dictionary. The latter may be done English-to-(language) *or* vice versa.

If your text, like mine, gives the first person verb endings in one chapter, the second person in the next, and the third person in the third, why not wait and combine all three tests; give parts of the first two as worksheets while you work on the third chapter, and then give a combined test. All you have to do is a little cut-and-paste job on the three chapter tests, and voilà!—you have adapted your testing to the block schedule.

Another quite welcome aspect of testing in the block is the increased time for oral tests. For example, I could never get through having all 28 or so students count aloud from 1 to 20 for me in the preblock class period; now it is a snap! It is now common for my students to come to me for the final few questions of their test, or go to the tape recorder area (a screened-off pocket in the classroom) to quietly speak a few sentences into the tape recorder. Or, using inside-outside circle (see Chapter 4), my students can perform a speech or a skit for myself and their classmates in a fraction of the time it used to take. Once again, variety and creativity make things easier on the students and on the teacher, with more learning and practice taking place than ever before.

Finally, why give a test at all if another product would display mastery of the same vocabulary or grammar concepts? Figure 5.3, on the next page, provides a list of products that might be used in place of a test grade occasionally, thereby avoiding frequent testing.

When it comes to the question, "What shall I place more emphasis on—grammar or communication?," let me share with you the study (July 1997) placed on FLTEACH, an Internet site for foreign language teachers. In it, two groups were taught a language. One group was encouraged to speak and was rarely corrected—just pure communication, with little or no attempt to impart language rules. The other group's instructors alternated speaking with a high emphasis on grammar practice. The results seem to speak in favor of grammar reinforcing speaking skills. While the first group spoke more promptly, at times their errors were so numerous as to make their responses completely incomprehensible; the second group spoke more slowly, sometimes stopping and starting over to correct or paraphrase their statements, but had fewer errors, resulting in better communication. In addition, their composition writing skill was substantially greater than the first group, and reading comprehension exams showed that the second group students were both faster and better in understanding materials (Abghari, 1997). This study seems to support a strong belief that grammar is necessary for communication, and both should be a formal part of classroom instruction.

For this reason, any good test should be a composite test. Moore (1994) supplies a suggested overall distribution of percentages in a language test, as agreed upon by a group of New York foreign language teachers: Culture 20 percent, Listening 25 percent, Speaking 25 percent, Reading 20 percent, Writing 10 percent = Total 100 percent. Contrast this test with the one supplied by your text; most of the texts I viewed at our last adoption year had little listening, little or no reading, and were primarily writing!

CULTURE

The New York teachers let the students submit portions of their portfolio for the culture segment of the test: one or two of their best pieces for the beginning and intermediate levels, and a project or two for the upper-level classes. Figure 5.4 presents the holistic grading criteria used by those teachers for the portfolio items.

FIGURE 5.3. PRODUCTS FOR USE IN LIEU OF A TEST GRADE

A letter	Editorial essay	Play
A lesson	Fact tile	Poetry
Advertisement	Fairy tale	Pop-up book
Animated movie	Film	Project cube
Annotated bibliography	Flip book	Puppet
Art gallery	Game	Puppet show
Block picture story	Illustrated story	Puzzle
Bulletin board	Interview	Radio program
Chart	Journal	Rebus story
Choral reading	Labeled diagram	Recipe
Clay sculpture	Learning center	Riddle
Collage	Letter to the editor	Role play
Collection	Map with legend	Skit
Comic strip	Mobile	Slogan
Computer program	Model	Song
Costume(s)	Mural	Survey
Crossword puzzle	Newspaper story	Tapes (audio)
Demonstration	Oral report	Television program
Detailed illustration	Painting	Timeline
Diorama	Pamphlet	Transparency
Diary	Papier mache	Travel brochure
Display	Photo essay	Venn diagram
Edibles	Picture story for children	Video

I use the form in Figure 5.4 for grading, but I also require the student to do a self-evaluation, which focuses on many of the same ideas (see Figure 5.2, p. 157). Students often are harsher on themselves than I am, but just as often they will validate errors in their work which I also see, which helps them accept the grade I assign more readily.

Here's a good tip for teachers who have decided what percentages of students' grades each performance category (culture, reading, writing, listening, and speaking) should represent: color code your gradebook. Take the five divisions and make each a different color of highlighter or marker or ink. Then, if, for example, you wanted 50% of the grades to be based on speaking activities, you can easily look at your gradebook and see if you are achieving your goal. It would also be easy to see what type of assignments a student was missing (a good memory jogger for those of us who use shorthand notations to describe assignments because of the small size of spaces in the gradebook).

FIGURE 5.4. HOLISTIC GRADING CRITERIA FOR PORTFOLIO ITEMS

Letter Grades	Criteria	Descriptors
Superior A+, A or A-	Outstanding in: presentation content, creativity Appropriate format Accurate information Several errors or faults, but none are grave	Coherence in presentation Sources well-documented Multiple sources Citations well-documented Well-organized Correct spelling & grammar
Satisfactory: B+, B or B-	Very good but not as creative as superior Errors in content Several weaknesses in presentation More errors or faults than superior	Not thoroughly researched Errors in documenting sources Insufficient sources Errors in spelling and in grammar
Unsatisfactory:	Many weaknesses Insufficient content Inadequate length Presentation sloppy Inaccurate information	Topic not well researched Few resources used Incomplete citations Many errors of spelling & grammar Insufficient evidence of work done

Source: Moore (1994)

LISTENING

With the portfolio as one portion of the exam and the choice made as to the activity that will form what percent of the total grade for the class, teachers must choose how to test the remaining portions: speaking, reading, listening, and writing. Valette (1977) suggests using authentic materials as much as possible for these portions. For the listening portion, most texts provide tapes of native speakers for testing purposes which could be used, or the teacher could read an advertisement or some other realia aloud, asking the students to respond either academically (multiple choice, true/false, matching, checklist, visual identification, complete open-ended statement, fill in words missing from text, writing main idea, or straight dictation) or realistically (paraphrase, act out response, respond orally, fill in a form or take a message, converse). As a change of pace, a video would also provide an alternative form of realistic listening experience, with both audio and visual information for the student to react to in the same ways.

SPEAKING

Speaking evaluation involves a lot of anxiety for students, and requires a lot of guidance from the teacher. First, the teacher should present students with examples of the type of speaking that will be required of them: are they to introduce themselves, describe a picture, or just answer questions? Give them a chance to practice a situation similar to the test: use Pairs/Interview with sets of questions to practice, for example, or Roundrobin to describe a picture, with each member of the group adding a sentence; or team them and have them introduce themselves or a partner as in Team Interview. Second, the teacher should acquaint the students with the evaluation form to be used for the speaking assessment (a sample form is found in Figure 5.5), and, because the descriptions are a bit vague, the teacher should model what type of answer would get a 4 or a 1. For example, the teacher should tell the students that a "jump start" answer such as: "Yo, ah, tiene, no, yo tengo..." would not receive the highest grade.

Look at the scale in Figure 5.5 on the next page; I have added a rather different category: "Effort to Communicate." This was in response to that well-known student ability to find the loophole in a grading system. Certain students found a generic answer or formula they could use over and over with success, such as "I'm not sure, but perhaps," "There are people in the picture/ video," or the psychoanalytic, "What do YOU think, Madame?." My "Effort to Communicate" category arose as an effort to torpedo such non-efforts and force a wider variety of responses.

Not all speaking needs to be graded with such an extensive scale. Consider using the following 5-point, holistic scale for everyday evaluations:

> 5: Answered after hearing question once. Gave a creative response, spoken with no hesitation.
> 4: Had to have the question repeated more slowly. Gave an appropriate response with little hesitation.
> 3: Needed question clarified or reworded. Gave an appropriate response, with frequent hesitations.
> 2: Needed many repetitions or rewordings. Gave a response that was very difficult to understand.
> 1: Misunderstood question. Gave an inappropriate response. Spoke only a word or two.
> 0: Did not try to understand. Did not answer.

FIGURE 5.5. SPEAKING EVALUATION CRITERIA

AMOUNT OF COMMUNICATION: The quality of information the student is able to convey.
0 = No information.
1 = Very little information, or inappropriate response.
2 = Some relevant information but only comprehensible to a native speaker accustomed to foreigners.
3 = A fair amount of information, mostly comprehensible to native speakers.
4 = Most or all information, without much hesitation.

COMPREHENSION: How easily the student understood the question or situation
0 = Did not try to understand.
1 = Misunderstood question.
2 = Answered question after two or more repetitions or rewordings.
3 = Answered after having question clarified or reworded.
4 = Answered question after hearing it once.

COMPREHENSIBILITY AND ACCURACY:
0 = Could not understand.
1 = Could only understand a few isolated words/ many errors.
2 = Could understand a few phrases/some serious pronunciation or grammatical errors.
3 = Could comprehend some short, simple sentences/ just a few minor errors.
4 = Could comprehend all or most of what the student said/ few or no errors.

FLUENCY:
0 = No student response.
1 = Very halting/ several starts and re-starts.
2 = Some smoothness in use of short word clusters.
3 = Hardly any unnatural pauses/ fairly effortless.
4 = Smooth and almost effortless delivery.

EFFORT TO COMMUNICATE:
0 = No student response.
1 = Resorts to one-word answers.
2 = Uses a very similar sentence or sentence structure, or a generic phrase.
3 = Uses appropriate vocabulary and phrases to get message across.
4 = Makes a huge effort to communicate and uses almost all possible verbal resources.

Obviously, the Russian teacher may be looking for solid pronunciation and a certain amount of vocabulary, and the Spanish teacher across the hall is looking more for effort to communicate and comprehensibility. This type of assessment allows a lot of room for the personality of the teacher, as well as that of the student. Adequate modeling during every classroom activity as well as before the assessment should take care of informing the students of their particular teacher's emphasis.

READING

Reading tests are simple to construct: find (or adapt) a short article, story, or conversation for the students to read, asking them to then summarize it, or paraphrase it. Have them choose a good title for the conversation (either constructing it themselves, or choosing from several options). Have students fill in blanks in the story/conversation, or suggest a logical continuation for the situation based on what they read, or show what happened by drawing a picture. On a more ordinary level, ask students to answer some basic comprehension questions.

WRITING

Rather than just adding the correct endings to verbs, written evaluations should ask the students to respond in writing to a situation, for example: in a hotel, you have been incorrectly charged for the following items…, write a letter to the manager; you are in a post office, ask for two stamps for postcards and mail a package to your mother in the United States; tell your best friend what you like about his or her family…. There are thousands of options!

USING TESTS AS LEARNING TOOLS

With a good test written, the evaluation scale chosen, and students well-informed about their teacher's expectations, the teacher now needs to consider how to administer a test and go over the results in a manner that continues the instructional process and involves the students actively. There are many methods discussed in Chapter 4 for active reviewing before the test, such as Pair/Drill, Graffiti, Roundrobin, Send-a-Problem, Numbered Heads Together, Turn-4-Review, TGT, and STAD, but Team Test is worth mentioning again.

In Team Test, students are given one copy of the test (or a portion of the test, or a test similar to the one you wish to give) to complete as a team before taking the actual test. They help each other understand what is being tested and how to complete each section. Reiterating the material reinforces their comprehension for both the bright and the slower students. However, Team Test need not be done as a review activity: in one variation, the team takes the test *after* the students take the test individually. In redoing the test as a group, students are validated for correct answers, and remediation comes from their peers about wrong answers. Even better, it forces them to go over the material one more time instead of just glancing at the grade at the top of the paper.

Even if group testing is done, however, it is the individual's performance that must be emphasized. Perhaps the solution is to incorporate in each student's score an evaluation of improvement. The suggested way to do this is to give an assignment that can be used to obtain a base score. This could be a practice test, a homework assignment, or a skit or composition. Taking that grade as the base, students are assigned additional points in this way:

> a test score of 5 percent or more below base score = 0 pt.
> 4 percent below to 4 percent above = 1 pt.
> 5 to 9 percent above = 2 pt.
> 10 percent above or a perfect score = 3 pt.

Also, a score from 95 to 99 percent total should never get less than 2 points. This would encourage even A/B students to better their scores. These points could be a portion of their final grade, or could be accumulated toward a goal such as a field trip, a movie, food, or something the students would like. If you have a market economy system of rewards in your class, these points could be converted into coupons or money to be spent. I am fond of using this method because it works well for students at every level. Even the lower-ability students with a 45 percent base score could, while still not passing the test, earn valuable points by increasing their score to a 55 or a 60. Instead of giving up because he or she knows passing is not possible, a student will strive for the improvement goal and the reward promised.

The teams themselves can be used to encourage the individual students. There are many, many ways to involve the group in striving to maximize each member's performance. Obviously, the first step is the assignment of duties such as Praiser and Checker, to show students that each person is important and accountable. Another method is to involve the group in the accumulation of improvement points. Research shows clearly that giving a group grade is a very bad idea, but setting up a group incentive system is quite acceptable.

Setting a group goal and having a celebration of some sort, or nonacademic reward for groups who achieve their goal, encourages teams to encourage each member to better his or her performance. Group celebrations may involve food, a movie, playing a favorite game, or doing homework on the front lawn. Perhaps a session of Think/Pair/ Share would provide you with a good idea of what students would consider a good reward for work well done.

Here are some other variations on group evaluations:

- Student receives his/her individual score plus bonus points based on all members' improvement.

- Student receives the individual score plus a bonus based on how the lowest-scoring member of the group performed.

- The individual receives a score and a bonus based on a group average. (Johnson, Johnson, & Holubec, 1993)

I have many reservations about the other four of methods presented by Johnson, Johnson, and Holubec: one randomly selected paper becomes the group's grade; the whole group receives its lowest member's score; the whole group receives its average score; or the group receives a grade based on the total points of all its members' tests. Although these four methods might encourage the group to perform better, they also penalize a group for the failure of the lowest common denominator in the group and could create considerable resentment. Using the three-point system to evaluate individual improvement shows the biggest results with the low scorers; they still have an F, but by improving, they contribute valuable points and receive team recognition of their effort. (Peer approval is the strongest motivator, after all!)

SELF-EVALUATION

And, finally, after peer approval, why not encourage a student to evaluate himself or herself.

Figure 5.6 (on the next page) is a modified form of the evaluation used in Maryland to help a student identify the areas of knowledge and his or her proficiency in each.

Figure 5.7 (p. 169) is an evaluation form that I like to use with my students for at least the first grading period at each level. It reinforces my classroom expectations, forces students to think about their performance, and provides me with an opportunity to agree or disagree with their assessment. It also is, in many cases, something positive the student can take home to communicate with a parent, or just look at for a moment of self-congratulation.

Figure 5.8 is a team assessment form. I require each team to do an assessment for every team assignment, to hand in the completed form with the project, or else complete it after they see my evaluation of their project.

FIGURE 5.8 TEAM ASSESSMENT FORM

TEAM EVALUATION

Talk among yourselves and give me an idea how you feel your team did, using this scale:

5 = Très bien   4 = Bien   3 = Pas mal   2 = Comme ci, comme ça   1 = Mal

Speaking French as much as possible	5	4	3	2	1
Helping each other	5	4	3	2	1
Checking for comprehension often	5	4	3	2	1
Staying on-task	5	4	3	2	1
Complimenting each other (no put-downs)	5	4	3	2	1

Other comments (on team OR on the assignment):

Figure 5.6. Self-Evaluation Form Used in Maryland

Read the descriptions and check the appropriate areas that indicate how you rate yourself.

LEVEL ONE: I can do the following:	Agree	Somewhat agree but need a lot of improvement	Can't do
Greet someone; ask the person how she/he feels			
Tell someone my name and age			
Tell someone a little about my family			
Question someone if it relates to me, my family, or my school			
Describe my best friends, male and female			
Understand and answer questions about my name, age, where I live, and things I like			
Read a simple short paragraph if it is about someone discussing him/herself, school, or friends			
Write a note to a pen pal telling about myself			
Write and describe a typical day from the time I get up to the time I go to bed			
Write the correct endings on verbs becasue I understand which endings go with specific subjects			
Read,write, and tell the time, day, and date			
Order something in a school store, a restaurant or cafe, a department store			
List three other tasks you can perform and are willing to demonstrate: a. b. c.			

(Figure is based on Prince George's County (MD) Public Schools Student Self-Assessment of Foreign Language Performance and is modified from Hancock (1994, pp. 209–10).)

FIGURE 5.7. EVALUATION FORM FOR A GRADING PERIOD

EVALUATION FORM: ___ Grading Period

NAME _____

WEEK ONE

Here's how I think I did this week in class:

  5 = Great 4 = Very good 3 = So-so 2 = Not so great 1 = Can we talk about a problem?

	STUDENT	TEACHER	COMMENTS
SPEAKING	5 4 3 2 1		
TEAMWORK	5 4 3 2 1		
VOLUNTEERING	5 4 3 2 1		

WEEK TWO

Here's how I think I did this week in class:

  5 = Great 4 = Very good 3 = So-so 2 = Not so great 1 = Can we talk about a problem?

	STUDENT	TEACHER	COMMENTS
SPEAKING	5 4 3 2 1		
TEAMWORK	5 4 3 2 1		
VOLUNTEERING	5 4 3 2 1		

WEEK THREE

Here's how I think I did this week in class:

  5 = Great 4 = Very good 3 = So-so 2 = Not so great 1 = Can we talk about a problem?

	STUDENT	TEACHER	COMMENTS
SPEAKING	5 4 3 2 1		
TEAMWORK	5 4 3 2 1		
VOLUNTEERING	5 4 3 2 1		

WEEK FOUR

Here's how I think I did this week in class:

  5 = Great 4 = Very good 3 = So-so 2 = Not so great 1 = Can we talk about a problem?

	STUDENT	TEACHER	COMMENTS
SPEAKING	5 4 3 2 1		
TEAMWORK	5 4 3 2 1		
VOLUNTEERING	5 4 3 2 1		

OTHER POSSIBILITIES

Finally, especially in upper-level classes, acquaint students with the forms some businesses use to evaluate job applicants' language abilities: the ACTFL scale, based on the national proficiency guidelines found in Chapter 1. These may be found at the following Internet addresses, along with explanations on their use:

Speaking

> http://www.sil.org/lingualinks/library/llearn/fre583/fre195/
> may380/index.htm

Listening

> http://www.sil.org/lingualinks/library/llearn/fre583/fre195/
> may264/index.htm

Writing

> http://www.sil.org/lingualinks/library/llearn/fre583/fre195/
> may427/index.htm

Reading

> http://www.sil.org/lingualinks/library/llearn/fre583/fre195/
> may411/index.htm

It is useful to have the students look at these, decide where they would fall on the scale, write down the strategies in which they feel they excel, plus the ones they feel they need to get more practice in. They could then set their own goals, and research vocabulary, or whatever else is needed to achieve them.

Other tests could also be given to students, perhaps even more than once, so they could see both how colleges or future employers would evaluate them and where their grammatical and vocabulary shortcomings lie. I have a book of several College Board Achievement Tests (CBAT) that I give my advanced classes as practice. Harrap's also has good books of self-administered and self-scored placement tests for French, German, and Spanish; perhaps there are some for other languages as well. It is also easy to obtain practice tests for both the SAT+ and the AP exams through a local bookstore or from the guidance counselors at your school. The AATF (American Association of Teachers of French) sponsors a yearly National French Exam with listening, grammar, and vocabulary in a multiple-choice format that would also allow students to see the level of effort and achievement this group deems desirable or typical for their level of language study.

Assessment comes in many forms. The block allows more time for variety in the forms of assessments used, and more opportunities to test students based upon the strengths of different learning styles, in order to determine that learning is taking place, and to reinforce that idea.

6

SAMPLE LESSON PLANS

"The time which we have at our disposal every day is elastic; the passions that we feel expand it, those that we inspire contract it; and habit fills up what remains."

Marcel Proust

This chapter of sample lesson plans borrowed from friends, off the Internet, and from observations made at other schools on the block schedule, should give you a good idea of what types of things and how much can be accomplished on a typical day in the block schedule. Whenever possible, I have provided the name of the text being used. You will find a variety of languages represented, as well as a variety of strand styles—from lessons centered around a single topic to those that jump from area to area. Some of these lesson plans cover a single day's span, and others cover an entire unit.

In addition to looking at these lesson plans, please reread Chapter 3, which discusses how to construct a good lesson plan, full of the variety that we must use to make the fullest and most successful use of the block schedule. Figure 6.1, on the next page, shows how multiple teaching methods may be used during a single block class period. Also, at the end of Chapter 4 are Web sites, which, at the time of printing, contain lesson plans from foreign language teachers who teach in the block, or that would be easily adaptable for the block classroom.

At the end of this chapter are comments from foreign language teachers on the block about lesson plans and the block schedule in general.

FIGURE 6.1. USING MULTIPLE TEACHING METHODS IN THE BLOCK

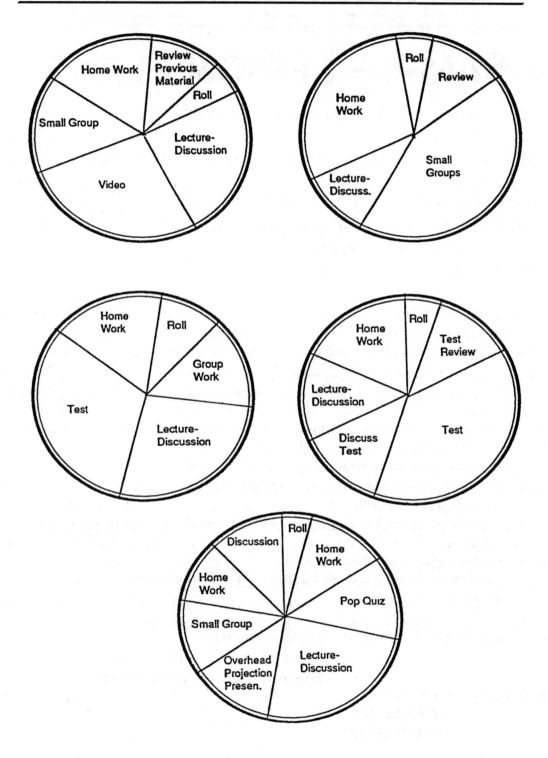

GENERAL LESSON PLAN FORMAT

Any Foreign Language
Multistrand Lesson

Opening activity: pair/share, question of the day, sponge activity Teacher does administrivia	5 min.
Teacher checks on success of opening activity, intros objective(s) for the day, etc.	5 min.
Review activity from text or workbook (or listening). Check orally or on board	10 min.
Introduce and practice new concept (teacher-directed)	10 min.
Practice new concept in written form (paired or teamed) Teacher monitors progress	10 min.

GROUP WORK: conversation cards
    group reading
    group listening
    group translation
        length of time depends on the type of work

Out-of-seat: TPR to learn things in classroom (lower levels)
    Scavenger hunt to find answers in classroom posters or realia (upper
    levels)
    (e.g., What city in France makes Coca-Cola? Bottle on shelf in classroom
        has answer)
    Spelling bee/vocabulary bee
    Beanbag: days of week, verb endings, etc.
    Inside/outside circle
Culture component: slides, video, postcards, culture from texts, magazines,
    Internet
Back to basics again: composition
    worksheet collected at end of hour OR due tomorrow
    Team review for test

Think of each block in thirds: review/intro new
                                  practice new in a variety of ways
                                  change of pace/more of what's new

Remember: **VARIETY**
            MOVEMENT
            ASSESSMENT

FRENCH LESSON PLANS

FRENCH I: OBSERVATION—HILLCREST H.S., SPRINGFIELD, MO 8-BLOCK SEPTEMBER, 1993

29 students

Seats arranged in a v-shape, two rows deep

Class began with activity period: News broadcast, short video on current events, discussion

9:50   Handed back quizzes from previous class & went over common errors

10:00   Grammar: Reviewed *-er* verb endings—10 min on board
10 minutes in book (also reviewed vocab and introduced new concept)

10:20   Listening practice with tape. Then, traded papers and checked them.

10:37   Book work: 6 students do one thing on board, rest of class do a different assignment at seat

10:45   Check papers, discuss board work

11:00   Assignment for tomorrow: 14 sentences

11:02   Asked them for scores on listening done earlier

11:07   Asked who wanted a pass for extra help during seminar; dismissed a little early because they all had classes in a different building next.

COMMENTS:

Loves block. Seminar period (schoolwide activity-cum-study hall) affords opportunity to catch up slow and/or absent students.

AUTHOR'S COMMENTS

This lesson plan is given as observed. It provides for VERY little student movement. Here are my suggestions to improve it:

10:00   Change teacher review to student review. Do review using Flyswatter, or student-made flashcards, or a team VERB RACE.
For a verb race, teacher has prepared cards or strips of paper with verbs on them. The first student in a team takes a card or strip, runs to the board and conjugates the verb. If the teacher says it is right, the student keeps the card as proof, and goes to the end of the line. The second student then selects a verb and runs to the front, etc. If the first student has it wrong, the team coaches him/her until it is done correctly, but the verb has to go back into the pile for another turn. The first team with no cards left in their pile wins.

11:00   To keep kids more actively involved, write sentences Roundrobin, or do Row Sentences (described in Chapter 4) while also reporting scores to the teacher!

EXAMPLE OF A 2-DAY "SINGLE-STRAND" LESSON ON THE PASSÉ COMPOSÉ (FRENCH 2 TEXT: *Discovering French* (Blanc) D.C. Heath)

Day 1

ACTIVITY	Teacher	Student	Time
1. Sponge activity. As students enter, assignment on board: "List five activities you did yesterday, i.e., Ecouter le prof…"	Opening paperwork	Think/Write	3 min.

2. Concept Attainment
  Four sentences on board. 2 are examples, 2 not.
    One more sentence on board
    One more sentence
  WITH PARTNERS: Discuss theory
    4 more sentences
    Check sentences
    2 more sentences
  TEAM 2 sets of partners: 2 more sentences
    4 more sentences
  Have team generate 2 sentences they feel are examples of this concept
  Team puts sentences on board
	Teacher posts
	Feedback
	Feedback
	Monitor
	Monitor
	Feedback
	Feedback
	Monitor
	Feedback
	Monitor
	
	Comment
		Think
		Guess
		Guess
		Discuss
		Discuss/guess
		
		Discuss/guess
		Discuss/guess
		Discuss/guess
		Discuss/write
		
		Read/think/
		  evaluate
			14 min.

3. Look at book section on passé composé Add this tense to verb card/notes	Lecture/read Monitor	Read Write	3 min.

4. Video (Discovering French 2.6)
  Show again; have students raise hand when they hear this new tense used
  Give script with verbs missing; fill in
	Show video
	
	Hand out papers
	Collect papers*
		Watch/listen
		Physical response
		
		Write
			10 min.

5. Think/Pair/Share
  Using verbs from Step 1, have students construct passé composé sentences
  With partner, tell two things did yesterday
	Monitor
	
	Monitor
		Think
		
		Speak/Listen
			5 min.

6. In text, look at how to make this tense negative p. 107
  Do book exercise # 6 p. 107
  Team/Check
	Talk
	Monitor
	Monitor
		Listen/Read
		Write
		Read aloud/
		  discuss
			10 min.

7. TEAM: Group translate Prévert poem "Déjeuner du Matin"	Hand out poem
	Monitor
		Assume roles:
		Reader/Check-
		  er/Praiser/
		  Writer
			15 min.

8. Listening activities D, E & F (G if time)	Run tape/
	  Monitor
	Feedback as
	  needed
		Listen/Write
		Speak
			12 min.

9. Write a postcard* in the passé composé Choose Paris, Tahiti, Maroc, or Nice	Explain assignment Monitor	Listen Write/Discuss	18 min.
*= assessment		TOTAL	90 min.

Day 2

ACTIVITY	TEACHER	STUDENT	TIME

1. Sponge activity: Say to partner Activity 5 p. 107
  One does evens, other odds, then reverse
  (Conversation: ask if did certain things, answer)
	Opening
	
	Monitor
		Think/Speak	8 min.

2. TEAMWORK: Look at vocab p. 106
(NOTE: vocab is adverbs: first…then…yesterday… finally…during…etc. used often with p.c. stories)
Brainstorm silly ways to remember the vocab
Share ideas with class
  Class votes on favorite ideas
  Groups draw ideas to help remember
	Pronounce
	  vocab
	
	Monitor
	
	Facilitate
	Facilitate
	Monitor
		Repeat
		
		Discuss
		
		Speak
		Evaluate
		Draw/discuss
			20 min.

3. TEAM: Roundrobin Activity 3 p. 106	Monitor	Write/ evaluate	5 min.
Cards, each with name of different person at top. Student writes one activity from list in book, passes card to next teammate who reads and corrects the first sentence, then adds another, until all in book are used up. (NOTE: this can be done as a race, but I do not as that's the next activity, also.) Hand in team cards*			

4. INDIVIDUAL: Crossword "race"	Hand out papers Give instructions	Listen Write	10 min.
5. SPONGE: Hand in crossword Pick up postcard/Read it/Return to writer Then read silently p. 108	Check crossword*	Watch teacher Read Read	5 min.
6. Workbook C 3 p. 124: Practice info from p. 108 (Writing questions in p.c.) Check by reading aloud in unison	Monitor	Write Speak	5 min.
7. INTERVIEWS: Have students write down five things they did last weekend Interview four classmates; see if can find a match Hand in list *	Monitor Monitor	Write Speak/Listen	10 min.
8. GROUPS (teacher-assigned, on cards that list group and assignment) Unscramble the stories pp. 112–13 Read and act out stories for class*	Distribute cards Monitor/ feedback	Group and begin Read/discuss Listen/watch	17 min.
9. HOMEWORK: Quiz tomorrow/ Review sheet to fill out	Explain	Begin review	10 min.
* assessments, not all are "graded" but all are corrected/given feedback			
NOTE: This unit used to take me over a week to cover; now I do it in two days (plus time on Day 3 for testing) with the class averaging higher grades. I have a lot of "organizing" to do before beginning class, but my function during class is primarily to monitor their progress. (See list of teacher activities!!)			

FRENCH 3—SINGLE-STRAND LESSON PLAN

Students entering classroom draw a slip of paper on which is written: Peasant, Bourgeois A, Bourgeois B, Noble, Intellectual, Prisoner, or Representative

Each finds his or her group according to this assignment, and one person from each group picks up a handout explaining their mission:
EXAMPLES:
Peasants, you are starving. You have had three hard winters followed by drought.

List the steps you will take to get help, and write a letter to the king.
1. What is the problem?
2. What is your solution? (be specific)
3. Who did you talk to before writing this letter, and what was the response?

Nobles, you can do ANYTHING you want today; what will you do? Prepare a timetable poster, listing, among other things, when you will get up, what amusements you will attend, what you will eat, how much you will spend, etc.

Students have approximately 20 minutes to discuss and prepare whatever their assignment is   20 min.

Staying in character, each group tells the others about their situation, and groups react to each other's situation. This activity usually creates group alliances and hatreds, and students have a good feel for the atmosphere at the beginning of the French Revolution (1789)   20 min.

Students then read the chapter in their text on the Revolution (in French, this time) and fill out a worksheet which requires them to find essential vocabulary from the chapter:
cahiers de doleance, les Etats-Generaux, le Tiers Etat, etc.
Students hand this in for a grade.   20 min.

Teacher shows a video on the French Revolution, introducing students to the main characters during the revolution (A & E's coverage of the Bicentennial celebration in France)   20 min.

Students learn La Marseillaise (words now have even more meaning!).
Extra credit for those who memorize it!   10 min.
Students leave the room, humming it.

NEXT DAY:
Graffiti: everything the group remembers about the Revolution!   10 min.
Hand back worksheets. Brief lecture in French   10 min.
Send-a-Question. Each group writes four questions on the Revolution, passes them to another group who answers them (see Chapter 4) 10 min.
Test over this tomorrow.
Video: Marie Antoinette (the revolution from her point of view)   40 min.
Get other text; work on conditional tense with partner   20 min.

MIDDLE SCHOOL FRENCH EXPLORATORY—SINGLE-STRAND

This is an actual First-Day-of-Class lesson plan

ACTIVITY	TEACHER	STUDENT	TIME (min.)
1. Teacher greets class, has them answer	Model/ speak	Listen/repeat	5
2. Students read Class Rules sheet	Take attendance	Read	5
3. Clock sheet sign-ups (see ch. 4) for paired activities	Explain rules Monitor	Listen Speak/write	5
4. Think/Pair/Share: Why they took French	Monitor List answers on board	Converse Discuss	10
5. Pronunciation practice, {a} and {i} sounds	Write on board	Read Pronounce	
LIST: garage, à la mode, corsage, ski, boutique, suite, automobile, fatigue, visa			
To check learning, try these: animal, Afrique, banane, giraffe, vanille, accident	Feedback	Guess/say	5
6. Students choose French names. After teacher okays the name, they make name tags.	Listen, write down	Read, pronounce Write	10
7. Wearing name tags, play Concentration. Students and teacher sit in a big circle and establish a 4-beat rhythm, 2 slaps on thighs, 2 finger snaps in air, slowly. Teacher starts: on leg slaps, says own name, on finger snaps, says the name of a student. Student repeats own name on slaps, and says the name of another on snaps…and so on. Everyone gets to know each other's name, and pronunciation and recognition are stressed.	Speak, listen	Speak, listen	15
8. Teacher introduces the numbers 1–10	Speak	Listen/repeat	5

9. Play slapjack: Group students by fours. Give each a deck of cards. One student turns over a card, while ALL say "un." This is repeated, as the group counts to 10. If, when they say "trois (three)," a 3 card is turned up, all quickly slap the pile, leaving hands down. The last to slap has to take all the cards dealt so far; so does anyone who slaps (first) at the wrong time. When all cards are gone, the winner has the least cards.	Monitor	Speak , listen
10. Assignment: Bring, in written form, 3 French words we use in English, for tomorrow.	Speak	Listen. Discuss if time

15

TOTAL: 80 min.

SPANISH LESSON PLANS

MIDDLE SCHOOL SPANISH—SINGLE-STRAND LESSON

ACTIVITY	TEACHER	STUDENT	TIME (min.)
1. Vocabulary review: HUNTING. Give a picture of a food item to every student but one. Students hold up theirs, as teacher names a food. If student without a picture can identify the correct picture, he or she takes it and a new student has no picture…and so on.	Speak Monitor	Listen React	15
2. New vocabulary: Drinks.	TPR presentation	Look, listen, repeat	5
3. Each takes a card with the name of a drink. Teacher comes by and student "orders" the drink from teacher.	Feedback	Speak	5
4. All pictures are now in a pot. Game: WITCHES BREW. Students take turns picking out a card. If they can name it in Spanish, they keep it. If they are wrong, the card goes back in. The one (or the team) with the most cards wins.	Monitor	Look, speak	20
5. LISTENING: Given a worksheet with a picture of a meal, and a list of food words, students circle all the foods they see in the picture.	Monitor	Read, respond	5
6. PAPER PLATES: Students draw a picture of a meal on a cheap white paper plate.	Monitor	Draw	10
7. Trade paper plates with someone and order that meal from them; they doublecheck to see that it was done correctly. Can be done paired or grouped.	Monitor	Look, speak, feedback	8
8. Begin workbook pages, due tomorrow.	Monitor	Read, write	12

SAMPLE SPANISH I OR II LESSON PLAN: SINGLE-STRAND ON COMPARISONS

1. Teacher takes grades for homework, general announcements, etc.   10 min.
   SPONGE while doing this: get an old magazine, cut out a picture of a
   person glue it to a paper, and label it with three adjectives from the
   chapter. Make sure the adjectives agree in gender and in number!

3. Vocabulary practice:
   a. Oral, with overhead or picture file. Practice adjectives: tall, short, thin,
      blond, etc.   5 min.
   b. Paired: get together with partner and show/describe the picture you
      cut out. Then, ask each other a question about the other person's   5 min.
      picture.
   c. Hand in pictures, and do crossword puzzle. Give extra-credit stamp for   10 min.
      perfect papers.

4. Oral demonstration of new grammar concept
   Student volunteers stand. Describe to the classroom (using gestures):
           Juan es alto (tall). Carlos es bastante alto (rather tall).
               Esteban es alto tambien (also tall).
   Then add: Juan es mas alto que Carlos (taller)
           Carlos es menos alto que Juan (less tall).
           Esteban es tan alto como Juan (as tall as).
   Repeat with more adjectives: dark-haired, thin, etc.   10 min.

5. Explanation: using chalkboard or overhead, explain regular comparisons, and irregular comparisons. Remind about adjective agreement.   10 min.

6. Group activity:
   a. Divide class in 6 groups. Assign each a station at the chalkboard.
      Choose one student helper from each group.
   b. Give each helper two characters to describe (i.e., the principal and the
      teacher, a classmate and a movie star, etc.)
   OR use the picture file and give each person a name. Choose pictures that
      very obviously illustrate tall, short, thin, fat, old, weak, pretty, etc. (I
      write the adjective on the back so that I can quickly match them up dur-
      ing the activity.) They each go to a station and write the names high on
      the board, with the adjective between them.
   c. Send the groups randomly to the stations so they don't start before it's
      time.
   d. Give them one minute to write a sentence using those two people +
      adjective correctly.
   e. Give each team with a correct sentence one point.
   f. Repeat four times, using different adjectives. If you wish, rotate the
      teams to a different spot also, but this is not necessary.
   g. Reward the winning team.
   h. Check for questions.   30 min.

7. Written assignment: worksheet as homework   10 min.

*(Adapted (several sections added) from a lesson plan by Cheryl Cowan, Roy J. Wasson High
School, found on the Internet.)*

SPANISH II: OBSERVATION—HILLCREST H.S., SPRINGFIELD, MO SEPTEMBER 1993

18 students

12:35 Conversation work with partners

12:43 Written sentence completion exercise, using *-ir* verbs

12:50 Each student reads favorite three sentences from written exercise as pronunciation practice

1:05 Listening activity. After, change papers and grade them. Teacher collected these for assessment.

1:10 Handout for tomorrow: verb crossword, then translate the verbs also while students worked on this, handed back papers: Quintain poem

    Line 1 their name

    Line 2 two adjectives to describe them

    Line 3 a comparison ("Como…")

    Line 4 word that describes them best

    Line 5 their name again

1:25 Teacher had volunteers read their poems.

1:32 More work time on handout.

COMMENTS ON BLOCK: (A/B SCHEDULE)

Has to skip a few "fun" things she used to do in order to keep up with other teachers in different sections

Reviews every day "a bit." Sees no big retention problem with a day off between each class.

Block means you have to go faster; two days' worth covered in one day.

Use a lot of variety.

SPANISH 2 LESSON PLAN

(Courtesy of Jocelyn Raught, Cactus Shadows HS, Cave Creek, Arizona)

Students tend to attain language in chunks, especially when it comes to tougher concepts like object pronouns, therefore, we have to give them short, usable "chunks" of meaningful language. I started the rhythmic approach to help the students learn the difference between the direct and the indirect: we chant the direct object in a 2-syllable sequence to match "direct," while the indirect pronouns are presented in a 3-syllable sequence to match "in-di-rect." The games and the oral interactive parts help the "chunk" acquisition so the kids start to use them.

Lesson:

I shall use capitals for the teacher talk, while the student repetition is lowercase. Dots represent pauses.

1. Tell the kids to listen well and repeat.
    ME—me…ME—me….TE—te…TE—te… ME TE—me te….ME TE—me te…
    Call on different individuals to repeat and then return to group:
    ME TE—me te …LO—lo …ME TE—me te …LO—lo … LA—la…ME TE—me te… LO LA—lo la….
    Put these 2-syllable parts together, and repeat many times. Alternate individuals with group.
    Add : NOS—nos….NOS—nos…OS—os…OS— os… NOS OS—nos os …
    ME TE—me te .. LO LA—lo la …NOS OS—nos os…
    Then say all together ME TE…LO LA…NOS OS….
    Add: LOS—los…LOS—los….LAS—las….LAS—las….LOS LAS—los las….
    Build up to : ME TE…LO LA….NOS OS……LOS LAS…

2. While presenting the pronouns, add hand clapping, finger snapping, swaying, etc. Make it sing-songy. The kids have fun and it's almost a tongue twister.

3. ORAL MODELING: Again, do not explain anything. Tell them to listen carefully. Model sentences replacing the direct object. Stress the direct object and pronoun so they may understand number, gender, and placement without explanation.
    Example: PABLO TIENE EL LIBRO…PABLO LO TIENE
    After about 5, the quicker students start to click, more after 10, etc. Then, as you say the sentence, allow the class as a whole to replace the direct object with a pronoun. When they seem ready, call on them individually.

4. SENTENCE LIST PRACTICE: Students see it and do it on their own. Have them underline the direct object in each of the first 5, and check as a group. Then have them write the sentence replacement, and check. Monitor by walking around. Have them exchange and check papers.

5. "LO TENGO" game: this is the biggest hit of all. I have 10 sets of cards with classroom vocabulary on it. Mine are in Spanish so I call the English name, but if you had pictures, you could call it in Spanish. Put the students in groups and have them lay the cards out on the floor so everyone in the group can see them. When I call out the name, the student that grabs it, holds it up and says , "Lo (la, las) tengo" gets to keep the card. If the student uses the wrong pronoun or grabs the wrong card, another can correct him or her, and take the card. This game is great because we use "lo tengo," etc. so much in our everyday speech.

This takes the biggest chunk of the block time.

On subsequent days, you can repeat the chant as needed, and add questions and classroom conversation: TU LAPIZ? LO TIENES??...si, lo tengo! Then incorporate other things including interests, hobbies, cultural realia....For example, EL FUTBOL? LO JUEGAS BIEN?... EL MOLE? LO ADMIRAS? etc.

You can add the grammatical explanation later, as some students want that linear thinking.

LATIN LESSON PLANS

SAMPLE LESSON PLAN: LATIN I

I. Roll, announcements, handling absences

    SPONGE: Write 4 sentences about yourself, all beginning with the word "Sum" (I am).

    Teacher collects these.   5 min.

II. Teacher review of the forms of "to be"—present tense only.   10 min.

III. Text: *Latin for Americans*, book one.

    Page 86, exercise A: drill on "to be" individual seat work, but try some on board afterward. Observations and generalizations from the class   10 min.

IV. Teacher models translation from English into Latin—page 86, exercise B   5 min.

V. Teacher reads chosen selections from part I of today's lesson, and students try to guess who is being described (Students are not allowed to tell on themselves when they hear their own selection.)   5 to 10 min.

V. "Translation trios"—Translation XV in the text.

    Students assigned to cooperative learning groups of three; have been together for the entire grading period.

    Teacher wanders/monitors as groups work.   20–30 min.

    Stops at 30 minutes. Efficient groups will be done; others will have homework.

VI. Ongoing notes on mythology from the day before: Roman view of the afterlife.   15 min.

(Adapted from a lesson plan by Roger Schoenstein, Wasson HS, found on Internet.)

LATIN II/III: OBSERVATION—HILLCREST H.S., SPRINGFIELD, MO SEPTEMBER 1993

Mixed-level class, 8 students in Level 2, 6 in Level 3

1:25 The 2's are reading a translation (assigned as homework) to review it before discussion, while teacher gives assignment to the 3's: translate lines 7–14 in a story in text

1:28 Teacher goes over translation with 2's while the 3's work independently on their translation

1:45 Told 2's to study vocabulary for test tomorrow

Worked with 3's to go over Lines 1–14 in story (1–6 were homework, 7–14 just completed in class)

2:00 Alternated translation work with an oral grammar review exercise—the 2's did possessives and the 3's did pluperfect tense

2:12 Students got dictionaries and tried to translate epigrams written on the board

2:22 Teacher read aloud from history text *501 Tidbits of Roman Antiquity*

Student discussion of the topic, applying it to modern life.

2:26 Handed out comic book-style readers; When bell rang, students put their books back

AUTHOR'S NOTE:

This lesson plan sounds boring, but due to the charismatic demeanor of the teacher, it was not. However, here are some suggestions to "spice it up":

1:45 Have the 2's make flashcards and do Pair/Drill or Send-a-Problem

2:00 Use whiteboards or a board race to review grammar

2:12 If didn't do a race at 2:00, make the translation a competition/race: fastest to complete three lines correctly gets to pick the next reading, etc.

JAPANESE LESSON PLAN

JAPANESE 1: OBSERVATION—HILLCREST H.S., SPRINGFIELD, MO SEPTEMBER 1993

NOTE: no text being used at this time. Teacher has Japanese aide who shares instructional duties.

20 students.

1. Aide introduced 15 new words using flashcard pictures, pronouncing them and having students repeat; TPR format means introducing them in threes, with frequent review of previously introduced items, varying the order of presentation.

2. Teacher introduced phrases, "I like," "I hate," and "Do you like…?"

   Asked the class if they liked the things pictured on cards held up by the aide: first as whole class, then asked individuals to respond.

   NOTE: used cards with students' names on them to call on students; put card on bottom of deck when done. Had a red card at the bottom; when it rose to the top, she shuffled the cards again and began anew.

3. GAME: Student comes to center of room, picks a card, and asks the teacher if she likes the item. If the teacher replies affirmatively, all the students switch seats, and the student in the middle tries to grab or steal someone's seat. If the teacher replies negatively, the student picks another card and tries again. If the student is able to steal a seat, a new student questions the teacher.

4. Dictation: teacher says the new vocabulary once again, and this time students write down the words.

   (NOTE: they have not yet seen them written; all work to this point has been oral)

   Aide distributes a vocab sheet, and students check to see how close they got to the actual spelling.

5. Homework from the previous lesson was to be ready to introduce a classmate to the class:

   Name, age, wants to be (profession), is in _____grade.

   First, students were given time to practice their introduction. Then, they introduce their partner. As they do this, the aide puts a few new vocab words on the board (16 in all).

6. End of hour: introduced the words on the board to learn for the next day. Also told them to study their "hirogana" as the quizzes over that weren't very good.

COMMENTS:

Give them homework that forces them to practice the vocab.

Don't throw too much at them in one period.

Need lots of variety.

GERMAN LESSON PLANS

FIRST-YEAR GERMAN—MULTISTRAND LESSON

Text: *German Today I* (1986). Chapter 5. The previous dialogue and chapter vocabulary has been learned already, hopefully.

10 min.	Teacher does administrative things; students study vocab in pairs.
15 min.	Warm-up drills: oral Sein, haben, weak verbs, tragen
	Ask each student to do at least one. Go to questions after drill, asking each student one also.
15 min.	Move to the dialogue: Welche Grosse trägst du? Model and have student repeat.
	Stress the vowels, especially the "a" in "trägst."
5 min	Change of pace: a vowel song.
5 min	Tape of dialogue.
20 min	Pair students; they choose roles and then let them practice 10–12 minutes and then have them do the dialogue from memory (Use Inside-Outside Circle—see Chapter 4—so they have to do the dialogue several times!)
5 min	Show the Alles Gute short video dialogue "Das sind meine Sachen." This reinforces clothing vocabulary and the "cin" words.
10 min	Wind down and have students, in groups, adapt the video dialogue into a short play, due the next day.

The next day students would have an oral test and then would trade the plays they wrote with another group, take time for a brief rehearsal, and then perform for the class.

(Adapted from a lesson by Jon Hoffman, Wasson HS, found on Internet)

GERMAN 2 LESSON:

Text: Deutsch aktuell 2

Warm-up. Use the Ruckblick for chapter, personalizing it as much as
        possible.   5 min.
    Tell your Partner activity. Teacher does administrivia.

Think/Pair/Share: Has anyone ever been to a coffee/espresso shop?
    What sorts of drinks are there? What do you like best?
    What sorts of people are there? What does the place look like?   5 min.

Every group stands when finished. One by one, each group shares
    some knowledge about American coffee shops, sitting when done.   5 min.

Teacher: (in German) Do you like coffee? Tea? Welchen Kaffee/Tee
    trinken sie gern und wo? Why do you go to coffee shops? (Warum
    sind sie beliebt: Getranke, Essen, Musik, Atmosphare?)   3 min.

Go to computer lab.   2 min.

Pair students and give each a worksheet to fill out. They will visit 2
    "sehr verschiedene und beliebte" Cafes in Vienna (Wien)...via Internet
    and fill out a worksheet:
    EXAMPLE:
    http://www.arosnet.se/werbeka/krog/krog.htm (Internationalen
        Netrestaurant)
        Klicken Sie rechts unten auf "Kaffee"
        Gehen Sie zur Mitte der Seite uber die Wiener
            Kaffeespezialitaten...
        Wortschatz: (Schlag-) obers = whipped cream.
    1. Welchen Kaffee/welche Getranke mochten Sie trinken?   20 min.
    2. Welchen Kaffee mochten Sie nicht trinken?

Back in classroom again, teacher collects the papers and the class dis-
    cusses the experience, using the list about American coffee shops on
    the board, and listing new vocab discovered, differences discovered,   15 min.
    etc.

Dialog: Ein Eis, bitte! Read, listen, practice with a partner.   15 min.

Regroup in groups of 3. Write a skit similar to the dialog, and learn it
    for tomorrow.   10 min.

LESSON PLAN—GERMAN 3/4

SPONGE: Write (in German) typical events in the life of a woman, beginning with birth. (Teacher takes roll, catches up absent student, etc.)   5 min.

Teacher makes large time line on board, and asks each group to add one event to the line. (Geburt, College, Heirat, u. a.)   10 min.

INTERNETAUFGABE:

   Class goes to computer lab with Internet access   2 min.

Students will look at a series of comical pictures showing a typical woman's life.

Worksheet: to be answered in German

   http://www.online.telecom.at/onlinec/women/women/oefl/
   phasen.html

   Wortschatz: mit Karacho = mit grosser Geschwindigkeit/hohem
   Tempo

  1. Welche Bilder finden Sie lustig?
  2. Welche Bilder finden Sie ernst?
  3. Gibt es mehr lustige oder mehr ernste Bilder?
  4. Glauben Sie, diese Geschichte ist _typisch_ fur das Leben einer
Frau?

     Wenn ja, welche Bilder?
     Wenn nein, welche Bilder?

  5. Finden Sie die Bildergeschichte insgesamt (overall) lustig, ernst
oder bittersüss?

     Warum?   20 min.

Falls Zeit, konnen Sie noch einen Kommentar an die Zeichnerin emailen (die Adresse folgt den Bildern)—this last was an extra credit sponge—for those who finish early

Back in class, students briefly discuss what they saw.   3 min.

They then, using scissors and old magazines, cut out pictures and construct a time line for a typical German woman, labeling each stage.   15 min.

When done, this is handed in and each student picks up a short reading (an autobiography) and begins translating it.

When all are done, teacher organizes students in groups of four, and they share translations, completing the reading.

To check on comprehension, students number off, and the teacher asks all the number threes a question, etc.   20 min.

HOMEWORK: Interview an older woman: Mom, aunt, grandma, neighbor, coworker.

Write a short story about the important aspects of her life: where born, when married, where attended school, etc.

For the rest of the hour, write questions to ask, and look up vocabulary words you will need to put on paper in German.

Write as much as you can, leaving spaces : She was born in (city)... in (year)...

NEXT DAY: Pair /Share stories...

   Then Inside-Outside Circle, saying them aloud (speaking/listening)
   Grammar work on common errors.
   Go on to next portion of chapter.

ADDITIONAL COMMENTS ON LESSON PLANNING

SOURCE: FLTEACH ARCHIVES

I overplan...fill up the time. Don't be left standing in front of 20 kids with no raw meat to throw them. I therefore have a lot of different things planned: a listening activity, a partner activity, short grammar drill (twice around the room with German adjective endings every day can be stimulating to left-brained types), etc. We can always sing our Preposition Songs if I end up with an extra minute or two.

But, my first corollary is to overlap activities. They've had a worksheet as homework, they've written the answers to the listening activities in the margin, they've interviewed five people about their favorite free time activity and written that in the extra three inches under the last exercise, they hand in the paper and pick up the next worksheet and read through the directions and get started. There is no wasted space, there is no wasted time.

I can only plan a couple of days at the most. But if you have a three-day wait before you can get a VCR, you're going to have to know you need it three days earlier, and that means you have to have some plans.—*source teacher unknown*

After 29 years teaching I know where the students get stuck. And I let them get stuck! From getting stuck we clear it up and then, "which, by the way, leads us to how we are going to say such and such." I depend a lot on what the students produce linguistically. I would rather stay home than enter my class without a clear idea of what I hope to accomplish and the manner and order in which I expect to accomplish it.—*Leonard*

It's great and liberating to work impromptu. But put that in a sequence as part of a unit where you must connect with previous knowledge and lay groundwork for upcoming knowledge, and it helps to know ahead of time how it all fits together...

Compare it to getting in the car for a trip. If you know your destination is somewhere north, you might eventually get there by taking roads that look interesting and seeing all the sights along the way. It's fun and can be low pressure until you've been on the road a few weeks and you're all beginning to wonder when you'll get there. On the other hand, knowing which freeways to use, which interchanges

AUGUST						
S	M	T	W	T	F	S
					1	2
3	4	5	6	7	8	9
10	11	12	13	14	15	16
17	18	19	20	21	22	23
24	25	26	27	28	29	30
31						

SEPTEMBER						
S	M	T	W	T	F	S
	1	2	3	4	5	6
7	8	9	10	11	12	13
14	15	16	17	18	19	20
21	22	23	24	25	26	27
28	29	30				

OCTOBER						
S	M	T	W	T	F	S
			1	2	3	4
5	6	7	8	9	10	11
12	13	14	15	16	17	18
19	20	21	22	23	24	25
26	27	28	29	30	31	

NOVEMBER						
S	M	T	W	T	F	S
						1
2	3	4	5	6	7	8
9	10	11	12	13	14	15
16	17	18	19	20	21	22
23	24	25	26	27	28	29
30						

DECEMBER						
S	M	T	W	T	F	S
	1	2	3	4	5	6
7	8	9	10	11	12	13
14	15	16	17	18	19	20
21	22	23	24	25	26	27
28	29	30	31			

10 am - 8 pm
10 am - 9 pm
10 am - 10 pm
10:30 am - 6 pm
10:30 am - 7 pm
10:30 am - 8 pm
10:30 am - 9 pm
11 am - 7 pm
Noon - 8 pm
Noon - 9 pm
4 pm - 10 pm
6 pm - 11 pm
Holiday in the Park Hours - TBD

Six Flags FIESTA TEXAS SAN ANTONIO
PREFERRED HOTELS

The Omni Hotel San Antonio
800-843-6664

SpringHill Suites
800-287-9400

Courtyard San Antonio North/Stone Oak Legacy
210-545-3100

Radisson Hill Country
210-509-9800

Quality Inn & Suites Fiesta Park
210-249-4800

SIXFLAGS.COM

© 2008 McDonald's. SIX FLAGS and all related indicia are trademarks of Six Flags Theme Parks Inc. ®, TM and © 2008. (s08) pp

admission ticket. Valid for up to six (6) tickets. Tickets valid only on day of purchase. Cash value 1/20 of a cent. Attractions, prices, shows, and operating schedules are subject to change without notice. Offer cannot be combined with other discount offers. Not valid at any other Six Flags Park. Coupon expires Sept. 14, 2008.

NLU 56096

Two Days for the Price of One!
Present this coupon at any Six Flags Fiesta Texas ticket booth any regular operating day and receive a free, next-day ticket with the purchase of a general admission at $46.99 + tax. Coupon is valid for up to six (6) discount admissions. Tickets purchased with this coupon are valid only on day of purchase and the following day. Cash value 1/20 of a cent. Attractions, prices, shows, and operating schedules are subject to change without notice. Offer cannot be combined with other discount offers. Not valid at any other Six Flags Park. Coupon expires Sept. 13, 2008.

NLU 922

$5 off any retail or photo pur
Make ANY single purchase of $25 or more from ANY
photo location and receive $5.00 OFF your total pu
Valid at participating locations. One coupon per
be sold or bartered. Valid during the 2008 o
Flags Theme Park in the United States
conjunction with any other discount off

Di

PAYS KIDS
PRICE!

TWO DAYS
FOR THE PRICE
OF ONE!

$5 OFF
RETAIL OR
PURCHASE!

i'm lovin' it

and offramps to take, you'll get to your destination and have time to enjoy it when you get there.—*Mary*

From a teacher who changed jobs, from a blocked school to a nonblocked one:

One thing I really liked about block scheduling is this: in the 50-minute classes I teach now, by the time I go over the new vocabulary and give them notes on the grammar topic and maybe do one or two oral exercises, it's time to leave and they don't really get much practice with their new material.

With the 90-minute classes, I could do all of that plus give them a written assignment to do individually or in groups. Then I could grade it before I saw them again and see if they were catching on to the new concept. I also liked the fact that I could spend quite a bit of class time reviewing for a test and still manage to give the test. Now all I can give them is 5 to 10 minutes to review and some of them feel pressed for time while they're taking the test.—*Linda R*

REFERENCES

BOOKS

ACTFL, *Standards for Foreign Language Learning: Preparing for the 21st Century.* Cost: $20.00 available from the ACTFL, 6 Executive Plaza, Yonkers, NY 10701-6801. Tel: (914) 963-8830; Fax : (914) 963-1275.

A Nation at risk: The imperative for educational reform. (April 1983). Washington, DC: National Commission on Excellence in Education.

Breaking ranks: Changing an American institution. Reston, VA: National Association of Secondary School Principals and the Carnegie Foundation for the Advancement of Teaching. Not cited in this text but influential on establishing a need for school reform.

Canady, R.L., & Rettig, M.D. (1995). *Block scheduling: A catalyst for change in high schools.* Larchmont, NY: Eye on Education.

Canady, R.L., & Rettig, M.D. (1996). *Teaching in the block: Strategies for engaging active learners.* Larchmont, NY: Eye on Education.

Evansville-Vanderburgh School Corporation, 1993. *Portfolio assessment in foreign language.* Evansville, IN.

Gunter, M.A., Estes, T., & Schwab, J. (1995). *Instruction: A models approach.* Needham Heights, MA: Simon and Schuster.

Hancock, C. (ed.) (1994). *Northeast Conference Reports: Teaching, testing and assessment.* Lincolnwood, IL: National Textbook Co.

Johnson, D.W., & Johnson, R. (1993). *Leading the cooperative school* (2nd ed.). Edina, MN: Interaction Book Co.

Johnson, D.W., Johnson, R., & Holubec, E. J. (1993). *Cooperation in the classroom* (6th ed.). Edina, MN: Interaction Book Co.

Joyce, B., & Weil, M. (1996). *Models of teaching* (5th ed.). Needham Heights, MA: Allyn and Bacon.

Kagan, S. (1995). *Cooperative learning: Resources for teachers.* San Juan Capistrano, CA: Resources for Teachers, Inc.

Larson, C.N., & Smalley, W.A. (1972). *Becoming Bilingual: A guide to language learning*. South Pasadena, CA: William Carey Library.

Moore, Z.T. (1994). "The portfolio and testing culture." In C. Hancock (ed.). *Northeast Conference Reports: Teaching, testing and assessment*. Lincolnwood, IL: National Textbook Co.

Rosensline, B., & Stevens, R. (1986). Teaching functions. In M.C. Wittrock (ed.), *Handbook of research on teaching* (3rd ed.). New York: Macmillan, pp. 376–391.

Slavin, R.E. (1986). *Using student team learning* (3rd ed.). Baltimore, MD: The Johns Hopkins Team Learning Project, Johns Hopkins University.

Valette, R.M. (1977). Modern language testing: A handbook. New York: Harcourt, Brace, Jovanovich.

Wisconsin Association of Foreign Language Teachers. (1995). *Redesigning high school schedules: A report of the Task Force on Block Scheduling by the Wisconsin Association of Foreign Language Teachers*. Madison, WI: WAFLT (can be found on ERIC on the Internet).

ARTICLES

Bartz, Walter H. (Winter 1997). *Foreign Language Network News*. Indianapolis, IN: Indiana Dept. of Education.

Birckbichler, Diane W., Robison, Robert E., & Robinson, Deborah W. (1995). "A collaborative approach to articulation and assessment." In *Broadening the frontiers of foreign language education: Report of the Central States Conference on the teaching of foreign languages*, G. Crouse (ed.). Lincolnwood, IL: National Textbook Co.

Carroll, Joseph M. (March 1994). "Organizing time to support learning." *The School Administrator*, 26–33.

Durham, C.R., Carmines, A., & Lewis, M. (September 1990). "Teaching for synthesis: A multifaceted, multi-language approach to Don Juan." *Newsletter*, vol. 28. Middlebury, VT: Northeast Conference on the Teaching of Foreign Languages, Inc.

Edwards, H.P. (1976). Evaluation of the French immersion program offered by the Ottawa Roman Catholic Separate School Board. *Canada Modern Language Review* 33, 137–142.

Elkins, G. (Spring 1996). " Making longer better: Staff development for block scheduling." Arlington, VA: ASCD Professional Development Newsletter.

Elkins, G. (April 1997). Workshop on *Effective teaching strategies for block schedules,* Indianapolis, IN.

Hottenstein, D.S. (Winter 1996). "Supporting block scheduling: A response to critics." *Alliance 1*(2), 11. Reston, VA: The National Alliance of High Schools, a division of the National Association of Secondary School Principals.

Houghton, D. (January 1997). *AATF National Bulletin.* Vol. 22, No. 3. Champaign, IL: American Association of Teachers of French, p. 6.

Lubiner, E., & Lubiner, A. (September 1990). "Sponge activities for the foreign language classroom." *Newsletter,* vol 28. Middlebury, VT: Northeast Conference on the Teaching of Foreign Languages, Inc.

Oxford, R.L. (1982). "Research on language loss: A review with implications for foreign language teaching." *Modern Language Journal* (66), 160–169.

Portela, B. (1996). *Preparing to teach foreign languages in a block 4 schedule.* Paper written for IPFW class EDU L520, provided to me by Ms. Portela via Internet.

Rieken, E., Kerby, W., & Mulhern, F. (1996). "Building better bridges: Middle school to high school articulation in foreign languages programs." *Foreign Language Annals 4,* 563–570.

Robison, Robert E. (May 1997). "Issues and trends in foreign language instruction." *NASSP Curriculum Report, 26*(5), 1–8.

Semb, G.B., Ellis, J.A., & Araujo, J. (1993). "Long-term memory for knowledge learned in school." *Journal of Educational Psychology, 85,* 305–316.

Sessoms, J.C. (1995) "Teachers' perceptions of three models of high school block scheduling." Unpublished doctoral dissertation, University of Virginia.

Slavin, R.E. (Feb. 1991). "Synthesis of research on cooperative learning," *Educational Leadership.*

Smythe, P.C., Jutras, G.C., Bramwell, J.R., & Gardner, R.C. (1973). "Second language retention over varying intervals." *Modern Language Journal* (57), 400–405.

Stern, H.H. (1976). "The Ottawa-Carleton French Project: Issues, conclusions and policy implications." *Canadian Modern Language Review* (33), 216–233.

Strasheim, L. (1983). "Coping with multi-level classes effectively and creatively." Fredericksburg, VA: Paper presented at the American Classical League Conference. Also available, ERIC Document Reproduction Service No. ED 232 454.

Tanner, B., Canady, R.L., & Rettig, M.D. (1995). "Scheduling time to maximize staff development opportunities." *Journal of Staff Development, 16*(4), 14–19.

Williamson, V.G. (1968). "A pilot program in teaching Spanish: An intensive approach." *Modern Language Journal* (52), 73–78.

WEB SITES

Abghari, Henry (July 1997). "Grammar and the communicative model" in FLTEACH archives: listserv.acsu.buffalo.edu/cgi-bin/wa?A2=ind9707&L=flteach&O=T&P=59970.

Curry, J. (1997). "Block scheduling research." An Internet site located at http://curry.edschool.Virginia.edu/~dhv3v/block/research/research.html.

FLTEACH archives. An Internet site located at listserv.acsu.buffalo.edu/archives/flteach.html

Paramskas, D. (August 1996). "Re: Coop learning/group idea." In FLTEACH Archives on Internet.

Reilly, T. (May 1988). "Maintaining foreign language skills." *ERIC Digest ED296573.* May be found on the Internet at www.ed.gov/databases/ERIC_Digests/.

Wichita North High School, "Block schedule." On Internet at www.feist.com/~north/ block.htm

Schoenstein, Roger. (March 1995). "Planning for a 90-minute block class." On the Internet at http://k12.oit.umass.edu/block/Block.Planning.txt. or at WassonHS@aol.com.

SOFTWARE

Total Recall, from Zoft Systems, PO Box 62763, Warner Robins, GA 31095; Tel. (912) 929-1570.